1st Workshop on NLP for Conversational AI 2019

Florence, Italy
1 August 2019

ISBN: 978-1-5108-9107-4

ACL 2019

NLP for Conversational AI

Proceedings of the 1st Workshop

August 1, 2019
Florence, Italy

Introduction

Welcome to the ACL 2019 Workshop on **NLP for Conversational AI**.

Ever since the invention of the intelligent machine, hundreds and thousands of mathematicians, linguists, and computer scientists have dedicated their career to empowering human-machine communication in natural language. Although the idea is finally around the corner with a proliferation of virtual personal assistants such as Siri, Alexa, Google Assistant, and Cortana, the development of these conversational agents remains difficult and there still remain plenty of unanswered questions and challenges.

Conversational AI is hard because it is an interdisciplinary subject. Initiatives were started in different research communities, from Dialogue State Tracking Challenges to NIPS Conversational Intelligence Challenge live competition and the Amazon Alexa prize. However, various fields within the NLP community, such as semantic parsing, coreference resolution, sentiment analysis, question answering, and machine reading comprehension etc. have been seldom evaluated or applied in the context of conversational AI.

The goal of this workshop is to bring together NLP researchers and practitioners in different fields, alongside experts in speech and machine learning, to discuss the current state-of-the-art and new approaches, to share insights and challenges, to bridge the gap between academic research and real-world product deployment, and to shed the light on future directions. "NLP for Conversational AI" will be a one-day workshop including keynotes, spotlight talks, posters, and panel sessions. In keynote talks, senior technical leaders from industry and academia will share insights on the latest developments of the field. An open call for papers will be announced to encourage researchers and students to share their prospects and latest discoveries. The panel discussion will focus on the challenges, future directions of conversational AI research, bridging the gap in research and industrial practice, as well as audience-suggested topics.

With the increasing trend of conversational AI, NLP4ConvAI 2019 is competitive. We received 68 submissions, and after a rigorous review process, we only accept 25. There are total 16 accepted regular workshop papers and 7 cross-submissions or extended abstracts. The workshop overall acceptance rate is about 36.8%.

We hope you will enjoy NLP4ConvAI 2019 at ACL and contribute to the future success of our community!

NLPConvAI 2019 Organizers
Tania Bedrax-Weiss, Google AI
Yun-Nung (Vivian) Chen, National Taiwan University
Dilek Hakkani-Tur, Amazon Alexa
Anuj Kumar, Facebook
Mike Lewis, Facebook AI
Thang-Minh Luong, Google Brain
Pei-Hao (Eddy) Su, PolyAI
Tsung-Hsien (Shawn) Wen, PolyAI

Organizers:

Tania Bedrax-Weiss, Google AI
Yun-Nung Chen, National Taiwan University
Dilek Hakkani-Tur, Amazon Alexa
Anuj Kumar, Facebook
Mike Lewis, Facebook AI
Thang-Minh Luong, Google Brain
Pei-Hao Su, PolyAI
Tsung-Hsien Wen, PolyAI

Program Committee:

Abhinav Arora, Anusha Balakrishnan, Pawel Budzianowski, Inigo Casanueva, Wenhu Chen, Ta-Chung Chi, Sam Coope, Nina Dethlefs, Mihail Eric, Ashish Garg, Daniela Gerz, Raghav Gupta, Adithya Gurram, Matt Henderson, Minlie Huang, Ting-Hao Huang, Simon Keizer, Shang-Wen Li, Bing Liu, Yi Luan, Gaurav Menghani, Mrinal Mohit, Seungwhan Moon, Jekaterina Novikova, Alexandros Papangelis, Julien Perez, Elahe Rahimtoroghi, Deepak Ramachandran, Abhinav Rastogi, Marek Rei, Lina M Rojas, Chinnadhurai Sankar, Pararth Shah, Georgios Spithourakis, Shang-Yu Su, Ming Sun, Trieu H Trinh, Gokhan Tur, Stefan Ultes, David Vandyke, Ivan Vendrov, Ivan Vulic, Peng Wang, Yi-Chia Wang, Zhuoran Wang, Jason Williams, Chien-Sheng Wu, Zi Yang, Yi-Ting Yeh, Tiancheng Zhao

Meta-Reviewers:

Tania Bedrax-Weiss, Google AI
Anuj Kumar, Facebook
Pei-Hao Su, PolyAI
Ivan Vulić, PolyAI
Tsung-Hsien Wen, PolyAI

Invited Speaker:

Yejin Choi, University of Washington
Jianfeng Gao, Microsoft Research AI Matt Henderson, PolyAI
Verena Rieser, Heriot-Watt University
Ruhi Sarikaya, Amazon Alexa
Jason Weston, Facebook

Table of Contents

Conference Program

14:00–15:30   **Afternoon Session I**

14:00–14:45   *Invited Talk 4*
Yejin Choi (University of Washington)

14:45–15:30   *Invited Talk 5: Putting Together the Threads of Conversational AI?*
Jason Weston (Facebook)

15:30–16:00   **Coffee Break and Poster Session III**

16:00–18:00   **Afternoon Session II**

16:00–16:45   *Invited Talk 6: Natural Self-Learning Contextual Conversational Systems*
Ruhi Sarikaya (Amazon Alexa)

16:45–17:45   *Panel Discussion*

17:45–18:00   *Closing Remarks*

Regular Workshop Papers

A Repository of Conversational Datasets
Matthew Henderson, Paweł Budzianowski, Iñigo Casanueva, Sam Coope, Daniela Gerz, Girish Kumar, Nikola Mrkšić, Georgios Spithourakis, Pei-Hao Su, Ivan Vulić and Tsung-Hsien Wen

A Simple but Effective Method to Incorporate Multi-turn Context with BERT for Conversational Machine Comprehension
Yasuhito Ohsugi, Itsumi Saito, Kyosuke Nishida, Hisako Asano and Junji Tomita

Augmenting Neural Response Generation with Context-Aware Topical Attention
Nouha Dziri, Ehsan Kamalloo, Kory Mathewson and Osmar Zaiane

Building a Production Model for Retrieval-Based Chatbots
Kyle Swanson, Lili Yu, Christopher Fox, Jeremy Wohlwend and Tao Lei

Cross-Submissions / Extended Abstracts

A Repository of Conversational Datasets

github.com/PolyAI-LDN/conversational-datasets

Matthew Henderson, Paweł Budzianowski, Iñigo Casanueva, Sam Coope,

Daniela Gerz, Girish Kumar, Nikola Mrkšić, Georgios Spithourakis,

Pei-Hao Su, Ivan Vulić, and Tsung-Hsien Wen

matt@poly-ai.com

PolyAI Limited, London, UK.

Abstract

Progress in Machine Learning is often driven by the availability of large datasets, and consistent evaluation metrics for comparing modeling approaches. To this end, we present a repository of conversational datasets consisting of hundreds of millions of examples, and a standardised evaluation procedure for conversational response selection models using *1-of-100 accuracy*. The repository contains scripts that allow researchers to reproduce the standard datasets, or to adapt the pre-processing and data filtering steps to their needs. We introduce and evaluate several competitive baselines for conversational response selection, whose implementations are shared in the repository, as well as a neural encoder model that is trained on the entire training set.

1 Introduction

Dialogue systems, sometimes referred to as conversational systems or conversational agents, are useful in a wide array of applications. They are used to assist users in accomplishing well-defined tasks such as finding and/or booking flights and restaurants (Hemphill et al., 1990; Williams, 2012; El Asri et al., 2017), or to provide tourist information (Henderson et al., 2014c; Budzianowski et al., 2018). They have found applications in entertainment (Fraser et al., 2018), language learning (Raux et al., 2003; Chen et al., 2017), and healthcare (Laranjo et al., 2018; Fadhil and Schiavo, 2019). Conversational systems can also be used to aid in customer service[1] or to provide the foundation for intelligent virtual assistants such as Amazon Alexa, Google Assistant, or Apple Siri.

Modern approaches to constructing dialogue systems are almost exclusively data-driven, supported by modular or end-to-end machine learning frameworks (Young, 2010; Vinyals and Le, 2015; Wen et al., 2015, 2017a,b; Mrkšić and Vulić, 2018; Ramadan et al., 2018; Li et al., 2018, *inter alia*). The research community, as in any machine learning field, benefits from large datasets and standardised evaluation metrics for tracking and comparing different models. However, collecting data to train data-driven dialogue systems has proven notoriously difficult. First, system designers must construct an ontology to define the constrained set of actions and conversations that the system can support (Henderson et al., 2014a,c; Mrkšić et al., 2015). Furthermore, task-oriented dialogue data must be labeled with highly domain-specific dialogue annotations (El Asri et al., 2017; Budzianowski et al., 2018). Because of this, such annotated dialogue datasets remain scarce, and limited in both their size and in the number of domains they cover. For instance, the recently published MultiWOZ dataset (Budzianowski et al., 2018) contains a total of 115,424 dialogue turns scattered over 7 target domains. Other standard task-based datasets are typically single-domain and smaller by several orders of magnitude: DSTC2 (Henderson et al., 2014b) contains 23,354 turns, Frames (El Asri et al., 2017) comprises 19,986 turns, and M2M (Shah et al., 2018) spans 14,796 turns.

An alternative solution is to leverage larger conversational datasets available online. Such datasets provide natural conversational structure, that is, the inherent context-to-response relationship which is vital for dialogue modeling. In this work, we present a *public* repository of three large and diverse conversational datasets containing hundreds of millions of conversation examples. Compared to the most popular conversational datasets used in prior work, such as length-restricted Twitter conversations (Ritter et al., 2010) or very technical domain-restricted technical chats from the Ubuntu

---

[1]For an overview, see poly-ai.com/blog/towards-ai-assisted-customer-support-automation

Proceedings of the 1st Workshop on NLP for Conversational AI, pages 1–10
Florence, Italy, August 1, 2019. ©2019 Association for Computational Linguistics

corpus (Lowe et al., 2015, 2017; Gunasekara et al., 2019), conversations from the three conversational datasets available in the repository are more natural and diverse. What is more, the datasets are large: for instance, after preprocessing around 3.7B comments from Reddit available in 256M conversational threads, we obtain 727M valid context-response pairs. Similarly, the number of valid pairs in the OpenSubtitles dataset is 316 million. To put these numbers into perspective, the frequently used Ubuntu corpus v2.0 comprises around 4M dialogue turns. Furthermore, our Reddit corpus includes 2 more years of data and so is substantially larger than the previous Reddit dataset of Al-Rfou et al. (2016), which spans around 2.1B comments and 133M conversational threads, and is not publicly available.

Besides the repository of large datasets, another key contribution of this work is the common evaluation framework. We propose applying consistent data filtering and preprocessing to public datasets, and a simple evaluation metric for response selection, which will facilitate direct comparisons between models from different research groups.

These large conversational datasets may support modeling across a large spectrum of natural conversational domains. Similar to the recent work on language model pretraining for diverse NLP applications (Howard and Ruder, 2018; Devlin et al., 2018; Lample and Conneau, 2019), we believe that these datasets can be used in future work to pre-train large general-domain conversational models that are then fine-tuned towards specific tasks using much smaller amounts of task-specific conversational data. We hope that the presented repository, containing a set of strong baseline models and standardised modes of evaluation, will provide means and guidance to the development of next-generation conversational systems.

The repository is available at `github.com/PolyAI-LDN/conversational-datasets`.

2 Conversational Dataset Format

Datasets are stored as Tensorflow record files containing serialized Tensorflow example protocol buffers (Abadi et al., 2015). The training set is stored as one collection of Tensorflow record files, and the test set as another. Examples are shuffled randomly (and not necessarily reproducibly) within the Tensorflow record files. Each example is deterministically assigned to either the train or test

set using a key feature, such as the conversation thread ID in Reddit, guaranteeing that the same split is created whenever the dataset is generated. By default the train set consists of 90% of the total data, and the test set the remaining 10%.

context/1	*Hello, how are you?*
context/0	*I am fine. And you?*
context	*Great. What do you think of the weather?*
response	*It doesn't feel like February.*

Figure 1: An illustrative Tensorflow example in a conversational dataset, consisting of a conversational context and an appropriate response. Each string is stored as a *bytes* feature using its UTF-8 encoding.

Each Tensorflow example contains a conversational context and a response that goes with that context, see e.g. figure 1. Explicitly, each example contains a number of string features:

- A **context** feature, the most recent text in the conversational context.

- A **response** feature, text that is in direct response to the context.

- A number of extra context features, **context/0**, **context/1** etc. going back in time through the conversation. They are named in reverse order so that **context/i** always refers to the ith most recent extra context, so that no padding needs to be done, and datasets with different numbers of extra contexts can be mixed.

- Depending on the dataset, there may be some extra features also included in each example. For instance, in Reddit the author of the context and response are identified using additional features.

3 Datasets

Rather than providing the raw processed data, we provide scripts and instructions to the users to generate the data themselves. This allows for viewing and potentially manipulating the pre-processing and filtering steps. The repository contains instructions for generating datasets with standard parameters split deterministically into train and test portions. These allow for defining reproducible evaluations in research papers. Section 5 presents benchmark results on these standard datasets for a variety of conversational response selection models.

Dataset creation scripts are written using Apache Beam and Google Cloud Dataflow (Akidau et al.,

	Built from	Training size	Testing size
Reddit	3.7 billion comments in threaded conversations	654,396,778	72,616,937
OpenSubtitles	over 400 million lines from movie and television subtitles (also available in other languages)	283,651,561	33,240,156
AmazonQA	over 3.6 million question-response pairs in the context of Amazon products	3,316,905	373,007

Table 1: Summary of the datasets included in the public repository. The Reddit data is taken from January 2015 to December 2018, and the OpenSubtitles data from 2018.

2015), which parallelizes the work across many machines. Using the default quotas, the Reddit script starts 409 workers to generate the dataset in around 1 hour and 40 minutes. This includes reading the comment data from the BigQuery source, grouping the comments into threads, producing examples from the threads, splitting the examples into train and test, shuffling the examples, and finally writing them to sharded Tensorflow record files.

Table 1 provides an overview of the Reddit, OpenSubtitles and AmazonQA datasets, and figure 3 in appendix A gives an illustrative example from each.

3.1 Reddit

Reddit is an American social news aggregation website, where users can post links, and take part in discussions on these posts. Reddit is extremely diverse (Schrading et al., 2015; Al-Rfou et al., 2016): there are more than 300,000 sub-forums (i.e., subreddits) covering various topics of discussion. These threaded discussions, available in a public *BigQuery* database, provide a large corpus of conversational contexts paired with appropriate responses. Reddit data has been used to create conversational response selection data by Al-Rfou et al. (2016); Cer et al. (2018); Yang et al. (2018). We share code that allows generating datasets from the Reddit data in a reproducible manner: with consistent filtering, processing, and train/test splitting. We also generate data using two more years of data than the previous work, 3.7 billion comments rather than 2.1 billion, giving a final dataset with 176 million more examples.

Reddit conversations are threaded. Each post may have multiple top-level comments, and every comment may have multiple children comments written in response. In processing, each Reddit thread is used to generate a set of examples. Each response comment generates an example, where the context is the linear path of comments that the comment is in response to.

Examples may be filtered according to the contents of the context and response features. The example is filtered if either feature has more than 128 characters, or fewer than 9 characters, or if its text is set to *[deleted]* or *[removed]*. Full details of the filtering are available in the code, and configurable through command-line flags.

Further back contexts, from the comment's parent's parent etc., are stored as extra context features. Their texts are trimmed to be at most 128 characters in length, without splitting words apart. This helps to bound the size of an individual example.

The train/test split is deterministic based on the thread ID. As long as all the input to the script is held constant (the input tables, filtering thresholds etc.), the resulting datasets should be identical.

The data from 2015 to 2018 inclusive consists of 3,680,746,776 comments, in 256,095,216 threads. In total, 727,013,715 Tensorflow examples are created from this data.

3.2 OpenSubtitles

OpenSubtitles is a growing online collection of subtitles for movies and television shows available in multiple languages. As a starting point, we use the corpus collected by Lison and Tiedemann (2016), originally intended for statistical machine translation. This corpus is regenerated every year, in 62 different languages.

Consecutive lines in the subtitle data are used to create conversational examples. There is no guarantee that different lines correspond to different speakers, or that consecutive lines belong to the same scene, or even the same show. The data nevertheless contains a lot of interesting examples for modelling the mapping from conversational contexts to responses.

Short and long lines are filtered, and some text

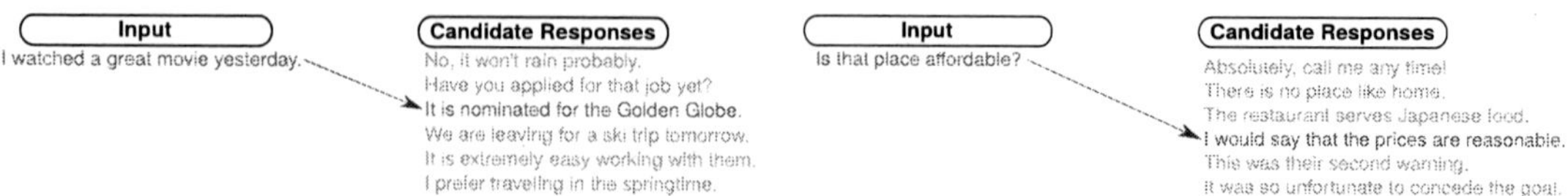

Figure 2: Two examples illustrating the conversational response selection task: given the input context sentence, the goal is to identify the relevant response from a large pool of candidate responses.

is filtered such as character names and auditory description text. The English 2018 data consists of 441,450,449 lines, and generates 316,891,717 examples. The data is split into chunks of 100,000 lines, and each chunk is used either for the train set or the test set.

3.3 AmazonQA

This dataset is based on a corpus extracted by Wan and McAuley (2016); McAuley and Yang (2016), who scraped questions and answers from Amazon product pages. This provides a corpus of question-answer pairs in the e-commerce domain. Some questions may have multiple answers, so one example is generated for each possible answer.

Examples with very short or long questions or responses are filtered from the data, resulting in a total of 3,689,912 examples. The train/test split is computed deterministically using the product ID.

4 Response Selection Task

The conversational datasets included in this repository facilitate the training and evaluation of a variety of models for natural language tasks. For instance, the datasets are suitable for training generative models of conversational response (Serban et al., 2016; Ritter et al., 2011; Vinyals and Le, 2015; Sordoni et al., 2015; Shang et al., 2015; Kannan et al., 2016), as well as discriminative methods of conversational response selection (Lowe et al., 2015; Inaba and Takahashi, 2016; Yu et al., 2016; Henderson et al., 2017).

The task of conversational response selection is to identify a correct response to a given conversational context from a pool of candidates, as illustrated in figure 2. Such models are typically evaluated using *Recall@k*, a typical metric in information retrieval literature. This measures how often the correct response is identified as one of the top k ranked responses (Lowe et al., 2015; Inaba and Takahashi, 2016; Yu et al., 2016; Al-Rfou et al., 2016; Henderson et al., 2017; Lowe et al., 2017; Wu et al., 2017; Cer et al., 2018; Chaudhuri et al.,

2018; Du and Black, 2018; Kumar et al., 2018; Liu et al., 2018; Yang et al., 2018; Zhou et al., 2018; Gunasekara et al., 2019; Tao et al., 2019). Models trained to select responses can be used to drive dialogue systems, question-answering systems, and response suggestion systems. The task of response selection provides a powerful signal for learning implicit semantic representations useful for many downstream tasks in natural language understanding (Cer et al., 2018; Yang et al., 2018).

The *Recall@k* metric allows for direct comparison between models. Direct comparisons are much more difficult for generative models, which are typically evaluated using perplexity scores or using human judgement. Perplexity scores are dependent on normalization, tokenization, and choice of vocabulary, while human judgement is expensive and time consuming.

When evaluating conversational response selection models on these datasets, we propose a *Recall@k* metric termed *1-of-100 accuracy*. This is *Recall@1* using 99 responses sampled from the test dataset as negatives. This *1-of-100 accuracy* metric has been used in previous studies: (Al-Rfou et al., 2016; Henderson et al., 2017; Cer et al., 2018; Kumar et al., 2018; Yang et al., 2018; Gunasekara et al., 2019). While there is no guarantee that the 99 randomly selected negatives will all be *bad* responses, the metric nevertheless provides a simple summary of model performance that has been shown to correlate with user-driven quality metrics (Henderson et al., 2017). For efficient computation of this metric, batches of 100 (context, response) pairs can be processed such that the other 99 elements in the batch serve as the negative examples.

Sections 4.1 and 4.2 present baseline methods of conversational response selection that are implemented in the repository. These baselines are intended to run quickly using a subset of the training data, to give some idea of performance and characteristics of each dataset. Section 4.3 describes a more competitive neural encoder model that is trained on the entire training set.

4.1 Keyword-based Methods

The keyword-based baselines use keyword similarity metrics to rank responses given a context. These are typical baselines for information retrieval tasks. The TF-IDF method computes inverse document frequency statistics on the training set, and scores responses using their tf-idf cosine similarity to the context (Manning et al., 2008).

The BM25 method builds on top of the tf-idf similarity, applying an adjustment to the term weights (Robertson and Zaragoza, 2009).

4.2 Vector-based Methods

The vector-based methods use publicly available neural net embedding models to embed contexts and responses into a vector space. We include the following five embedding models in the evaluation, all of which are available on Tensorflow Hub:

> **USE** the Universal Sentence Encoder from Cer et al. (2018)
>
> **USE-LARGE** a larger version of the Universal Sentence Encoder
>
> **ELMO** the Embeddings from Language Models approach from Peters et al. (2018).
>
> **BERT-SMALL** the deep bidirectional transformer model of Devlin et al. (2018).
>
> **BERT-LARGE** a larger deep bidirectional transformer model.

There are two vector-based baseline methods, one for each of the above models. The SIM method ranks responses according to their cosine similarity with the context vector. This method relies on pretrained models and does not use the training set at all.

The MAP method learns a linear mapping on top of the response vector. The final score of a response with vector $\mathbf{y}$ given a context with vector $\mathbf{x}$ is the cosine similarity $\langle \cdot, \cdot \rangle$ of the context vector with the mapped response vector:

$$\langle \mathbf{x}, (W + \alpha I) \cdot \mathbf{y} \rangle \tag{1}$$

where W, α are learned parameters and I is the identity matrix. This allows learning an arbitrary linear mapping on the context side, while the residual connection gated by α makes it easy for the model to interpolate with the SIM baseline. Vectors are L2-normalized before being fed to the MAP method, so that the method is invariant to scaling.

The W and α parameters are learned on a random sample of 10,000 examples from the training set, using the dot product loss from Henderson et al. (2017). A sweep over learning rate and regularization parameters is performed using a held-out development set. The final learned parameters are used on the evaluation set.

The combination of the three embedding models with the two vector-based methods results in the following six baseline methods: USE-SIM, USE-MAP, USE-LARGE-SIM, USE-LARGE-MAP, ELMO-SIM, and ELMO-MAP.

4.3 Encoder Model

We also train and evaluate a neural encoder model that maps the context and response through separate sub-networks to a shared vector space, where the final score is a dot-product between a vector representing the context and a vector representing the response as per Henderson et al. (2017); Cer et al. (2018); Kumar et al. (2018); Yang et al. (2018). This model is referred to as POLYAI-ENCODER in the evaluation.

Full details of the neural structure are given in Henderson et al. (2019). To summarize, the context and response are both separately passed through sub-networks that:

1. split the text into unigram and bigram features

2. convert unigrams and bigrams to numeric IDs using a vocabulary of known features in conjunction with a hashing strategy for unseen features

3. separately embed the unigrams and bigrams using large embedding matrices

4. separately apply self-attention then reduction over the sequence dimension to the unigram and bigram embeddings

5. combine the unigram and bigram representations, then pass them through several dense hidden layers

6. L2-normalize the final hidden layer to obtain the final vector representation

Both sub-networks are trained jointly using the dot-product loss of Henderson et al. (2017), with label smoothing and a learned scaling factor.

5 Evaluation

All the methods discussed in section 4 are evaluated on the three standard datasets from section 3,

	Reddit	OpenSubtitles	AmazonQA
TF-IDF	26.7	10.9	51.8
BM25	27.6	10.9	52.3
USE-SIM	36.6	13.6	47.6
USE-MAP	40.8	15.8	54.4
USE-LARGE-SIM	41.4	14.9	51.3
USE-LARGE-MAP	47.7	18.0	61.9
ELMO-SIM	12.5	9.5	16.0
ELMO-MAP	19.3	12.3	33.0
BERT-SMALL-SIM	17.1	13.8	27.8
BERT-SMALL-MAP	24.5	17.5	45.8
BERT-LARGE-SIM	14.8	12.2	25.9
BERT-LARGE-MAP	24.0	16.8	44.1
POLYAI-ENCODER	**61.3**	**30.6**	**84.2**

Table 2: *1-of-100 accuracy* results for keyword-based baselines, vector-based baselines, and the encoder model for each of the three standard datasets. The latest evaluation results are maintained in the repository. Results are computed on a random subset of 50,000 examples from the test set (500 batches of 100).

and the results are presented in table 2. In this evaluation, all methods use only the (immediate) context feature to score the responses, and do not use other features such as the extra contexts.

The keyword-based TF-IDF and BM25 are broadly competitive with the vector-based methods, and are particularly strong for AmazonQA, possibly because rare words such as the product name are informative in this domain. Learning a mapping with the MAP method gives a consistent boost in performance over the SIM method, showing the importance of learning the mapping from context to response versus simply relying on similarity. This approach would benefit from more data and a more powerful mapping network, but we have constrained the baselines so that they run quickly on a single computer. The Universal Sentence Encoder model outperforms ELMo in all cases.

The POLYAI-ENCODER model significantly outperforms all of the baseline methods. This is not surprising, as it is trained on the entire training set using multiple GPUs for several hours. We welcome other research groups to share their results, and we will be growing the table of results in the repository.

6 Conclusion

This paper has introduced a repository of conversational datasets, providing hundreds of millions examples for training and evaluating conversational response selection systems under a standard evaluation framework. Future work will involve introducing more datasets in this format, more competitive baselines, and more benchmark results. We welcome contributions from other research groups in all of these directions.

References

Martín Abadi, Ashish Agarwal, Paul Barham, Eugene Brevdo, Zhifeng Chen, Craig Citro, Greg S. Corrado, Andy Davis, Jeffrey Dean, Matthieu Devin, Sanjay Ghemawat, Ian Goodfellow, Andrew Harp, Geoffrey Irving, Michael Isard, Yangqing Jia, Rafal Jozefowicz, Lukasz Kaiser, Manjunath Kudlur, Josh Levenberg, Dan Mané, Rajat Monga, Sherry Moore, Derek Murray, Chris Olah, Mike Schuster, Jonathon Shlens, Benoit Steiner, Ilya Sutskever, Kunal Talwar, Paul Tucker, Vincent Vanhoucke, Vijay Vasudevan, Fernanda Viégas, Oriol Vinyals, Pete Warden, Martin Wattenberg, Martin Wicke, Yuan Yu, and Xiaoqiang Zheng. 2015. TensorFlow: Large-scale machine learning on heterogeneous systems. Software available from tensorflow.org.

Tyler Akidau, Robert Bradshaw, Craig Chambers,

Slava Chernyak, Rafael J. Fernández-Moctezuma, Reuven Lax, Sam McVeety, Daniel Mills, Frances Perry, Eric Schmidt, and Sam Whittle. 2015. The dataflow model: A practical approach to balancing correctness, latency, and cost in massive-scale, unbounded, out-of-order data processing. *Proceedings of the VLDB Endowment*, 8.

Rami Al-Rfou, Marc Pickett, Javier Snaider, Yun-Hsuan Sung, Brian Strope, and Ray Kurzweil. 2016. Conversational contextual cues: The case of personalization and history for response ranking. *CoRR*, abs/1606.00372.

Paweł Budzianowski, Tsung-Hsien Wen, Bo-Hsiang Tseng, Iñigo Casanueva, Stefan Ultes, Osman Ramadan, and Milica Gašić. 2018. MultiWOZ - A large-scale multi-domain wizard-of-oz dataset for task-oriented dialogue modelling. In *Proceedings of EMNLP*.

Daniel Cer, Yinfei Yang, Sheng-yi Kong, Nan Hua, Nicole Limtiaco, Rhomni St. John, Noah Constant, Mario Guajardo-Cespedes, Steve Yuan, Chris Tar, Yun-Hsuan Sung, Brian Strope, and Ray Kurzweil. 2018. Universal sentence encoder. *CoRR*, abs/1803.11175.

Debanjan Chaudhuri, Agustinus Kristiadi, Jens Lehmann, and Asja Fischer. 2018. Improving response selection in multi-turn dialogue systems by incorporating domain knowledge. In *Proceedings of CoNLL*.

Hongshen Chen, Xiaorui Liu, Dawei Yin, and Jiliang Tang. 2017. A survey on dialogue systems: Recent advances and new frontiers. *CoRR*, abs/1711.01731.

Jacob Devlin, Ming-Wei Chang, Kenton Lee, and Kristina Toutanova. 2018. BERT: Pre-training of deep bidirectional transformers for language understanding. *CoRR*, abs/1810.04805.

Wenchao Du and Alan Black. 2018. Data augmentation for neural online chats response selection. In *Proceedings of SCAI*.

Layla El Asri, Hannes Schulz, Shikhar Sharma, Jeremie Zumer, Justin Harris, Emery Fine, Rahul Mehrotra, and Kaheer Suleman. 2017. Frames: A corpus for adding memory to goal-oriented dialogue systems. In *Proceedings of SIGDIAL*.

Ahmed Fadhil and Gianluca Schiavo. 2019. Designing for health chatbots. *CoRR*, abs/1902.09022.

Jamie Fraser, Ioannis Papaioannou, and Oliver Lemon. 2018. Spoken conversational AI in video games: Emotional dialogue management increases user engagement. In *Proceedings of IVA*.

Chulaka Gunasekara, Jonathan K Kummerfeld, Lazaros Polymenakos, and Walter S Lasecki. 2019. DSTC7 task 1: Noetic end-to-end response selection.

Charles T. Hemphill, John J. Godfrey, and George R. Doddington. 1990. The ATIS Spoken Language Systems Pilot Corpus. In *Proceedings of the Workshop on Speech and Natural Language*, HLT '90.

Matthew Henderson, Rami Al-Rfou, Brian Strope, Yun-Hsuan Sung, László Lukács, Ruiqi Guo, Sanjiv Kumar, Balint Miklos, and Ray Kurzweil. 2017. Efficient natural language response suggestion for Smart Reply. *CoRR*, abs/1705.00652.

Matthew Henderson, Blaise Thomson, and Jason D. Wiliams. 2014a. The Second Dialog State Tracking Challenge. In *Proceedings of SIGDIAL*, pages 263–272.

Matthew Henderson, Blaise Thomson, and Jason Williams. 2014b. The Second Dialog State Tracking Challenge. In *Proceedings of SIGDIAL*.

Matthew Henderson, Blaise Thomson, and Steve Young. 2014c. Word-based dialog state tracking with recurrent neural networks. In *Proceedings of SIGDIAL*.

Matthew Henderson, Ivan Vulić, Daniela Gerz, Iñigo Casanueva, Paweł Budzianowski, Sam Coope, Georgios Spithourakis, Tsung-Hsien Wen, Nikola Mrkšić, and Pei-Hao Su. 2019. Training neural response selection for task-oriented dialogue systems. In *Proceedings of ACL*.

Jeremy Howard and Sebastian Ruder. 2018. Universal language model fine-tuning for text classification. In *ACL*, pages 328–339.

Michimasa Inaba and Kenichi Takahashi. 2016. Neural utterance ranking model for conversational dialogue systems. In *Proceedings of SIGDIAL*.

Anjuli Kannan, Karol Kurach, Sujith Ravi, Tobias Kaufmann, Andrew Tomkins, Balint Miklos, Greg Corrado, László Lukács, Marina Ganea, Peter Young, and Vivek Ramavajjala. 2016. Smart Reply: Automated response suggestion for email. In *Proceedings of KDD*.

Girish Kumar, Matthew Henderson, Shannon Chan, Hoang Nguyen, and Lucas Ngoo. 2018. Question-answer selection in user to user marketplace conversations. In *Proceedings of IWSDS*.

Guillaume Lample and Alexis Conneau. 2019. Cross-lingual language model pretraining. *CoRR*, abs/1901.07291.

Liliana Laranjo, Adam G. Dunn, Huong Ly Tong, Ahmet Baki Kocaballi, Jessica Chen, Rabia Bashir, Didi Surian, Blanca Gallego, Farah Magrabi, Annie Y.S. Lau, and Enrico Coiera. 2018. Conversational agents in healthcare: A systematic review. *Journal of the American Medical Informatics Association*, 25(9):1248–1258.

Xiujun Li, Sarah Panda, Jingjing Liu, and Jianfeng Gao. 2018. Microsoft dialogue challenge: Building end-to-end task-completion dialogue systems. *CoRR*, abs/1807.11125.

Pierre Lison and Jörg Tiedemann. 2016. Opensubtitles2016: Extracting large parallel corpora from movie and TV subtitles.

Bing Liu, Tong Yu, Ian Lane, and Ole J Mengshoel. 2018. Customized nonlinear bandits for online response selection in neural conversation models. In *Proceedings of AAAI*.

Ryan Lowe, Nissan Pow, Iulian Serban, Laurent Charlin, Chia-Wei Liu, and Joelle Pineau. 2017. Training end-to-end dialogue systems with the Ubuntu dialogue corpus. *Dialogue & Discourse*, 8(1).

Ryan Lowe, Nissan Pow, Iulian Serban, and Joelle Pineau. 2015. The Ubuntu dialogue corpus: A large dataset for research in unstructured multi-turn dialogue systems. In *Proceedings of SIGDIAL*.

Christopher D. Manning, Prabhakar Raghavan, and Hinrich Schütze. 2008. *Introduction to Information Retrieval*. Cambridge University Press.

Julian McAuley and Alex Yang. 2016. Addressing complex and subjective product-related queries with customer reviews. In *Proceedings of the 25th International Conference on World Wide Web*, WWW '16, Republic and Canton of Geneva, Switzerland. International World Wide Web Conferences Steering Committee.

Nikola Mrkšić and Ivan Vulić. 2018. Fully statistical neural belief tracking. In *Proceedings of ACL*.

Nikola Mrkšić, Diarmuid Ó Séaghdha, Blaise Thomson, Milica Gašić, Pei-Hao Su, David Vandyke, Tsung-Hsien Wen, and Steve Young. 2015. Multi-domain dialog state tracking using recurrent neural networks. In *Proceedings of ACL*, pages 794–799.

Matthew E. Peters, Mark Neumann, Mohit Iyyer, Matt Gardner, Christopher Clark, Kenton Lee, and Luke Zettlemoyer. 2018. Deep contextualized word representations. In *Proceedings of NAACL*.

Osman Ramadan, Paweł Budzianowski, and Milica Gasic. 2018. Large-scale multi-domain belief tracking with knowledge sharing. In *ACL*.

Antoine Raux, Brian Langner, Alan W. Black, and Maxine Eskénazi. 2003. LET's GO: Improving spoken dialog systems for the elderly and non-natives. In *Proceedings of EUROSPEECH*.

Alan Ritter, Colin Cherry, and Bill Dolan. 2010. Unsupervised modeling of Twitter conversations. In *Proceedings of NAACL-HLT*.

Alan Ritter, Colin Cherry, and William B. Dolan. 2011. Data-driven response generation in social media. In *Proceedings of EMNLP*, Stroudsburg, PA, USA. Association for Computational Linguistics.

Stephen Robertson and Hugo Zaragoza. 2009. The probabilistic relevance framework: BM25 and beyond. *Foundations and Trends in Information Retrieval*, 3(4).

Nicolas Schrading, Cecilia Ovesdotter Alm, Ray Ptucha, and Christopher Homan. 2015. An analysis of domestic abuse discourse on Reddit. In *Proceedings of EMNLP*.

Iulian Serban, Ryan Lowe, Laurent Charlin, and Joelle Pineau. 2016. Generative deep neural networks for dialogue: A short review. *CoRR*, abs/1611.06216.

Pararth Shah, Dilek Hakkani-Tür, Bing Liu, and Gokhan Tür. 2018. Bootstrapping a neural conversational agent with dialogue self-play, crowdsourcing and on-line reinforcement learning. In *Proceedings of NAACL-HLT*.

Lifeng Shang, Zhengdong Lu, and Hang Li. 2015. Neural responding machine for short-text conversation. *CoRR*, abs/1503.02364.

Alessandro Sordoni, Michel Galley, Michael Auli, Chris Brockett, Yangfeng Ji, Margaret Mitchell, Jian-Yun Nie, Jianfeng Gao, and Bill Dolan. 2015. A neural network approach to context-sensitive generation of conversational responses. *CoRR*, abs/1506.06714.

Chongyang Tao, Wei Wu, Can Xu, Wenpeng Hu, Dongyan Zhao, and Rui Yan. 2019. Multi-representation fusion network for multi-turn response selection in retrieval-based chatbots. In *Proceedings of WSDM*.

Oriol Vinyals and Quoc V. Le. 2015. A neural conversational model. *CoRR*, abs/1506.05869.

Mengting Wan and Julian McAuley. 2016. Modeling ambiguity, subjectivity, and diverging viewpoints in opinion question answering systems. In *ICDM*, pages 489–498.

Tsung-Hsien Wen, Milica Gasic, Nikola Mrkšić, Pei-Hao Su, David Vandyke, and Steve Young. 2015. Semantically conditioned LSTM-based natural language generation for spoken dialogue systems. In *Proceedings of EMNLP*.

Tsung-Hsien Wen, Yishu Miao, Phil Blunsom, and Steve J. Young. 2017a. Latent intention dialogue models. In *Proceedings of ICML*.

Tsung-Hsien Wen, David Vandyke, Nikola Mrkšić, Milica Gašić, Lina M. Rojas-Barahona, Pei-Hao Su, Stefan Ultes, and Steve Young. 2017b. A network-based end-to-end trainable task-oriented dialogue system. In *Proceedings of EACL*.

Jason D. Williams. 2012. A belief tracking challenge task for spoken dialog systems. In *Proceedings of the NAACL HLT Workshop on Future directions and needs in the Spoken Dialog Community*.

Yu Wu, Wei Wu, Chen Xing, Ming Zhou, and Zhoujun Li. 2017. Sequential matching network: A new architecture for multi-turn response selection in retrieval-based chatbots. In *Proceedings of ACL*.

Yinfei Yang, Steve Yuan, Daniel Cer, Sheng-Yi Kong, Noah Constant, Petr Pilar, Heming Ge, Yun-hsuan Sung, Brian Strope, and Ray Kurzweil. 2018. Learning semantic textual similarity from conversations. In *Proceedings of The Workshop on Representation Learning for NLP*.

Steve Young. 2010. Still talking to machines (cognitively speaking). In *Proceedings of INTER-SPEECH*.

Zhou Yu, Ziyu Xu, Alan W Black, and Alexander Rudnicky. 2016. Strategy and policy learning for non-task-oriented conversational systems. In *Proceedings of SIGDIAL*.

Xiangyang Zhou, Lu Li, Daxiang Dong, Yi Liu, Ying Chen, Wayne Xin Zhao, Dianhai Yu, and Hua Wu. 2018. Multi-turn response selection for chatbots with deep attention matching network. In *Proceedings of ACL*.

A   Appendix

Reddit

context/2	*Could someone there post a summary of the insightful moments.*
context/1	*Basically L2L is the new deep learning.*
context/0	*What's "L2L" mean?*
context	*"Learning to learn", using deep learning to design the architecture of another deep network: https://arxiv.org/abs/1606.04474*
response	*using deep learning with SGD to design the learning algorithms of another deep network **
context_author	*goodside*
response_author	*NetOrBrain*
subreddit	*MachineLearning*
thread_id★	*5h6yvl*

OpenSubtitles

context/9	*So what are we waiting for?*
context/8	*Nothing, it...*
context/7	*It's just if...*
context/6	*If we've underestimated the size of the artifact's data stream...*
context/5	*We'll fry the ship's CPU and we'll all spend the rest of our lives stranded in the Temporal Zone.*
context/4	*The ship's CPU has a name.*
context/3	*Sorry, Gideon.*
context/2	*Can we at least talk about this before you connect...*
context/1	*Gideon?*
context/0	*You still there?*
context	*Oh my God, we killed her.*
response	*Artificial intelligences cannot, by definition, be killed, Dr. Palmer.*
file_id★	*lines-emk*

AmazonQA

context	*i live in singapore so i would like to know what is the plug cos we use those 3 pin type*
response	*it's a 2 pin U.S. plug, but you can probably get an adapter , very good hair dryer!*
product_id★	*B003XNYHWS*

Figure 3: Examples from the three datasets. Each example is a mapping from feature names to string features. Features with a star ★ are used to compute the deterministic train/test split.

A Simple but Effective Method to Incorporate Multi-turn Context with BERT for Conversational Machine Comprehension

Yasuhito Ohsugi   **Itsumi Saito**   **Kyosuke Nishida**   **Hisako Asano**   **Junji Tomita**
NTT Media Intelligence Laboratories, NTT Corporation
`yasuhito.ohsugi.va@hco.ntt.co.jp`

Abstract

Conversational machine comprehension (CMC) requires understanding the context of multi-turn dialogue. Using BERT, a pre-training language model, has been successful for single-turn machine comprehension, while modeling multiple turns of question answering with BERT has not been established because BERT has a limit on the number and the length of input sequences. In this paper, we propose a simple but effective method with BERT for CMC. Our method uses BERT to encode a paragraph independently conditioned with each question and each answer in a multi-turn context. Then, the method predicts an answer on the basis of the paragraph representations encoded with BERT. The experiments with representative CMC datasets, QuAC and CoQA, show that our method outperformed recently published methods (+0.8 F1 on QuAC and +2.1 F1 on CoQA). In addition, we conducted a detailed analysis of the effects of the number and types of dialogue history on the accuracy of CMC, and we found that the gold answer history, which may not be given in an actual conversation, contributed to the model performance most on both datasets.

1 Introduction

Single-turn machine comprehension (MC) has been studied as a question answering method (Seo et al., 2016; Chen et al., 2017; Yu et al., 2018; Lewis and Fan, 2019). Conversational artificial intelligence (AI) such as Siri and Google Assistant requires answering not only a single-turn question but also multi-turn questions in a dialogue. Recently, two datasets, QuAC (Choi et al., 2018) and CoQA (Reddy et al., 2018), were released to answer sequential questions in a dialogue by comprehending a paragraph. This task is called conversational machine comprehension (CMC) (Huang et al., 2019), which requires understanding the context of multi-turn dialogue that consists of the question and answer history.

Learning machine comprehension models requires a lot of question answering data. Therefore, transfer learning from pre-training language models based on a large-scale unlabeled corpus is useful for improving the model accuracy. In particular, BERT (Devlin et al., 2018) achieved state-of-the-art results when performing various tasks including the single-turn machine comprehension dataset SQuAD (Rajpurkar et al., 2016). BERT takes a concatenation of two sequences as input during pre-training and can capture the relationship between the two sequences. When adapting BERT for MC, we use a question and a passage as input and fine-tune the pre-trained BERT model to extract an answer from the paragraph. However, BERT can accept only two sequences of 512 tokens and thus cannot handle CMC naively.

Zhu et al. (2018) proposed a method for CMC that is based on an architecture for single-turn MC and uses BERT as a feature-based approach. To convert CMC into a single-turn MC task, the method uses a reformulated question, which is the concatenation of the question and answer sequences in a multi-turn context with a special token. It then uses BERT to obtain contextualized embeddings for the reformulated question and paragraph, respectively. However, it cannot use BERT to capture the interaction between each sequence in the multi-turn context and the paragraph.

In this paper, we propose a simple but effective method for CMC based on a fine-tuning approach with BERT. Our method consists of two main steps. The first step is contextual encoding where BERT is used for independently obtaining paragraph representations conditioned with the current question, each of the previous questions, and each of the previous answers. The second step

Proceedings of the 1st Workshop on NLP for Conversational AI, pages 11–17
Florence, Italy, August 1, 2019. ©2019 Association for Computational Linguistics

is answer span extraction, where the start and end position of the current answer are predicted based on the concatenation of the paragraph representations encoded in the previous step.

The contributions of this paper are as follows:

- We propose a novel method for CMC based on fine-tuning BERT by regarding the sequences of the questions and the answers as independent inputs.

- The experimental results show that our method outperformed published methods on both QuAC and CoQA.

- We found that the gold answer history contributed to the model performance most by analyzing the effects of dialogue history.

2 Task Definition

In this paper, we define the CMC task as follows:

- **Input**: Current question Q_i, paragraph P, previous questions $\{Q_{i-1}, ..., Q_{i-k}\}$, and previous answers $\{A_{i-1}, ..., A_{i-k}\}$

- **Output**: Current answer A_i and type T_i

where i and k denote the turn index in the dialogue and the number of considered histories (turns), respectively. Answer A_i is a span of paragraph P. Type T_i is *SPAN*, *YES*, *NO*, or *UNANSWERABLE*.

3 Pre-trained Model

BERT is a powerful language representation model (Devlin et al., 2018), which is based on bi-directional Transformer encoder (Vaswani et al., 2017). BERT can obtain language representation by unsupervised pre-training with a huge data corpus and by supervised fine-tuning, and it can achieve outstanding results in various NLP tasks such as sentence pair classification, single sentence tagging, and single-turn machine comprehension.

Here, we explain how to adapt BERT for single-turn machine comprehension tasks such as SQuAD (Rajpurkar et al., 2016). In SQuAD, a question and a paragraph containing the answer are given, and the task is to predict the answer text span in the paragraph. In the case of using BERT for SQuAD, after the special classification token [CLS] is added in front of the question, the question and the paragraph are concatenated with

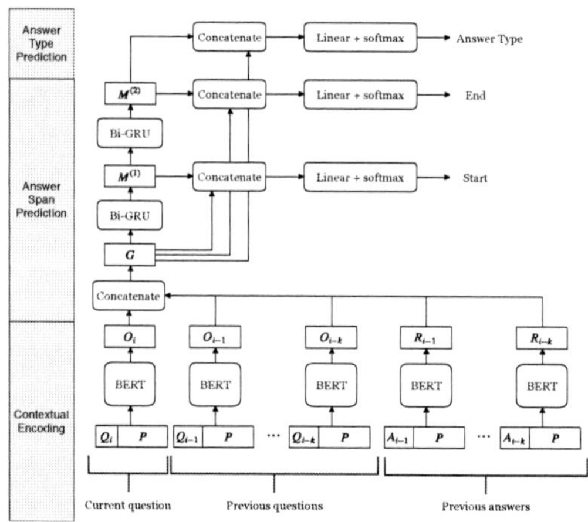

Figure 1: Our model

special tokens [SEP] into one sequence. The sequence is inputted to BERT with segment embeddings and positional embeddings. Then, the final hidden state of BERT is converted to the probabilities of answer span by a linear layer and softmax function. The fined-tuned BERT for the SQuAD dataset can capture the relationship between one question and one paragraph so that BERT achieved state-of-the-art performance on the SQuAD. However, BERT itself cannot be used for a task requiring multiple queries or multiple paragraphs, because BERT can accept only two segments in one input sequence. This limitation can be a problem for the CMC task because there are multi-turn questions about the same paragraph.

4 Proposed Method

In the CMC task, it is necessary to consider not only the current question Q_i but also the question history $\{Q_{i-1}, ..., Q_{i-k}\}$ and the answer history $\{A_{i-1}, ..., A_{i-k}\}$. We propose a method of modeling the current question, question history, and answer history by using BERT (Figure 1). Our method consists of two steps: contextual encoding and answer span prediction. On top of that, answer type is predicted only in the case of CoQA (see Section 4.3).

4.1 Contextual Encoding

In this step, we use BERT to encode not only the relationship between the current question and the paragraph but also the relationship between the history and the paragraph. We define the method of extracting features by using BERT as follows,

$$z = f(\text{BERT}(x, y|\theta)), \tag{1}$$

where x, y, and z denote the input query sequence, input paragraph sequence, and output feature, respectively. The function $\text{BERT}(\cdot)$ outputs BERT's d-dimensional final hidden states with parameters θ, and the function $f(\cdot)$ extracts features corresponding to the segment of the paragraph in the final hidden states. Namely, if input paragraph text y has T tokens, then, $z \in \mathbb{R}^{d \times T}$. This step consists of three parts, and each part shares the BERT parameters θ. First, we encode the current question as follows,

$$O_i = f(\text{BERT}(Q_i, P|\theta)). \tag{2}$$

Second, we encode the question history $\{Q_{i-1}, ..., Q_{i-k}\}$ in the same manner.

$$O_{i-l} = f(\text{BERT}(Q_{i-l}, P|\theta)), \tag{3}$$

where l denotes the index of the previous context. Last, we encode the answer history $\{A_{i-1}, ..., A_{i-k}\}$. Note that previous answer A_{i-l} is given as text, even if the current answer is predicted as the span of the paragraph. The encoded feature can be obtained as follows,

$$R_{i-l} = f(\text{BERT}(A_{i-l}, P|\theta)). \tag{4}$$

4.2 Answer Span Prediction

In this step, the current answer span is predicted. Let s_i and e_i represent the start index and the end index, respectively. First, the output features of the previous step are concatenated as follows,

$$G = [O_i; O_{i-1}; ...; O_{i-k}; R_{i-1}; ...; R_{i-k}], \tag{5}$$

where $[;]$ is vector concatenation across row and $G \in \mathbb{R}^{(2k+1)d \times T}$. Then, G is passed to BiGRU over tokens and converted to $M^{(1)} \in \mathbb{R}^{2d \times T}$. To predict the start index s_i, the probability distribution is calculated by,

$$p^{\text{s}} = \text{softmax}\left(w_1^\top [G; M^{(1)}] + b_1\right), \tag{6}$$

where w_1 and $b_1 \in \mathbb{R}^{(2k+3)d}$ are trainable vectors. Next, to predict the end index e_i, $M^{(1)}$ is passed to another BiGRU over tokens and converted to $M^{(2)} \in \mathbb{R}^{2d \times T}$. Then, the probability distribution is calculated by

$$p^{\text{e}} = \text{softmax}\left(w_2^\top [G; M^{(2)}] + b_2\right), \tag{7}$$

where w_2 and $b_2 \in \mathbb{R}^{(2k+3)d}$ are trainable vectors.

4.3 Answer Type Prediction

Some questions should be simply answered as "yes" or "no" and not answered as a rationale text. To address these questions, the probability of the answer type is calculated as follows,

$$p^{\text{ans}} = \left[\text{softmax}\left(w_3^\top [G; M^{(2)}] + b_3\right)\right]_{e_i}, \tag{8}$$

where w_3 and $b_3 \in \mathbb{R}^{(2k+3)d}$ are trainable vectors and e_i is the end index of the predicted span.

4.4 Fine-tuning and Inference

In the fine-tuning phase, we regard the sum of the negative log likelihood of the true start and end indices as training loss,

$$L = -\frac{1}{N} \sum_{l=1}^{N} \left[\log(p_{y_l^1}^{\text{s}}) + \log(p_{y_l^2}^{\text{e}})\right], \tag{9}$$

where N, y_l^1, and y_l^2 denote the number of examples, true start, and true end indices of the l-th example, respectively. If answer type prediction is necessary, we add the cross entropy loss of the answer type to the training loss. In the inference phase, the answer span (s_i, e_i) is calculated by dynamic programming, where the values of p^{s} and p^{e} are maximum and $1 \leq s_i \leq e_i \leq T$.

5 Experiment

In this section, we evaluate our method on two conversational machine comprehension datasets, QuAC (Choi et al., 2018) and CoQA (Reddy et al., 2018).

5.1 Datasets and Evaluation Metrics

Although CoQA is released as an abstractive CMC dataset, Yatskar (2018) shows that the extractive approach is also effective for CoQA. Thus, we also use our extractive approach on CoQA. To handle answer types in CoQA, we predict the probability distribution of the answer type (*SPAN, YES, NO, and UNANSWERABLE*) and replace the predicted span with "yes", "no", or "unknown" tokens except for the "SPAN" answer type. In QuAC, the unanswerable questions are handled as an answer span (P contains a special token), and the type prediction for yes/no questions is not evaluated on the leaderboard. Therefore, we skip the answer type prediction step.

13

	In-domain					Out-of-domain		In-domain	Out-of-domain	
	Child.	Liter.	Mid-High.	News	Wiki	Reddit	Science	overall	overall	Overall
DrQA + PGNet	64.2	63.7	67.1	68.3	71.4	57.8	63.1	67.0	60.4	65.1
BiDAF++ (3-ctx)	66.5	65.7	70.2	71.6	72.6	60.8	67.1	69.4	63.8	67.8
FlowQA (1-ans)	73.7	71.6	76.8	79.0	80.2	67.8	76.1	76.3	71.8	75.0
SDNet (single)	75.4	73.9	77.1	80.3	**83.1**	69.8	76.8	78.0	73.1	76.6
BERT w/ 2-ctx	**76.0**	**77.0**	**80.5**	**82.1**	83.0	**72.5**	**79.6**	**79.8**	**75.9**	**78.7**
ConvBERT (single)	-	-	-	-	-	-	-	87.7	84.6	86.8
Google SQuAD 2.0 + MMFT (single)	-	-	-	-	-	-	-	88.5	86.0	87.8

Table 1: The results on the CoQA test set of single models (F_1 score). Our BERT w/ 2-ctx model ranked 13th among all unpublished and published models (including ensemble) on the leaderboard at the submission time (April 13, 2019). The ConvBERT and the Google SQuAD 2.0 + MMFT are the current state-of-the-art models, but they are unpublished.

As evaluation metrics for CoQA, we use the F_1 score. CoQA contains seven domains as paragraph contents: childrens stories, literature, middle and high school English exams, news articles, Wikipedia articles, science articles, and Reddit articles. We report F_1 for each domain and the overall domains. On the other hand, as evaluation metrics of QuAC, we use not only F_1 but also the human equivalence score for questions (HEQ-Q) and for dialogues (HEQ-D) (Choi et al., 2018). HEQ-Q represents the percentage of exceeding the model performance over the human evaluation for each question, and HEQ-D represents the percentage of exceeding the model performance over the human evaluation for each dialogue.

5.2 Comparison Systems

We compare our model (BERT w/ k-ctx) with the baseline models and published models. For QuAC, we use the reported scores of BiDAF++ w/ k-ctx (Choi et al., 2018) and FlowQA (Huang et al., 2019). For CoQA, the comparison system is DrQA+PGNet (Reddy et al., 2018), BiDAF++ w/ x-ctx, FlowQA, and SDNet (Zhu et al., 2018). Note that the scores of BiDAF++ w/ x-ctx on CoQA are reported by Yatskar (2018). In addition, we use gold answers as the answer history, except for the investigation of the effect of answer history. More information on our implementation is available in Appendix A.

5.3 Results

Does our model outperform published models on both QuAC and CoQA? Table 1 and Table 2 show the results on CoQA and QuAC, respectively. On CoQA, our model outperformed all of the published models regarding the overall F_1 score. Although our model was compa-

	F_1	HEQ-Q	HEQ-D
BiDAF++ (2-ctx)	60.1	54.8	4.0
FlowQA (2-ans)	64.1	59.6	5.8
BERT w/ 2-ctx	**64.9**	**60.2**	**6.1**
ConvBERT (single)	68.0	63.5	9.1
Bert-FlowDelta (single)	67.8	63.6	12.1

Table 2: The results on the QuAC test set of single models. Our BERT w/ 2-ctx model ranked 1st among all unpublished and published models on the leaderboard at the submission time (March 7, 2019). The ConvBERT and Bert-FlowDelta are the current state-of-the-art models, but they are unpublished.

	# contexts	CoQA	QuAC
BERT w/ 0-ctx	0	72.8	55.0
BERT w/ 1-ctx	1	79.2	63.4
BERT w/ 2-ctx	2	79.6	**65.4**
BERT w/ 3-ctx	3	79.6	65.3
BERT w/ 4-ctx	4	79.4	64.8
BERT w/ 5-ctx	5	**79.7**	64.5
BERT w/ 6-ctx	6	79.5	64.9
BERT w/ 7-ctx	7	**79.7**	64.4

Table 3: The results with the number of previous contexts on the development set of QuAC and CoQA (F_1 score)

rable with SDNet for the Wikipedia domain, our model outperformed SDNet for the other domains. On QuAC, our model also obtained the best score among the published models for all of the metrics and obtained state-of-the-art scores on March 7th, 2019.

Our method uses the paragraph representations independently conditioned with each question and each answer. This model structure is suitable for the pre-trained BERT, which was trained with two input segments. Therefore, our model was able to capture the interaction between a dialogue history and a paragraph, and it achieved high accuracy.

	CoQA	QuAC
BERT w/ 0-ctx	72.8	55.0
BERT w/ 2-ctx (gold ans.)	**79.6**	**65.4**
w/o question history	78.0	64.7
w/o answer history	77.7	59.3
BERT w/ 2-ctx (predicted ans.)	77.2	56.7

Table 4: Ablation study on the development set of QuAC and CoQA (F_1 score)

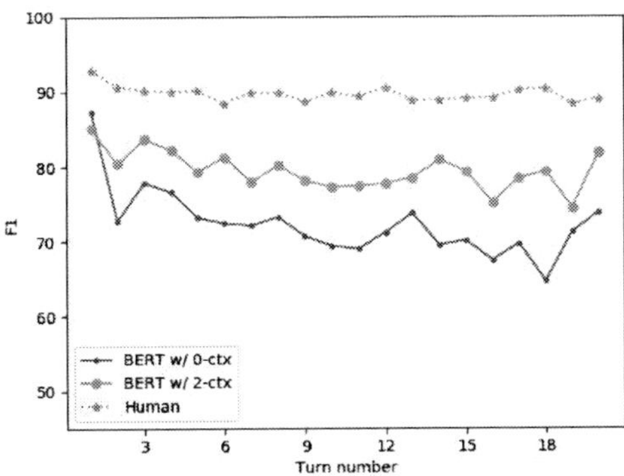

Figure 2: The F_1 scores with turn number on CoQA development set

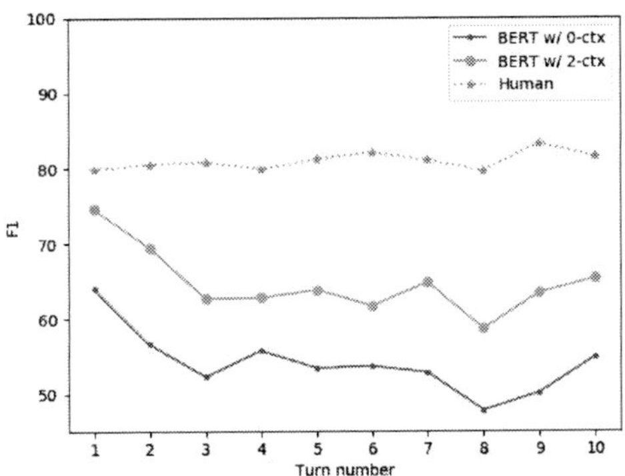

Figure 3: The F_1 scores with turn number on QuAC development set

Does our model improve the performance when the number of previous contexts increases? Table 3 shows the results with the number of previous contexts. On both of the datasets, it was effective to use previous contexts. However, on CoQA, the number of contexts had little effect on the score even if the long context was considered. On QuAC, the best score was obtained in the case of using two contexts, and the score decreased with more than two contexts. As Yatskar (2018) mentioned, the topics in a dialogue shift more frequently on QuAC than on CoQA. Thus, the previous context on QuAC can include the context that is unrelated to the current question, and this unrelated context can decrease the score. This result suggests that it is important to select context that is related to the current question and not use the whole context in any cases.

Which is more important, the question history or the answer history? Table 4 shows the contribution of the dialogue history. We can see from the results that the model performance decreased significantly when we removed the gold answer history on QuAC. In dataset collection, CoQA allows the asker to see the evidence paragraph. On the other hand, the asker in QuAC cannot see the evidence paragraph. As a result, questions in QuAC are far from the phrases in the passage and are less effective in improving the model performance. For CoQA, the model could substitute the question history for the gold answer history. The model performance did not decrease significantly when we remove the answer history.

Does our model maintain the performance when using the predicted answer history? In actual conversation, the gold answer history may not be given in the CMC model. In this experiment, we trained the models with the gold answer history and evaluated the model with the predicted answer history.

As shown in Table 4, when using the predicted answer history, the model performance decreased significantly on QuAC. This result also suggests that the model can substitute the question history for the gold answer history in CoQA. We think the CMC setting where the history of questions posed by an asker that does not see the evidence paragraph is given and the gold answer is not given for input is a more realistic and important setting.

Does our model performance approach human performance as the dialogue progresses? We calculated F_1 scores over the turns, where the data in each turn contained more than 100 question/answer pairs. Figure 2 and Figure 3 show that the score was lower than human performance over all turns on both datasets and that the score with context was higher than that without context on both datasets, except for the first question on CoQA. This result indicates that there is still room for improvement with long turn questions.

6 Related Work

QuAC (Choi et al., 2018) and CoQA (Reddy et al., 2018) were released as the CMC dataset. On QuAC, the answers are extracted from source paragraph as spans. On CoQA, the answers are free texts based on span texts extracted from the source paragraph. On these datasets, the baseline models were based on conventional models for single-turn machine comprehension such as BiDAF (Seo et al., 2016) and DrQA (Chen et al., 2017). For QuAC, Choi et al. (2018) extended BiDAF (an extractive machine comprehension model) to BiDAF++ w/ x-ctx by concatenating word embeddings of the source paragraph and embeddings of previous answer span indexes. For CoQA, Reddy et al. (2018) proposed DrQA+PGNet as an abstractive method by concatenating previous questions and previous answers with special tokens. However, most of the recently published methods about CoQA were extractive approaches, since the abstractive answers on CoQA are based on span texts in the paragraph and Yatskar (2018) shows that the extractive approach is also effective for CoQA. Huang et al. (2019) proposed FlowQA for both QuAC and CoQA by stacking bidirectional recurrent neural networks (RNNs) over the words of the source paragraph and unidirectional RNNs over the conversational turns. Zhu et al. (2018) proposed SDNet for CoQA by regarding the concatenation of previous questions and answers as one query.

Most recently, BERT (Devlin et al., 2018) was proposed as a contextualized language representation that is pre-trained on huge unlabeled datasets. By fine-tuning a supervised dataset, BERT obtained state-of-the-art scores on various tasks including single-turn machine reading comprehension datasets such as SQuAD (Rajpurkar et al., 2016). Since the relationship between words can be captured in advance, pre-training approaches such as BERT and GPT-2 (Radford et al., 2019) can be useful especially for tasks with a small amount of supervised data. For QuAC and CoQA, many approaches on the leaderboard[1,2] use BERT, including SDNet. However, SDNet uses BERT as contextualized word embedding without updating the BERT parameters. This is one of the differences between SDNet and our model.

---

¹ https://quac.ai/
² https://stanfordnlp.github.io/coqa/

7 Conclusion

In this paper, we propose a simple but effective method based on a fine-tuning approach with BERT for a conversational machine comprehension (CMC) task. Our method uses questions and answers simply as the input of BERT to model the interaction between the paragraph and each dialogue history independently and outperformed published models on both QuAC and CoQA.

From detailed analysis, we found that the gold answer history, which may not be given in real conversational situations, contributed to the model performance most on both datasets. We also found that the model performance on QuAC decreased significantly when we used predicted answers instead of gold answers. On the other hand, we can substitute the question history for the gold answer history on CoQA. For future work, we will investigate a more realistic and more difficult CMC setting, where the history of questions posed by the asker that does not see the evidence paragraph is given and the gold answer is not given for input. We will also investigate how to obtain related and effective context for the current question in the previous question and answer history.

References

Danqi Chen, Adam Fisch, Jason Weston, and Antoine Bordes. 2017. Reading wikipedia to answer open-domain questions. In *Proceedings of the 55th Annual Meeting of the Association for Computational Linguistics (Volume 1: Long Papers)*, pages 1870–1879, Vancouver, Canada. Association for Computational Linguistics.

Eunsol Choi, He He, Mohit Iyyer, Mark Yatskar, Wen-tau Yih, Yejin Choi, Percy Liang, and Luke Zettlemoyer. 2018. Quac: Question answering in context. In *Proceedings of the 2018 Conference on Empirical Methods in Natural Language Processing*, pages 2174–2184. Association for Computational Linguistics.

Jacob Devlin, Ming-Wei Chang, Kenton Lee, and Kristina Toutanova. 2018. BERT: pre-training of deep bidirectional transformers for language understanding. *CoRR*, abs/1810.04805.

Hsin-Yuan Huang, Eunsol Choi, and Wen tau Yih. 2019. FlowQA: Grasping flow in history for conversational machine comprehension. In *International Conference on Learning Representations*.

Diederik P. Kingma and Jimmy Ba. 2015. Adam: A method for stochastic optimization. In *3rd International Conference on Learning Representations*,

ICLR 2015, San Diego, CA, USA, May 7-9, 2015, Conference Track Proceedings.

Mike Lewis and Angela Fan. 2019. Generative question answering: Learning to answer the whole question. In *International Conference on Learning Representations*.

Alec Radford, Jeff Wu, Rewon Child, David Luan, Dario Amodei, and Ilya Sutskever. 2019. Language models are unsupervised multitask learners.

Pranav Rajpurkar, Jian Zhang, Konstantin Lopyrev, and Percy Liang. 2016. Squad: 100,000+ questions for machine comprehension of text. In *Proceedings of the 2016 Conference on Empirical Methods in Natural Language Processing*, pages 2383–2392. Association for Computational Linguistics.

Siva Reddy, Danqi Chen, and Christopher D. Manning. 2018. Coqa: A conversational question answering challenge. *CoRR*, abs/1808.07042.

Min Joon Seo, Aniruddha Kembhavi, Ali Farhadi, and Hannaneh Hajishirzi. 2016. Bidirectional attention flow for machine comprehension. *CoRR*, abs/1611.01603.

Ashish Vaswani, Noam Shazeer, Niki Parmar, Jakob Uszkoreit, Llion Jones, Aidan N Gomez, Ł ukasz Kaiser, and Illia Polosukhin. 2017. Attention is all you need. In I. Guyon, U. V. Luxburg, S. Bengio, H. Wallach, R. Fergus, S. Vishwanathan, and R. Garnett, editors, *Advances in Neural Information Processing Systems 30*, pages 5998–6008. Curran Associates, Inc.

Mark Yatskar. 2018. A qualitative comparison of coqa, squad 2.0 and quac. *CoRR*, abs/1809.10735.

Adams Wei Yu, David Dohan, Quoc Le, Thang Luong, Rui Zhao, and Kai Chen. 2018. Fast and accurate reading comprehension by combining self-attention and convolution. In *International Conference on Learning Representations*.

Chenguang Zhu, Michael Zeng, and Xuedong Huang. 2018. Sdnet: Contextualized attention-based deep network for conversational question answering. *CoRR*, abs/1812.03593.

A Implementation Details

We used the BERT-base-uncased model implemented by PyTorch [3]. We used a maximum sequence length of 384, document stride of 128, maximum query length of 64, and maximum answer length of 30. The optimizer was Adam (Kingma and Ba, 2015) with a learning rate of 3e-5, $\beta_1 = 0.9$, $\beta_2 = 0.999$, L2 weight decay of 0.01, learning rate warmup over the first 10 % of training steps, and linear decay of the learning rate. The number of training epochs was 2. The batch size of training was 8 or 12. In the case of QuAC, we used dialogs whose paragraphs have under 5,000 characters. In the case of CoQA, we followed Huang et al. (2019) and regarded a span with maximum F_1 overlap with respect to given abstractive answers as gold answers during training. We used four NVIDIA Tesla V100 32GB GPUs.

---

[3] `https://github.com/huggingface/pytorch-pretrained-BERT`

Augmenting Neural Response Generation with Context-Aware Topical Attention

Nouha Dziri   **Ehsan Kamalloo**   **Kory W. Mathewson**   **Osmar Zaiane**

Department of Computing Science
University of Alberta
{dziri,kamalloo,korym,zaiane}@cs.ualberta.ca

Abstract

Sequence-to-Sequence (Seq2Seq) models have witnessed a notable success in generating natural conversational exchanges. Notwithstanding the syntactically well-formed responses generated by these neural network models, they are prone to be acontextual, short and generic. In this work, we introduce a Topical Hierarchical Recurrent Encoder Decoder (THRED), a novel, fully data-driven, multi-turn response generation system intended to produce contextual and topic-aware responses. Our model is built upon the basic Seq2Seq model by augmenting it with a hierarchical joint attention mechanism that incorporates topical concepts and previous interactions into the response generation. To train our model, we provide a clean and high-quality conversational dataset mined from Reddit comments. We evaluate THRED on two novel automated metrics, dubbed Semantic Similarity and Response Echo Index, as well as with human evaluation. Our experiments demonstrate that the proposed model is able to generate more diverse and contextually relevant responses compared to the strong baselines.

1   Introduction

With the recent success of deep neural networks in natural language processing tasks such as machine translation (Sutskever et al., 2014) and language modeling (Mikolov et al., 2010), there has been growing research interest in building data-driven dialogue systems. Fortunately, innovation in deep learning architectures and the availability of large public datasets have produced fertile ground for the data-driven approaches to become feasible and quite promising. In particular, the Sequence-to-Sequence (Seq2Seq) neural network model (Sutskever et al., 2014) has witnessed substantial breakthroughs in improving the perfor-

mance of conversational agents. Such a model succeeds in learning the backbone of the conversation but lacks any aptitude for producing context-sensitive and diverse conversations. Instead, generated responses are dull, short and carry little information (Li et al., 2016a). Instinctively, humans tend to adapt conversations to their interlocutor not only by looking at the last utterance but also by considering information and concepts covered in the conversation history (Danescu-Niculescu-Mizil and Lee, 2011). Such adaptation increase the smoothness and engagement of the generated responses. We speculate that incorporating conversation history and topic information with our novel model and method will improve generated conversational responses. In this work, we introduce a novel, fully data-driven, multi-turn response generation system intended to produce context-aware and diverse responses. Our model builds upon the basic Seq2Seq model by combining conversational data and external knowledge information trained through a hierarchical joint attention neural model. We find that our method leads to both diverse and contextual responses compared to the literature strong baselines. We also introduce two novel quantitative metrics for dialogue model development, dubbed Semantic Similarity and Response Echo Index. While the former measures the capability of the model to be consistent with the context and to maintain the topic of the conversation, the latter assesses how much our approach is able to generate unique and plausible responses which are measurably distant from the input dataset. Used together, they provide a means to reduce burden of human evaluation and allow rapid testing of dialogue models. We show that such metrics correlate well with human judgment, making a step towards a good automatic evaluation procedure.

The key contributions of this work are:

18

Proceedings of the 1st Workshop on NLP for Conversational AI, pages 18–31
Florence, Italy, August 1, 2019. ©2019 Association for Computational Linguistics

- We devise a fully data-driven neural conversational model that leverages conversation history and topic information in the response generation process through a hierarchical joint attention mechanism; making the dialogue more diverse and engaging.

- We introduce two novel automated metrics: Semantic Similarity and Response Echo Index and we show that they correlate well with human judgment.

- We collect, parse and clean a conversational dataset from Reddit comments[1].

2   Related Work

Neural generative models have been improved through several techniques. (Serban et al., 2016) built upon the Seq2Seq work by introducing a Hierarchical Recurrent Encoder-Decoder neural network (HRED) that accounts for the conversation history. (Li et al., 2016b) used deep reinforcement learning to generate highly-rewarded responses by considering three dialogue properties: ease of answering, informativeness and coherence. (Zhang et al., 2018) addressed the challenge of personalizing the chatbot by modeling human-like behaviour. They presented a persona-based model that aims to handle the speaker consistency by integrating a speaker profile vector representation into the the Seq2Seq model. (Xing et al., 2017) used a similar idea but added an extra probability value in the decoder to bias the overall distribution towards leveraging topic words in the generated responses. Their architecture does not focus on capturing conversation history. All of these improvements are motivated by the scarcity of diversity and informativeness of the responses. Our work follows on from these works with the additional aim of generating context-aware responses by using a hierarchical joint attention model. An important line of research that we also address in this work is automatically evaluating the quality of dialogue responses. In dialogue systems, automated metrics tend to be borrowed from other NLP tasks such as BLEU (Papineni et al., 2002) from machine translation and ROUGE (Lin, 2004) from text summarization. Yet, such metrics fail, mainly because they are focusing on the word-level overlap between the machine-generated answer and the human-generated answer, which can be inconsistent with what humans deem a plausible and interesting response. (Liu et al., 2016) have showed that these metrics correlate very weakly with human evaluation. Indeed, word-overlapping metrics achieve best results when the space of responses is small and lexically overlapping which is not the case for dialogue systems responses. Significant works have looked into this challenge. Examples include ADEM (Lowe et al., 2017), an evaluation model that learns to score responses from an annotated dataset of human responses scores. (Venkatesh et al., 2018) proposed a number of metrics based on user experience, coherence, and topical diversity and have showed that these metrics can be used as a proxy for human evaluation. However, engagement and coherence metrics are estimated via recruiting evaluators. In this work, we propose directly calculable approximations of human evaluation grounded in conversational theories of accommodation and affordance (Danescu-Niculescu-Mizil and Lee, 2011).

3   Topical Hierarchical Recurrent Encoder Decoder

Topical Hierarchical Recurrent Encoder Decoder (THRED) can be viewed as a hybrid model that conditions the response generation on conversation history captured from previous utterances and on topic words acquired from a Latent Dirichlet Allocation (LDA) model (Blei et al., 2003). The proposed approach extends the standard Seq2Seq model by leveraging topic words in the process of response generation and accounting for conversation history. Figure 1 illustrates our model. We detail below the components of our model.

3.1   Message Encoder

Let a sequence of N utterances within a dialogue $D = \{U_1, ..., U_N\}$. Every utterance $U_i = \{w_{i,1}, ..., w_{i,L_i}\}$ contains a random variable L_i of sequence of words where $w_{i,k}$ represents the word embedding vector at position k in the utterance U_i. The message encoder sequentially accepts the embedding of each word in the input message U_i and updates its hidden state at every time step t by a bidirectional GRU-RNN (Cho et al., 2014) according to:

$$h_{i,t} = GRU(h_{i,t-1}, w_{i,t}), \forall t \in \{1, \ldots, L_i\} \quad (1)$$

where $h_{i,t-1}$ represents the previous hidden state.

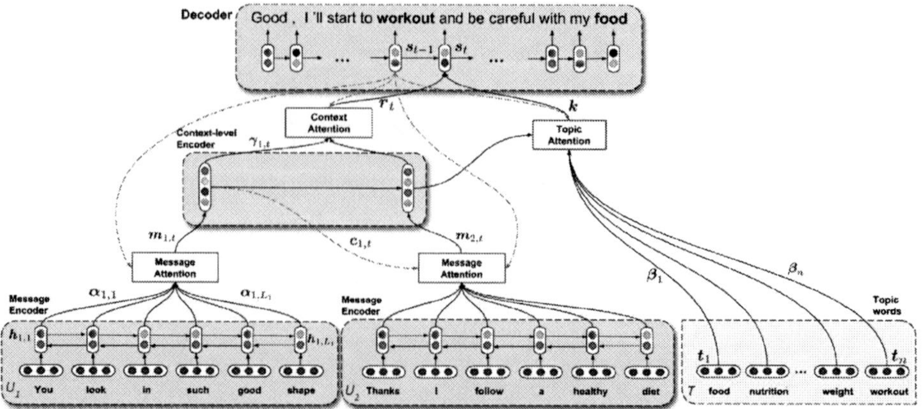

Figure 1: THRED model architecture in which we jointly model two specifications that presumably make the task of response generation successful: context-awareness (modeled by **Context Attention**) and diversity (modeled by **Topic Attention**).

3.2 Message Attention

Different parts of the conversation history have distinct levels of importance that may influence the response generation process. The message attention in THRED operates by putting more focus on the salient input words with regard to the output. It computes, at step t, a weight value $\alpha_{i,j,t}$ for every encoder hidden state $h_{i,j}$ and linearly combines them to form a vector $m_{i,t}$ according to Bahdanau attention mechanism (Bahdanau et al., 2015). Formally, $m_{i,t}$ is calculated as:

$$m_{i,t} = \sum_{j=1}^{L_i} \alpha_{i,j,t}\, h_{i,j}, \ \forall i \in \{1, \ldots, N\} \quad (2)$$

where $\alpha_{i,j,t}$ is computed as:

$$\alpha_{i,j,t} = \frac{\exp(e_{i,j,t})}{\sum_{k=1}^{L_i} \exp(e_{i,k,t})} \ ;$$

$$e_{i,j,t} = \eta(s_{t-1}, h_{i,j}, c_{i-1,t})$$

where s_{t-1} represents the hidden state of the decoder (further details are provided later), $c_{i,t}$ delineates the hidden state of the context-level encoder (computed in Equation (3)) , η is a multi-layer perceptron having tanh as activation function. Unlike the Bahdanau attention mechanism, the attentional vector $m_{i,t}$ is based on both the hidden states of the decoder and the hidden states of the context-level encoder. We are motivated by the fact that $c_{i,t}$ may carry important information that could be missing in s_{t-1}. In summary, the attentional vector $m_{i,t}$ is an order-sensitive information of all the words in the sentence, attending to more important words in the input messages.

3.3 Context-Level Encoder

The context-level encoder takes as input each utterance representation $(m_{1,t}, \ldots, m_{N,t})$ and calculates the sequence of recurrent hidden states as shown in Equation (3):

$$c_{i,t} = GRU(c_{i-1,t}, m_{i,t}), \forall i \in \{1, \ldots, N\} \quad (3)$$

where $c_{i-1,t}$ delineates the previous hidden state of the context-level encoder and N represents the number of utterances in the conversation history. The resulted $c_{i,t}$ vector summarizes all past information that have been processed up to position i.

3.4 Context-Topic Joint Attention

Context Attention: On top of the context-level encoder, a context attention is added to attend to important utterances in the conversation history. Precisely, the context attention assigns weights $(\gamma_{1,t}, ..., \gamma_{N,t})$ to $(c_{1,t}, ..., c_{N,t})$ and forms a vector r_t as

$$r_t = \sum_{j=1}^{N} \gamma_{j,t} c_{j,t} \quad (4)$$

where:

$$\gamma_{j,t} = \frac{\exp(e'_{j,t})}{\sum_{i=1}^{N} \exp(e'_{i,t})} \ ; \quad (5)$$

$$e'_{i,t} = \eta(s_{t-1}, c_{i,t})$$

Topic Attention: In order to infuse the response with information relevant to the input messages, we enhance the model with topic information. We assign a topic T to the conversation context using a pre-trained LDA model (Hoffman et al., 2010). LDA is a probabilistic topic model

20

that appoints multiple topics for the dialogue history. The LDA parameters were estimated using the collapsed Gibbs sampling algorithm (Zhao et al., 2011). We provide further details on how we train this model in the supplementary material. In our case, the conversation history is a short document, so we believe that the most probable topic will be sufficient to model the dialogue. After acquiring topic words for the entire history, we pick the n highest probable words under T (we choose $n = 100$ in our experiments). The topic words $\{t_1, \cdots, t_n\}$ are then linearly combined to form a fixed-length vector k. The weight values are calculated as the following:

$$\beta_{i,t} = \frac{\exp(\eta(s_{t-1}, t_i, c_{N,t}))}{\sum_{j=1}^{n} \exp(\eta(s_{t-1}, t_j, c_{N,t}))} \qquad (6)$$

where $i \in \{1, \cdots, n\}$, $c_{N,t}$ is the last hidden state of the context-level encoder, and s_{t-1} is the $t-1^{th}$ hidden state in the decoder. The topic attention uses additionally the last hidden state of the context-level encoder $c_{N,t}$ in order to diminish the repercussion of impertinent topic words and feature the relevant ones to the message. Unlike (Xing et al., 2017), our model employs the final context-level encoder hidden state $c_{N,t}$ in order to account for conversation history in the generated response. In summary, the topic words are summarized as a topic vector k representing prior knowledge for response generation. The key idea of this approach is to affect the generation process by avoiding the need to learn the same conversational pattern for each utterance but instead enriching the responses with topics and words related to the subject of the message even if the words were never used before.

3.5 Decoder

The decoder is responsible for predicting the response utterance U_{m+1} given the previous utterances and the topic words. Following (Xing et al., 2017), we biased the generation probability towards generating the topic words in the response. In particular, we added an extra probability to the standard generation probability, enforcing the model to account for the topical tokens. Consequently, the generation probability is defined as the following:

$$p(w_i) = p_V(w_i) + p_K(w_i) \qquad (7)$$

where K and V represent respectively topic vocabulary and response vocabulary; p_V and p_K are defined as follows:

$$p_V(w_i) = \frac{1}{M} \exp(\sigma_V(s_i, w_{i-1}))$$

$$p_K(w_i) = \frac{1}{M} \exp(\sigma_K(s_i, w_{i-1}, r_i))$$

where $s_i = GRU(w_{i-1}, s_{i-1}, r_i, k)$, σ is a tanh and M is calculated as follows:

$$M = \sum_{v \in V} \exp\left(\sigma_V(s_i, w_{i-1})\right)$$
$$+ \sum_{v' \in K} \exp\left(\sigma_K(s_i, w_{i-1}, r_i)\right)$$

4 Datasets

One of the main weaknesses of dialogue systems is caused by the paucity of high-quality conversational dataset. The well-known OpenSubtitles dataset (Tiedemann, 2012) lacks speaker annotations, thus making it more difficult to train conversation systems which demand high quality speaker and conversation level tags. Therefore, the assumption of treating consecutive utterances as turn exchanges uttered by two persons (Vinyals and Le, 2015) could not be viable. To enable the study of high-quality and large-scale dataset for dialogue modeling, we have collected a corpus of 35M conversations drawn from the Reddit data[2], where each dialogue is composed of three turn exchanges. The Reddit dataset is composed of posts and comments, where each comment is annotated with rich meta data (i.e., author, number of replies, user's comment karma, etc.)[3]. To harvest the dataset, we curated 95 English subreddits out of roughly 1.1M public subreddits[4]. Our choice was based on the top-ranked subreddits that discuss topics such as news, education, business, politics and sports. We processed Reddit for a 12 month-period ranging from December 2016 until December 2017. For each post, we retrieved all comments and we recursively followed the chain of replies of each comment to recover the entire conversation. Reddit dataset is often semantically well-structured and is not filled with spelling errors thanks to moderator's efforts. Therefore, we do not perform any spelling correction procedure. Due to resource limitations, we randomly sampled 6M dialogues as training data, 700K dialogues as development data, and 40K dialogues as test data.

---

[2]https://files.pushshift.io/reddit/
[3]https://github.com/reddit-archive/
reddit/wiki/JSON
[4]As of February 2019

21

For OpenSubtitles, we trained the models on the same size of data as for Reddit.

5 Experiments

In this section, we focus on the task of evaluating the next utterance given the conversation history. We compare THRED against three open-source baselines, namely Standard Seq2Seq with attention mechanism (Bahdanau et al., 2015), HRED (Serban et al., 2016), and Topic-Aware (TA) Seq2Seq (Xing et al., 2017). As done in (Li et al., 2016b), for Standard Seq2Seq and TA-Seq2Seq, we concatenate the dialogue history to account for context in a multi-turn conversation. All experiments are conducted on two datasets (i.e., Reddit and OpenSubtitles). We report results on OpenSubtitles in the supplementary material.

5.1 Quantitative Evaluation

In the following subsections, we introduce two metrics that can impartially evaluate THRED and compare against the different baselines. These metrics were tested on 5000 dialogues randomly sampled from the test dataset. It is worth mentioning that we present word perplexity (PPL) on the test data in Table 4 (along with diversity metric). However, we do not believe that it represents a good measure for assessing the quality of responses (Serban et al., 2017). This is because perplexity captures how likely the responses are under a generation probability distribution, and does not measure the degree of diversity and engagingness in the responses.

5.2 Semantic Similarity

A good dialogue system should be capable of sustaining a coherent conversation with a human by staying on topic and by following a train of thoughts (Venkatesh et al., 2018). Semantic Similarity (SS) metric estimates the correspondence between the utterances in the context and the generated response. The intuition behind this metric is that plausible responses should be consistent with the context and should maintain the topic of the conversation. Our response generator THRED along with the baselines generate an utterance based on the two previous utterances in the dialogue (i.e., Utt1 and Utt2). We compute the cosine distance between the embedding vectors of the test utterances (Utt.1 and Utt.2) and the generated responses from the different models (i.e., THRED,

TA-Seq2Seq, HRED and Seq2Seq). Therefore, a low score denotes a high coherence. More precisely, for each triple in the test dataset, we test two scenarios: (1) we compute the SS of each generated response with respect to the most recent utterance in the conversation (Utt.2) and (2) we compute the SS of each generated response with respect to the second most recent utterance (Utt.1). To render the semantic representation of an utterance, we leverage Universal Sentence Encoder (Cer et al., 2018) wherein a sentence is projected to a fixed dimensional embedding vector.

However, dull and generic responses such as *"i'm not sure"* tend to be semantically close to many utterances, hindering the effectiveness of the metric. To cope with this negative effect, we manually compiled a set of 60 dull responses and computed the SS score by multiplying the cosine distance with the following penalty factor (akin to length penalty in (Wu et al., 2016)):

$$P = 1 + \log \frac{2 + L'}{2 + L''}$$

where L' indicates the length of the response after dropping stop words and punctuation and L'' stands for the length of non-dull part of the response after dropping stop words. The intuition here is that the longer utterances, with nearly the same similarity, communicate the intention unequivocally since it takes more words to convey the same meaning.

The penalized Semantic Similarity score is therefore defined as:

$$SS(utt_{i,j}, resp_i) = P \times (1 - cos(\vec{utt}_{i,j}, \vec{resp}_i))$$

where i represents the index for the dialogue in the test dataset and j denotes the index of the utterance in the conversation history. The results conducted on Reddit dataset are shown in Table 2. We can observe that THRED is able to generate responses which follow the topic and semantics of the input utterances. In particular, the responses generated by THRED tend to be closer to the context of the conversation (Utt.1 and Utt.2) compared to the responses generated from the baslines. To ensure the statistical significance of THRED, we conducted Student's t-test over the average values of SS metric. THRED outperforms all baselines ($p < 0.001$) especially when the comparison is made against the most recent utterance (Utt.2). On the other hand, THRED is level with compared models in semantic distance with respect to the second most recent utterance (Utt.1). This makes

Context	Generated Responses
(Reddit) sanctions are an act of war → why do you think that ?	**THRED:** because it's really a *theory* that supports *terrorism* . and this has an effect on the idea of a *regime* that isn't the same as a *government* (*Excellent, Good, Excellent, Good, Excellent*)
	HRED: because the war is n't a war . it 's a war . (*Good, Poor, Poor, Poor, Poor*)
	Seq2Seq: because it 's an unpopular opinion , and that 's why it 's a bad thing to say . (*Good, Poor, Excellent, Good, Good*)
	TA-Seq2Seq: because it's a war . (*Good, Poor, Excellent, Poor, Good*)

Table 1: One cherry-picked dialogue out of 150 conversations along with the generated responses from all models. Human judgments are provided in the brackets. The blue arrow specifies a dialogue exchange and the highlighted words in red represent the topic words acquired from the pre-trained LDA model.

Stat.	THRED	Seq2Seq	HRED	TA-Seq2Seq
SS with respect to Utt.1				
μ	**0.680**	0.694	0.755	0.692
σ	0.200	0.236	0.283	0.252
SS with respect to Utt.2				
μ	**0.649****	0.672	0.720	0.702
σ	0.212	0.236	0.292	0.253

Table 2: Mean μ and standard deviation σ of SS scores for the responses generated from different models with respect to the most recent utterance (Utt.2) and the second most recent utterance (Utt.1) from conversation history on the Reddit test dataset (** indicates statistical significance over the second best method with p-value < 0.001).

Metric	THRED	Seq2Seq	HRED	TA-Seq2Seq
$SS_{Utt.1}$	0.008	0.009	0.001	0.006
$SS_{Utt.2}$	0.010	0.008	0.007	0.005

Table 3: Standard deviation of mean SS scores over the 5 different partitions of Reddit test dataset.

sense because in a multi-turn dialogue, speakers are more likely to address the last utterance spoken by the interlocutor, which is why THRED tends to favour the most recent utterance over an older one. Additionally, the roughly similar distances for both utterances in Standard Seq2Seq and TA-Seq2Seq exhibit that by concatenating context as single input, these models cannot distinguish between early turns and late turns. Similarly, the results achieved on OpenSubtitles dataset (See Figure 4 in the supplementary material) illustrate that THRED succeeds in staying on topic and in accounting for contextual information.

5.2.1 Reliability Assurance

In order to ensure that the SS measurement is stable and void of random error, we investigate whether the SS metric is able to yield the same previous results regardless of a specific test dataset. Following (Papineni et al., 2002), the test dataset is randomly partitioned to 5 disjoint subsets (i.e., each one consists of 1000 test dialogues). Then, we compute standard deviation of SS over each dataset. The results, showcased in Table 3, indicate low standard deviation on the subdatasets, denoting that the SS metric is a consistent and re-

liable measure to compare different dialogue models.

5.3 Response Echo Index

The goal of the Response Echo Index (REI) metric is to detect overfitting to the training dataset. More specifically, we want to measure the extent to which the responses generated by our model repeat the utterances appearing in the training data. Our approach is close to sampling and finding the nearest neighbour in image generative models (Theis et al., 2016). We randomly sampled 10% of the training data of both OpenSubtitles and Reddit. The nearest neighbour is determined via Jaccard similarity function. Each utterance is represented by lemmatized bag-of-words where stop words and punctuation marks are omitted. In effect, REI is defined as:

$$REI\left(resp_i\right) = \max_{utt_m \in \mathbb{T}_{0.1}} \mathcal{J}\left(\overline{resp_i}, \overline{utt_m}\right)$$

where $\bar{t}$ is the normalized form of text t, $\mathbb{T}_{0.1}$ denotes the sampled training data, and $\mathcal{J}$ represents Jaccard function. REI is expected to be low since the generated responses should be distant from the nearest neighbor. According to the results, presented in Figure 2, the REI scores of the responses generated from THRED are the lowest compared to the rest of the models. Such observation leads us to the conclusion that THRED is able to generate unique responses which appear to be drawn from the input distribution, while being measurably far from the input dataset. This strength in THRED is attributed to the topic attention and incorporating topic words in response generation.

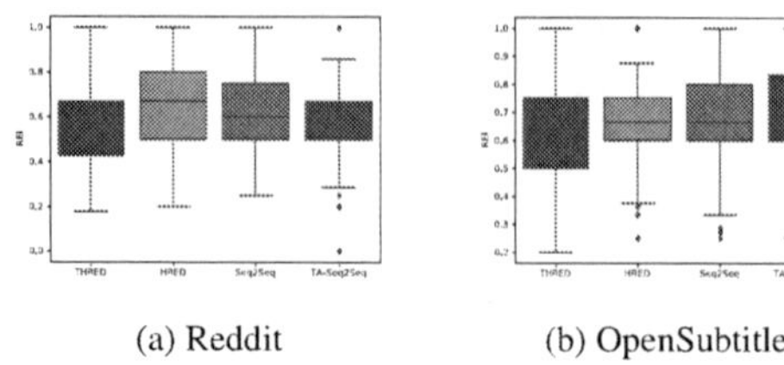

(a) Reddit   (b) OpenSubtitles

Figure 2: Performance results of the generated responses from different models based on REI. From left to right, the labels in horizontal axis are THRED, HRED, Seq2Seq, TA-Seq2Seq.

Due to the same reason, standard Seq2Seq and HRED fall short.

5.4 Degree of Diversity & Perplexity

To account further for diversity in generated responses, following (Li et al., 2016a), we calculated $distinct$-1 and $distinct$-2 by counting unique unigrams and bigrams, normalized by the number of generated words. The results, given in Table 4, on Reddit indicate that THRED yields content rich and diverse responses, mainly ascribed to incorporating new topic words into response generation. Further, in perplexity, THRED performs slightly better.

5.5 Human Evaluation

Besides the quantitative measures, 4-scale and side-by-side human evaluation were carried out. Five human raters were recruited for the purpose of evaluating the quality of the responses. They were fluent, native English speakers and well-instructed for the judgment task to ensure quality rating. We showed every judge 300 conversations (150 dialogues from Reddit and 150 dialogues from OpenSubtitles) and two generated responses for each dialogue: one generated by THRED model and the other one generated by one of our baselines. The source models were unknown to the evaluators. The responses were ordered in a random way to avoid biasing the judges. Additionally, Fleiss' Kappa score is used to gauge the reliability of the agreement between human evaluators (Shao et al., 2017). An example of generated responses from the Reddit dataset are provided in Table 1 For the 4-scale human evaluation, judges were asked to judge the responses from Bad (0) to Excellent (3). Additional details are provided in the supplementary material. The results of this experiment, conducted on Reddit, are detailed in Table 5. The lablers with a high

Method	**PPL**	*distinct-1*	*distinct-2*
Seq2Seq	62.12	0.0082	0.0222
HRED	63.00	0.0083	0.0182
TA-Seq2Seq	62.40	0.0098	0.0253
THRED	**61.73**	**0.0103**	**0.0347**

Table 4: Performance results of diversity and perplexity metrics of all the models on the Reddit test dataset. THRED surpasses all the baselines with a gain of 5% in $distinct$-1 and 37% in $distinct$-2 over TA-Seq2Seq (second best).

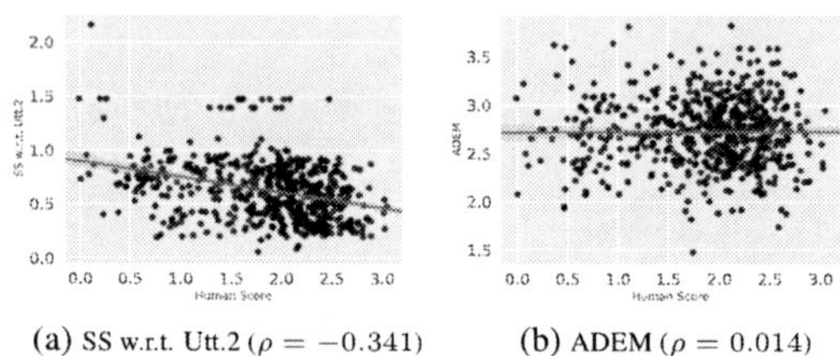

(a) SS w.r.t. Utt.2 ($\rho = -0.341$)   (b) ADEM ($\rho = 0.014$)

Figure 3: Scatter plots illustrating correlation between automated metrics and human judgment (Pearson correlation coefficient is reported in the brackets). In order to better visualize the density of the points, we added stochastic noise generated by Gaussian distribution $\mathcal{N}(0, 0.1)$ to the human ratings (i.e., horizontal axis) at the cost of lowering correlation, as done in (Lowe et al., 2017).

consensus degree rated 32.9% and 36.9% of the THRED responses in OpenSubtitles and Reddit respectively as Excellent, which is greatly larger than all baselines (up to 11.6% and 22.7% respectively). Apart from the 4-scale rating, we conducted the evaluations side-by-side to measure the gain in THRED over the strong baselines. Specific comparison instructions are included in the supplementary material. The results, illustrated in Table 5, suggest that THRED is substantially superior to all baselines in producing informative and plausible responses from human's perspective. The high Kappa scores imply that a major agreement prevails among the lablers. In particular, THRED beats the strong baselines in 52% of the test data in Reddit (the percentage is achieved by averaging the win ratio). However, for the rest of the cases, THRED is equally good with the baselines in 25% in Reddit (calculated similarly based on Table 5). Hence, the ratio of cases where THRED is better than or equal with the baselines in terms of quality is 77% in Reddit.

5.5.1 Automated metric vs. Human evaluation

We also carried out an analysis on the correlation between the human evaluator ratings and our

Side-by-Side	Wins	Losses	Equally Good	Equally Bad	Kappa
THRED vs Seq2Seq	**47.5%**±4.4%	19.1%±3.3%	28.5%±3.1%	4.9%±1.8%	0.80
THRED vs HRED	**51.7%**±4.6%	20.1%±3.4%	20.9%±3.1%	7.2%±2.3%	0.75
THRED vs TA-Seq2Seq	**55.7%**±4.1%	13.5%±2.6%	24.7%±3.0%	6.1%±1.8%	0.77
4-scale	**Excellent**	**Good**	**Poor**	**Bad**	**Kappa**
Seq2Seq	22.7%±2.6%	47.2%±3.5%	22.5%±3.5%	7.6%±2.7%	0.80
HRED	14.5%±2.8%	46.7%±3.8%	31.3%±3.8%	7.5%±2.5%	0.84
TA-Seq2Seq	17.1%±2.4%	44.8%±3.5%	30.1%±3.2%	8.0%±2.3%	0.72
THRED	**36.9%**±3.0%	51.1%±2.9%	10.3%±2.4%	1.7%±1.5%	0.84

Table 5: Side-by-side human evaluation along with 4-scale human evaluation of dialogue utterance prediction on Reddit dataset (mean preferences ±90% confidence intervals).

quantitative scores. The Semantic Similarity metric, which requires no pre-training, reaches a Pearson correlation of -0.341 with respect to the most recent utterance (Utt.2) on Reddit. A negative correlation is anticipated here since the higher human ratings correspond to the lower semantic distance. This compares with values of 0.351 for Automatic User Ratings (Venkatesh et al., 2018) and 0.436 for ADEM (Lowe et al., 2017) from recent models which required large amounts of training data and computation. The correlations are visualized as scatter plots in Figure 3. In addition, we assessed ADEM on our test datasets using the pre-trained weights[5], provided by the authors. ADEM achieves low correlation with human judgment ($\rho = 0.014$ on Reddit and $\rho = 0.034$ on OpenSubtitles) presumably since the quality of its predicted scores highly depends on the corpus on which the model is trained.

5.6 Comparing Datasets

Finally, we investigate the impact of training datasets on the quality of the responses generated by THRED and all baselines. Table 6 has results which support that our cleaner, well-parsed Reddit dataset generates significantly improved responses over our metrics of interest. In particular, we contrast the two datasets in terms of human judgment and the automated metrics among all the models. Regarding human assessment, we took the mean evaluation rating (MER) per response in the test data to draw the comparison between the datasets. As demonstrated in Table 6 (see more details in Figure 6 in the Appendix), the human evaluators scored generated responses from the Reddit dataset higher than utterances generated from the OpenSubtitles dataset, which is true not only

[5] https://github.com/mike-n-7/ADEM

Method	OpenSubtitles		Reddit	
	μ	σ	μ	σ
Human MER	1.681	0.639	**1.868**	0.624
SS w.r.t. Utt.1	0.642	0.167	**0.631**	0.270
SS w.r.t. Utt.2	0.662	0.209	**0.599****	0.262
REI	0.667	0.205	**0.546****	0.201

Table 6: Mean μ and standard deviation σ over metrics per dataset to fare Reddit against OpenSubtitles. (** indicates statistical significance with p-value < 0.001)

in THRED, but in all models. Consequently, the training data plays a crucial role in generating high-quality responses. Morever, in OpenSubtitles, the assumption of spotting a conversation, as stated in Section 4, tends to include extraneous utterances in the dialogue, impeding the response generation process. While such presumption may seem valid in dealing with two-turn dialogues, it can aggravate the quality of conversations in multi-turn dialogues.

6 Conclusion

In this work, we introduce the Topical Hierarchical Recurrent Encoder Decoder (THRED) model for generating topically consistent responses in multi-turn open conversations. We demonstrate that THRED significantly outperforms current state-of-the-art systems on quantitative metrics and human judgment. Additionally, we evaluate our new model and existing models with two new metrics which prove to be good measures for automatically evaluating the quality of the responses. Finally, we present a parsed and cleaned dataset based on conversations from Reddit which improves generated responses. We expect more advanced work to be done in the area of chit-chat dialogue to improve the models, training data, and means of evaluation.

References

Dzmitry Bahdanau, Kyunghyun Cho, and Yoshua Bengio. 2015. Neural machine translation by jointly learning to align and translate. *international conference on learning representations*.

David M Blei, Andrew Y Ng, and Michael I Jordan. 2003. Latent dirichlet allocation. *Journal of machine Learning research*, 3(Jan):993–1022.

Daniel Cer, Yinfei Yang, Sheng yi Kong, Nan Hua, Nicole Lyn Untalan Limtiaco, Rhomni St. John, Noah Constant, Mario Guajardo-Cspedes, Steve Yuan, Chris Tar, Yun hsuan Sung, Brian Strope, and Ray Kurzweil. 2018. Universal sentence encoder. *arXiv preprint arXiv:1803.11175*.

Kyunghyun Cho, Bart van Merrienboer, Caglar Gulcehre, Dzmitry Bahdanau, Fethi Bougares, Holger Schwenk, and Yoshua Bengio. 2014. Learning phrase representations using rnn encoder–decoder for statistical machine translation. In *Proceedings of the 2014 Conference on Empirical Methods in Natural Language Processing (EMNLP)*, pages 1724–1734.

Cristian Danescu-Niculescu-Mizil and Lillian Lee. 2011. Chameleons in imagined conversations: A new approach to understanding coordination of linguistic style in dialogs. In *Proceedings of the 2nd Workshop on Cognitive Modeling and Computational Linguistics*, pages 76–87. Association for Computational Linguistics.

Matthew Hoffman, Francis R Bach, and David M Blei. 2010. Online learning for latent dirichlet allocation. In *advances in neural information processing systems*, pages 856–864.

Jiwei Li, Michel Galley, Chris Brockett, Jianfeng Gao, and Bill Dolan. 2016a. A diversity-promoting objective function for neural conversation models. In *Proceedings of the 2016 Conference of the North American Chapter of the Association for Computational Linguistics: Human Language Technologies*, pages 110–119.

Jiwei Li, Will Monroe, Alan Ritter, Dan Jurafsky, Michel Galley, and Jianfeng Gao. 2016b. Deep reinforcement learning for dialogue generation. In *Proceedings of the 2016 Conference on Empirical Methods in Natural Language Processing*, pages 1192–1202.

Chin-Yew Lin. 2004. Rouge: A package for automatic evaluation of summaries. *Text Summarization Branches Out*.

Chia-Wei Liu, Ryan Lowe, Iulian Vlad Serban, Michael Noseworthy, Laurent Charlin, and Joelle Pineau. 2016. How not to evaluate your dialogue system: An empirical study of unsupervised evaluation metrics for dialogue response generation. In *Proceedings of the 2016 Conference on Empirical Methods in Natural Language Processing*, pages 2122–2132.

Ryan Lowe, Michael Noseworthy, Iulian Vlad Serban, Nicolas Angelard-Gontier, Yoshua Bengio, and Joelle Pineau. 2017. Towards an automatic turing test: Learning to evaluate dialogue responses. In *Proceedings of the 55th Annual Meeting of the Association for Computational Linguistics (Volume 1: Long Papers)*, volume 1, pages 1116–1126.

Thang Luong, Hieu Pham, and Christopher D. Manning. 2015. Effective approaches to attention-based neural machine translation. In *Proceedings of the 2015 Conference on Empirical Methods in Natural Language Processing*, pages 1412–1421.

Tomas Mikolov, Martin Karafiát, Lukas Burget, Jan Cernockỳ, and Sanjeev Khudanpur. 2010. Recurrent neural network based language model. In *Interspeech*, volume 2, page 3.

Kishore Papineni, Salim Roukos, Todd Ward, and Wei-Jing Zhu. 2002. Bleu: a method for automatic evaluation of machine translation. In *Proceedings of the 40th annual meeting on association for computational linguistics*, pages 311–318. Association for Computational Linguistics.

Iulian Vlad Serban, Alessandro Sordoni, Yoshua Bengio, Aaron C Courville, and Joelle Pineau. 2016. Building end-to-end dialogue systems using generative hierarchical neural network models. In *AAAI*, pages 3776–3784.

Iulian Vlad Serban, Alessandro Sordoni, Ryan Lowe, Laurent Charlin, Joelle Pineau, Aaron C Courville, and Yoshua Bengio. 2017. A hierarchical latent variable encoder-decoder model for generating dialogues. In *AAAI*, pages 3295–3301.

Louis Shao, Stephan Gouws, Denny Britz, Anna Goldie, Brian Strope, and Ray Kurzweil. 2017. Generating high-quality and informative conversation responses with sequence-to-sequence models. In *Proceedings of the 2017 Conference on Empirical Methods in Natural Language Processing*, pages 2210–2219.

Ilya Sutskever, Oriol Vinyals, and Quoc V. Le. 2014. Sequence to sequence learning with neural networks. *neural information processing systems*, pages 3104–3112.

Lucas Theis, Aron van den Oord, and Matthias Bethge. 2016. A note on the evaluation of generative models. *international conference on learning representations*.

Jörg Tiedemann. 2012. Parallel data, tools and interfaces in opus. In *LREC*, volume 2012, pages 2214–2218.

Anu Venkatesh, Chandra Khatri, Ashwin Ram, Fenfei Guo, Raefer Gabriel, Ashish Nagar, Rohit Prasad, Ming Cheng, Behnam Hedayatnia, Angeliki Metallinou, Rahul Goel, Shaohua Yang, and Anirudh Raju. 2018. On evaluating and comparing conversational agents. *arXiv preprint arXiv:1801.03625*.

Oriol Vinyals and Quoc Le. 2015. A neural conversational model. *arXiv preprint arXiv:1506.05869*.

Yonghui Wu, Mike Schuster, Zhifeng Chen, Quoc V Le, Mohammad Norouzi, Wolfgang Macherey, Maxim Krikun, Yuan Cao, Qin Gao, Klaus Macherey, et al. 2016. Google's neural machine translation system: Bridging the gap between human and machine translation. *arXiv preprint arXiv:1609.08144*.

Chen Xing, Wei Wu, Yu Wu, Jie Liu, Yalou Huang, Ming Zhou, and Wei-Ying Ma. 2017. Topic aware neural response generatio. In *AAAI*, pages 3351–3357.

Saizheng Zhang, Emily Dinan, Jack Urbanek, Arthur Szlam, Douwe Kiela, and Jason Weston. 2018. Personalizing dialogue agents: I have a dog, do you have pets too? *arXiv preprint arXiv:1801.07243*.

Wayne Xin Zhao, Jing Jiang, Jianshu Weng, Jing He, Ee-Peng Lim, Hongfei Yan, and Xiaoming Li. 2011. Comparing twitter and traditional media using topic models. In *ECIR 2011 Proceedings of the 33rd European Conference on Advances in Information Retrieval - Volume 6611*, pages 338–349.

A Supplementary Material

A.1 Experimental Setup

The model parameters are learned by optimizing the log-likelihood of the utterances via Adam optimizer with a learning rate of 0.0002; we followed (Luong et al., 2015) for decaying the learning rate. The dropout rate is set to 0.2 for both the encoder and the decoder to avoid overfitting. For all the baselines, we experimented hidden state units with the size of 1024. For our model, we tested with encoder and decoder hidden state units of size 800, the same for the context encoder. During inference, we experimented with the standard beam search with the beam width 5 and the length normalization $\alpha = 1$ (Wu et al., 2016). We noticed that applying the length normalization resulted in a more diverse and longer sentences but at the expense of the semantic coherence of the response in some cases.

Training LDA model: We trained two LDA models[6]: one trained on OpenSubtitles and the other one trained on Reddit. Both of them were trained on 1M dialogues. We set the number of topics to 150, α to $\frac{1}{150}$ and γ to 0.01. We filtered out stop words and universal words. We also discarded the 1000 words with the highest frequency from the topic words.

A.2 Human Evaluation Procedure

For the 4-scale human evaluation, judges were asked to judge the responses from Bad (0) to Excellent (3). Excellent (score 3): The response is very appropriate, on topic, fluent, interesting and shows understanding of the context. Good (score 2): The response is coherent with the context but it is not diverse and informative. It may imply the answer. Poor (score 1): The response is interpretable and grammatically correct but completely off-topic. Bad (score 0): The response is grammatically broken and it does not provide an answer. Regarding the side-by-side evaluation, humans were asked to favor response 1 over response 2 if: (1) response 1 is relevant, logically consistent to the context, fluent and on topic; or (2) Both responses 1 and 2 are relevant, consistent and fluent but response 1 is more informative than response 2. If judges cannot tell which one is better, they can rate the responses as Equally good or Equally Bad.

---

[6]We used LDA model developed in Gensim library.

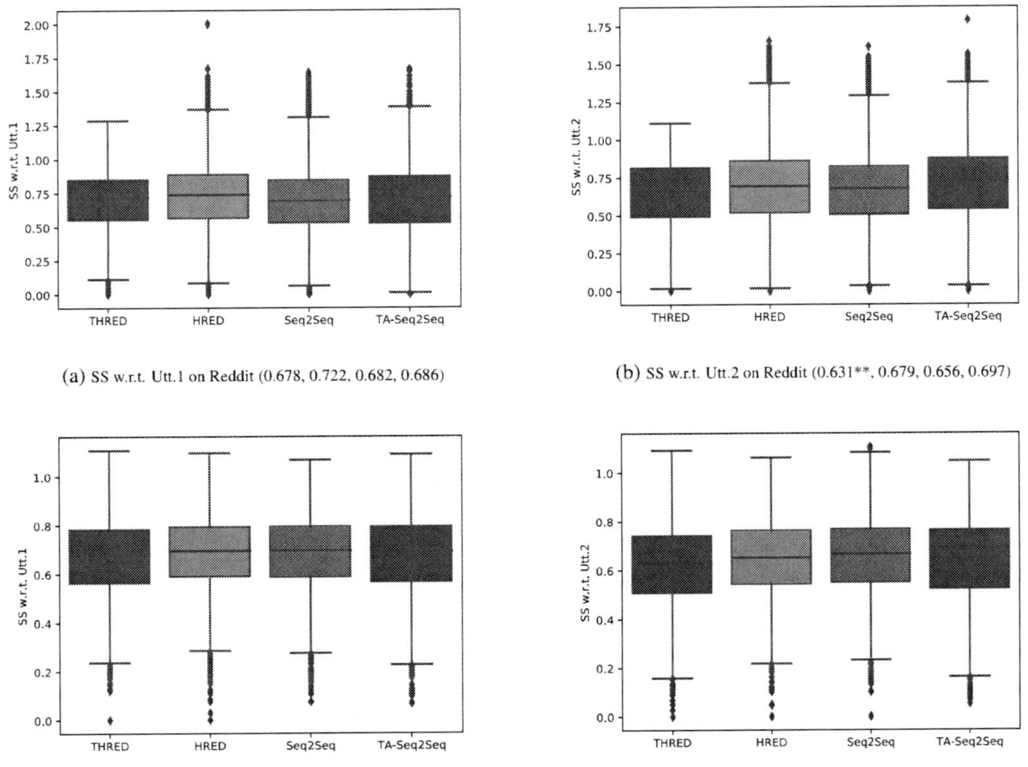

(a) SS w.r.t. Utt.1 on Reddit (0.678, 0.722, 0.682, 0.686) (b) SS w.r.t. Utt.2 on Reddit (0.631**, 0.679, 0.656, 0.697)

(c) SS w.r.t. Utt.1 on OpenSubtitles (0.679, 0.694, 0.696, 0.690) (d) SS w.r.t. Utt.2 on OpenSubtitles (0.628**, 0.653, 0.667, 0.653)

Figure 4: Box plots showcasing the performance of the generated responses from different models based on the Semantic Similarity metric with respect to Utt.1 and Utt.2 (complementary to Table 2). From left to right, the labels in horizontal axis are THRED, HRED, Seq2Seq and TA-Seq2Seq. THRED surpasses all baselines in similarity with Utt.2, and works mildly better in similarity with Utt.1. The median for every box plot is also reported between brackets. The order of the values is the same as the order of the methods.

CONTEXT	GENERATED RESPONSES
(OpenSubtitles) the giant observatory in hawaii are like time machines capturing the faint light that has travelled towards us through all of cosmic history → the deeper they look into space the farther back they see in time	**THRED:** as the stars move into space they see the rising sun and the stars rise above the clouds (*Excellent, Excellent, Good, Excellent, Poor*) **HRED:** this is the first time we have ever seen (*Poor, Poor, Bad, Good, Bad*) **Seq2Seq:**the stars and stars of the moon are the stars and stars of the stars and stars and stars and stars and stars and stars (*Poor, Bad, Bad, Bad, Poor*) **TA-Seq2Seq:** they have been searching for a long time for a long time (*Good, Poor, Good, Good, Good*)
(OpenSubtitles) and closer to home in baltimore prominent psychiatrist and the author of a newly released book on insanity disappeared mysteriously last night after a lecture at the university → former mental patient james cole is wanted for questioning regarding dr cole 's disappearance	**THRED:** authorities warn that cole has a history of violence and advise anyone to notify authorities (*Excellent, Excellent, Excellent, Excellent, Excellent*) **HRED:** they have been unable to identify him (*Good, Poor, Poor, Good, Poor*) **Seq2Seq:**cole cole is cole is cole(*Poor, Bad, Bad, Bad, Bad*) **TA-Seq2Seq:** authorities warn that cole has been kidnapped (*Poor, Good, Good, Good, Good*)

Table 7: One cherry-picked dialogues out of 150 conversations along with the generated responses from all models. Human judgments are provided in the brackets. The blue arrow specifies a dialogue exchange and the highlighted words in red represent the topic words acquired from the pre-trained LDA model.

Method	OpenSubtitles			Reddit		
	PPL	*distinct-1*	*distinct-2*	**PPL**	*distinct-1*	*distinct-2*
Seq2Seq	74.37	0.0112	0.0258	62.12	0.0082	0.0222
HRED	74.65	0.0079	0.0219	63.00	0.0083	0.0182
TA-Seq2Seq	75.92	0.0121	0.0290	62.40	0.0098	0.0253
THRED	**73.61**	**0.0157** *(+30%)*	**0.0422** *(+45%)*	**61.73**	**0.0103** *(+5%)*	**0.0347** *(+37%)*

Table 8: Complete performance results of diversity and perplexity on Reddit test data and OpenSubtitles test data (complementary to Table 4). The numbers in the bracket indicate the gain of *distinct*-1 and *distinct*-2 over the second best method (i.e., TA-Seq2Seq).

Side-by-Side	Wins	Losses	Equally Good	Equally Bad	Kappa
THRED vs Seq2Seq	**54.0%**±**4.2%**	18.4%±3.4%	17.2%±3.0%	10.4%±2.3%	0.75
THRED vs HRED	**51.6%**±**4.4%**	19.5%±3.5%	18.4%±2.9%	10.5%±2.4%	0.72
THRED vs TA-Seq2Seq	**64.0%**±**4.3%**	14.4%±3.1%	14.1%±2.5%	7.5%±2.1%	0.90
4-scale Rating	**Excellent**	**Good**	**Poor**	**Bad**	**Kappa**
Seq2Seq	**8.4%**±**2.2%**	48.9%±3.9%	33.2%±3.7%	9.5%±3.1%	0.89
HRED	**11.6%**±**2.4%**	41.5%±3.4%	36.9%±3.9%	10.0%±2.8%	0.79
TA-Seq2Seq	**9.5%**±**2.1%**	42.3%±3.7%	34.7%±3.9%	13.6%±3.7%	0.92
THRED	**32.9%**±**3.6%**	49.2%±3.3%	16.8%±3.0%	1.1%±0.9%	0.83

Table 9: Side-by-side human evaluation along with 4-scale human evaluation of dialogue utterance prediction on OpenSubtitles dataset (mean preferences ±90% confidence intervals). Results on Reddit dataset are reported in Table 5.

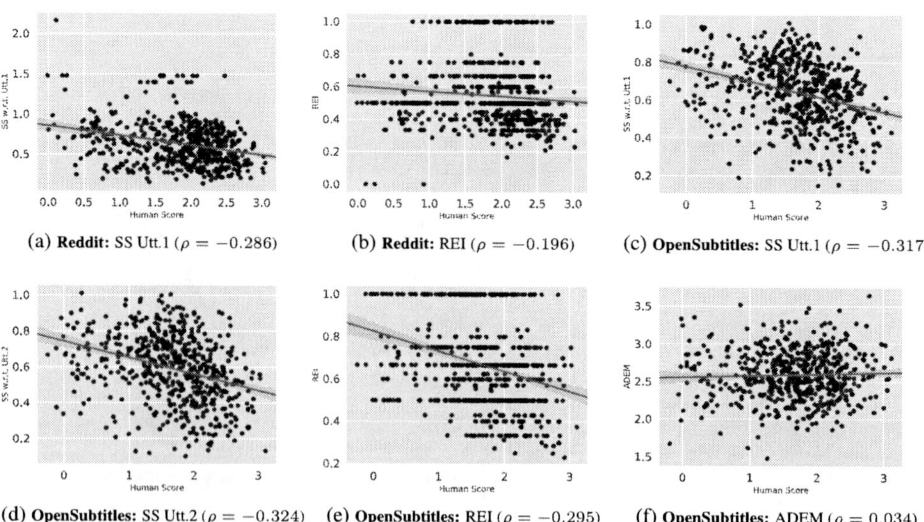

(a) **Reddit**: SS Utt.1 ($\rho = -0.286$)   (b) **Reddit**: REI ($\rho = -0.196$)   (c) **OpenSubtitles**: SS Utt.1 ($\rho = -0.317$)

(d) **OpenSubtitles**: SS Utt.2 ($\rho = -0.324$)   (e) **OpenSubtitles**: REI ($\rho = -0.295$)   (f) **OpenSubtitles**: ADEM ($\rho = 0.034$)

Figure 5: Scatter plots illustrating correlation between automated metrics and human judgment (Pearson correlation coefficient is reported in the brackets).

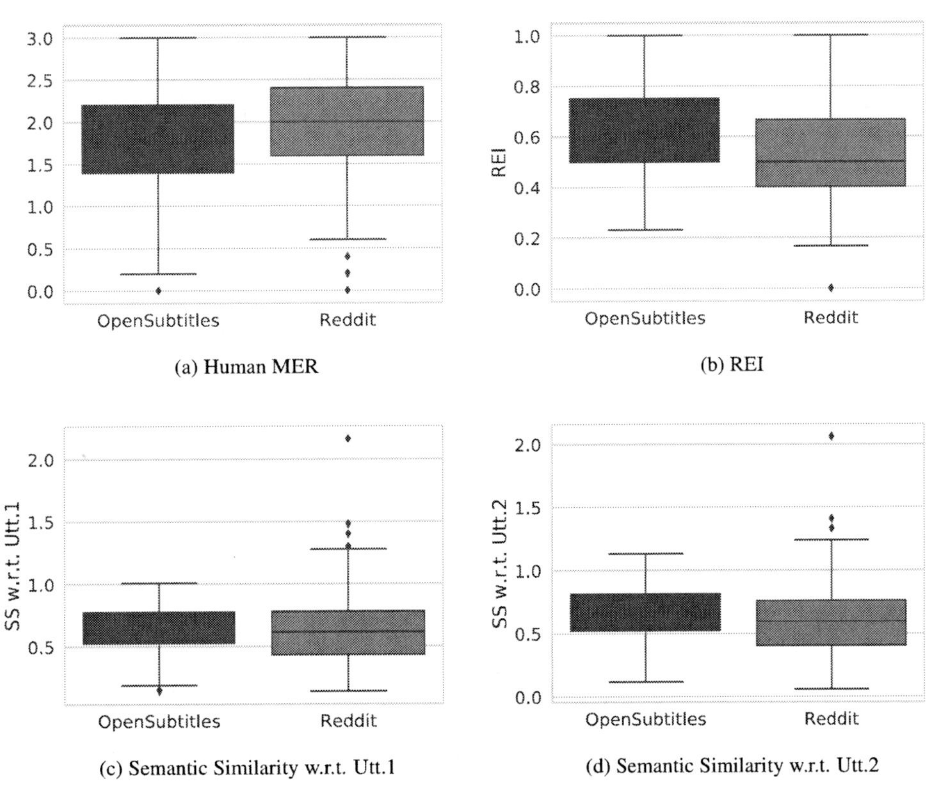

(a) Human MER   (b) REI

(c) Semantic Similarity w.r.t. Utt.1   (d) Semantic Similarity w.r.t. Utt.2

Figure 6: Box plots demonstrating the detailed comparison between OpenSubtitles and Reddit datasets. The metrics are calculated for all models in the cherry-picked data (150 samples for OpenSubtitles and 150 samples for Reddit). The results here complement what we found in Table 6 in which only mean and standard deviation are reported per metric.

Building a Production Model for Retrieval-Based Chatbots

Kyle Swanson[1†], Lili Yu[2], Christopher Fox[2], Jeremy Wohlwend[2], Tao Lei[2]
[1]Massachusetts Institute of Technology
[2]ASAPP, Inc.
swansonk@mit.edu
{liliyu, cdfox, jeremy, tao}@asapp.com

Abstract

Response suggestion is an important task for building human-computer conversation systems. Recent approaches to conversation modeling have introduced new model architectures with impressive results, but relatively little attention has been paid to whether these models would be practical in a production setting. In this paper, we describe the unique challenges of building a production retrieval-based conversation system, which selects outputs from a whitelist of candidate responses. To address these challenges, we propose a dual encoder architecture which performs rapid inference and scales well with the size of the whitelist. We also introduce and compare two methods for generating whitelists, and we carry out a comprehensive analysis of the model and whitelists. Experimental results on a large, proprietary help desk chat dataset, including both offline metrics and a human evaluation, indicate production-quality performance and illustrate key lessons about conversation modeling in practice.

1 Introduction

Predicting a response given conversational context is a critical task for building open-domain chatbots and dialogue systems. Recently developed conversational systems typically use either a generative or a retrieval approach for producing responses (Wang et al., 2013; Ji et al., 2014; Vinyals and Le, 2015; Serban et al., 2015; Li et al., 2016; Xing et al., 2016; Deb et al., 2019). While both of these approaches have demonstrated strong performance in the literature, retrieval methods often enjoy better control over response quality than generative approaches. In particular, such methods select outputs from a *whitelist* of candidate responses, which can be pre-screened and revised for desired qualities such as sentence fluency and diversity.

Most previous work on retrieval models has concentrated on designing neural architectures to improve response selection. For instance, several works have improved model performance by encoding multi-turn conversation context instead of single-turn context (Serban et al., 2015; Zhou et al., 2016; Wu et al., 2017). More recent efforts (Zhou et al., 2018; Zhang et al., 2018) have explored using more advanced architectures, such as the Transformer (Vaswani et al., 2017), to better learn the mapping between the context and the candidate responses.

Relatively little effort, however, has been devoted to the practical considerations of using such models in a real-world production setting. For example, one critical consideration rarely discussed in the literature is the inference speed of the deployed model. While recent methods introduce rich computation, such as cross-attention (Zhou et al., 2018), to improve the modeling between the conversational context and candidate response, the model outputs must be re-computed for every pair of context and response. As a consequence, these models are not well-suited to a production setting where the size of the response whitelist can easily extend into the thousands.

Another critical concern is the whitelist selection process and the associated retrieval evaluation. Most prior work have reported Recall@k on a small set of randomly selected responses which include the true response sent by the agent (Lowe et al., 2015; Zhou et al., 2016, 2018; Wu et al., 2017; Zhang et al., 2018). However, this oversimplified evaluation may not provide a useful indication of performance in production, where the whitelist is not randomly selected, is significantly larger, and may not contain the target response.

In this paper, we explore and evaluate model

[†]Work done primarily while an intern at ASAPP, Inc.

Proceedings of the 1st Workshop on NLP for Conversational AI, pages 32–41
Florence, Italy, August 1, 2019. ©2019 Association for Computational Linguistics

and whitelist design choices for building retrieval-based conversation systems in production. We present a dual encoder architecture that is optimized to select among as many as 10,000 responses within a couple tens of milliseconds. The model makes use of a fast recurrent network implementation (Lei et al., 2018) and multi-headed attention (Lin et al., 2017) and achieves over a 4.1x inference speedup over traditional encoders such as LSTM (Hochreiter and Schmidhuber, 1997). The independent dual encoding allows pre-computing the embeddings of candidate responses, thereby making the approach highly scalable with the size of the whitelist. In addition, we compare two approaches for generating the response candidates, and we conduct a comprehensive analysis of our model and whitelists on a large, real-world help desk dataset, using human evaluation and metrics that are more relevant to use in a production setting.

2 Related Work

This paper extends the line of work on conversational retrieval models for multi-turn response selection (Lowe et al., 2015; Al-Rfou et al., 2016; Zhou et al., 2016, 2018; Wu et al., 2016, 2017; Yan et al., 2016; Lu et al., 2017; Zhang et al., 2018; Shalyminov et al., 2018; Deb et al., 2019; Yang et al., 2019). Our model is most similar to Lowe et al. (2015), who construct the context of the conversation by concatenating all previous utterances. They use an RNN to separately encode the context and each candidate response, and they then compute a matching score between the context and response representations to determine the best response for that context.

Other recent work has explored more complex methods of incorporating information from the context of a conversation. Serban et al. (2015) and Zhou et al. (2016) employ a hierarchical architecture in which they encode the context using RNNs at both the word level and the utterance level. In contrast to these models, which generate a single context encoding, Wu et al. (2017) designed a network that matches a response to each utterance in the context individually.

While many of the models cited above implement their RNNs with an LSTM (Hochreiter and Schmidhuber, 1997), we instead use an SRU (Lei et al., 2018). SRU uses light recurrence, which makes it highly parallelizable, and Lei et al. (2018)

showed that it trains 5-9x faster than cuDNN LSTM. SRU also exhibits a significant speedup in inference time compared to LSTM (by a factor of 4.1x in our experiments), which is particularly relevant in a production setting. Furthermore, Lei et al. (2018) showed that SRU matches or exceeds the performance of models using LSTMs or the Transformer architecture (Vaswani et al., 2017) on a number of NLP tasks, meaning significant speed gains can be achieved without a drop in performance.

Despite the abundance of prior work on retrieval models for dialogue, whitelist selection has received relatively little attention. Since practical use of conversational models has typically not been addressed, most models are evaluated on their ability to select the correct response from a small list of randomly sampled responses (Lowe et al., 2015). Another option, from Wu et al. (2017), is to use *Apache Lucene*[1] to select a list of response candidates relevant to each context. However, neither method produces a single whitelist that can be used for every context and reviewed for quality. The closest work to ours is Lu et al. (2017), who build a whitelist using a k-means clustering of responses. We extend this work by doing a more comprehensive analysis of different whitelist selection methods, and we further analyze the effect of whitelist size on performance.

3 Model Architecture

Next we describe the architecture of our retrieval model. The two inputs to the model are a context c, which is a concatenation of all utterances in the conversation, and a candidate response r. In the context, we use special tokens to indicate whether each utterance comes from the customer or the agent. The model outputs a score $s(c, r)$ indicating the relevance of the response to the context. The model architecture is described in detail below and is illustrated in Figure 1.

3.1 Dual Encoders

At the core of our model are two neural encoders f_c and f_r to encode the context and the response, respectively. These encoders have identical architectures but learn separate weights.

Each encoder takes a sequence of tokens $w = \{w_1, w_2, \ldots, w_n\}$ as input, which is either a con-

---

[1] http://lucene.apache.org/

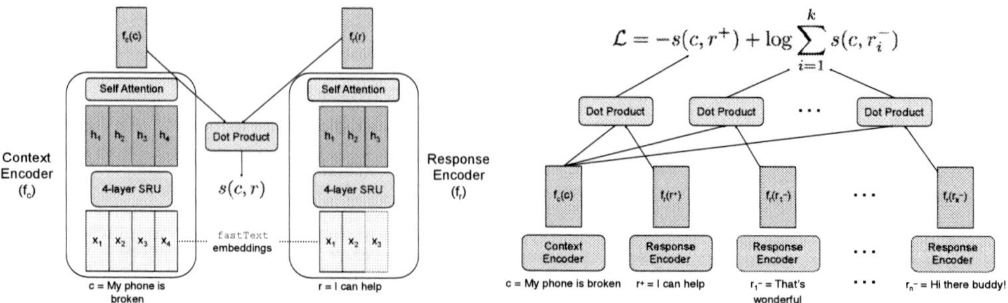

Figure 1: (Left) The dual encoder architecture, which takes as input a context c and a response r and computes the score $s(c, r)$. (Right) Computing the model's loss based on the scores between a context c, the actual agent response r^+, and k randomly sampled agent responses $r_1^-, \ldots, r_k^-$.

text or a response. Due to the prevalence of typos in both user and agent utterances in real chats, we use `fastText` (Bojanowski et al., 2016) as the word embedding method. `fastText` learns both word-level and character-level features and is therefore more robust to misspellings. We pre-trained `fastText`[2] embeddings on a corpus of 15M utterances from help desk conversations and then fixed the embeddings while training the neural encoders.

Each encoder consists of a recurrent neural network followed by a multi-headed attention layer (Lin et al., 2017) to perform pooling. We use multi-layer, bidirectional SRUs as the recurrent network. Each layer of the SRU involves the following computation:

$$
\begin{aligned}
\mathbf{f}_t &= \sigma(\mathbf{W}_f \mathbf{x}_t + \mathbf{v}_f \odot \mathbf{c}_{t-1} + \mathbf{b}_f) \\
\mathbf{c}_t &= \mathbf{f}_t \odot \mathbf{c}_{t-1} + (1 - \mathbf{f}_t) \odot (\mathbf{W}\mathbf{x}_t) \\
\mathbf{r}_t &= \sigma(\mathbf{W}_r \mathbf{x}_t + \mathbf{v}_r \odot \mathbf{c}_{t-1} + \mathbf{b}_r) \\
\mathbf{h}_t &= \mathbf{r}_t \odot \mathbf{c}_t + (1 - \mathbf{r}_t) \odot \mathbf{x}_t
\end{aligned}
\tag{1}
$$

where σ is the sigmoid activation function, $\mathbf{W}, \mathbf{W}_f, \mathbf{W}_r \in \mathbb{R}^{d_h \times d_e}$ are learned parameter matrices, and $\mathbf{v}_f, \mathbf{v}_r, \mathbf{b}_f, \mathbf{b}_v \in \mathbb{R}^{d_h}$ are learned parameter vectors.

The multi-headed attention layer compresses the encoded sequence $\mathbf{h} = \{\mathbf{h}_1, \mathbf{h}_2, \ldots, \mathbf{h}_n\}$ into a single vector. For each attention head i, attention weights are generating with the following computation:

$$
\boldsymbol{\alpha}^{(i)} = \texttt{softmax}(\sigma(\mathbf{h}^T \mathbf{W}_a^{(i)})\mathbf{v}_a^{(i)})
\tag{2}
$$

where σ is a non-linear activation function, $\mathbf{W}_a^{(i)} \in \mathbb{R}^{d_h \times d_a}$ is a learned parameter matrix, and $\mathbf{v}_a^{(i)} \in \mathbb{R}^{d_a}$ is a learned parameter vector.

The encoded sequence representation is then pooled to a single vector for each attention head i by summing the attended representations:

$$
\widetilde{\mathbf{h}}^{(i)} = \sum_{j=1}^{n} \alpha_j^{(i)} \mathbf{h}_j .
\tag{3}
$$

Finally, the pooled encodings are averaged across the n_h attention heads:

$$
\widetilde{\mathbf{h}} = \frac{1}{n_h} \sum_{i=1}^{n_h} \widetilde{\mathbf{h}}^{(i)} .
\tag{4}
$$

The output of the encoder is the vector $f(w) = \widetilde{\mathbf{h}}$.

3.2 Scoring

To determine the relevance of a response r to a context c, our model computes a matching score between the context encoding $f_c(c)$ and the response encoding $f_r(r)$. This score is simply the dot product of the encodings:

$$
s(c, r) = f_c(c) \cdot f_r(r) .
\tag{5}
$$

3.3 Training

We optimize the model to maximize the score between the context c and the response r^+ actually sent by the agent while minimizing the score between the context and each of k random ("negative") responses $r_1^-, \ldots, r_k^-$. This is accomplished by training the model to minimize the cross-entropy loss:

$$
\mathcal{L} = -s(c, r^+) + \log \sum_{i=1}^{k} s(c, r_i^-) .
\tag{6}
$$

Although negative responses could be sampled separately for each context-response pair, we instead use a method inspired by Logeswaran and Lee (2018) and share a set of negative responses across all examples in a batch. Specifically, for each batch, we sample k responses from the set of all agent responses (weighted according to response frequency), and we use those k responses as the negative responses for every context-response pair in the batch. This has the benefit of reducing the number of responses that need to be encoded in each batch of size b from $\mathcal{O}(bk)$ to $\mathcal{O}(b+k)$, thereby significantly accelerating training.

3.4 Whitelist Generation

After training, we experimented with two methods of creating the whitelist from which our model selects responses at inference time. For each method, we created both a 1,000 response whitelist and a 10,000 response whitelist. Having a whitelist with any more than 10,000 responses would likely make a manual review infeasible.

Frequency-Based Method. Responses that are sent frequently are more likely to be relevant in multiple conversations and are less likely to contain errors. Therefore, one method of building a high-quality whitelist is simply to collect messages that are sent often. We created frequency-based whitelists by selecting the 1,000 or 10,000 most common agent responses, after accounting for minor variations in capitalization, punctuation, and whitespace.

Clustering-Based Method. Although selecting responses based on frequency may help guarantee quality, manual examination of the frequency whitelists showed that they contained many redundant responses. Therefore, we experimented with a clustering-based whitelist selection method in the hope of reducing redundancy and increasing response diversity. Specifically, we encoded all agent responses using our response encoder f_r and then used k-means clustering with $k = 1,000$ or $k = 10,000$ to cluster the responses. We then selected the most common response from each cluster to create the whitelists.

4 Experiments and Results

We evaluated our model and whitelists on a large, proprietary help desk chat dataset using several offline metrics and a human evaluation. We particularly emphasize metrics relevant to produc-

tion, such as inference speed and Recall@k from a large candidate set. The human evaluation illustrates how our model and whitelists compare to each other and to the responses sent by a real human agent.

4.1 Data

The help desk chat dataset used in our experiments consists of 15M utterances from 595K conversations. We randomly split the conversations into train, validation, and test sets with 80%, 10%, and 10% of the conversations, respectively. Since each conversation includes several agent responses, each of which produces a context-response example, our dataset consists of 6.6M training examples, 828K validation examples, and 828K test examples. Additional dataset statistics are provided in Table 1. An example chat conversation can be seen in Table 2.

4.2 Model Details

We implemented the dual encoder model using PyTorch (Paszke et al., 2017). We use pre-trained `fastText` embeddings of dimension $d_e = 300$, a 4-layer bidirectional SRU[3] with hidden size $d_h = 300$, and multi-headed attention with 16 heads and a hidden size of $d_a = 64$. The batch size was 200 and we used $k = 200$ negative responses for each positive response. To ensure quick encoding even for long inputs, contexts were restricted to the 500 most recent tokens and responses were restricted to the 100 most recent tokens[4]. The model was optimized using Adam (Kingma and Ba, 2014) with the Noam learning rate schedule from Vaswani et al. (2017). The model was trained for 30 epochs, with each epoch limited to 10,000 training batches (2M training examples). Training took about 32 hours on a single Tesla V100 GPU.

4.3 Results and Analysis

AUC and AUC@p. To determine the model's ability to use context to distinguish between true responses and negative responses, we use the metrics AUC and AUC@p. AUC is the area under the receiver operating characteristic curve when using the score $s(c, r)$ to determine whether each re-

---

[3]SRU code available at `https://github.com/taolei87/sru/tree/master/sru`

[4]A context with 500 tokens contains 39 utterances on average, which is typically more than enough to understand the topic of conversation. Almost all responses are shorter than 100 tokens.

Conversations	594,555
Utterances	15,217,773
Customer utterances	6,943,940
Agent utterances	8,273,833
Mean conversation length (# utterances)	25.60
Mean utterance length (# tokens)	12.70
Mean customer utterance length (# tokens)	7.53
Mean agent utterance length (# tokens)	17.15

Table 1: Summary statistics for the propriety help desk dataset.

Example Conversation
Customer: I would like to pay my bill can you help me
Agent: I can definitely help you to pay your bill. Are we going to work with the account logged in now?
Customer: Yes it still says there is no money on my account
Agent: I understand that. I have reviewed your account and its shows here that the payment has been posted and you're all good until next month service.
Customer: Oh ok thank you for all your help
Agent: You're welcome. Anything for a valued customer like you!

Table 2: A sample conversation from the propriety help desk chat dataset. The sample has been lightly edited to remove proprietary information.

Metric	Validation	Test
AUC	0.991	0.977
AUC@0.1	0.925	0.885
AUC@0.05	0.871	0.816
AUC@0.01	0.677	0.630

Table 3: AUC and AUC@p of our model on the propriety help desk dataset.

Candidates	R@1	R@3	R@5	R@10
10	0.892	0.979	0.987	1
100	0.686	0.842	0.894	0.948
1,000	0.449	0.611	0.677	0.760
10,000	0.234	0.360	0.421	0.505

Table 4: Recall@k from n response candidates for different values of n using random whitelists. Each random whitelist includes the correct response along with $n-1$ randomly selected responses.

sponse is the true response or a negative response. AUC@p is the area under the portion of the ROC curve where the false positive rate is $\leq p$, renormalized so that the maximum AUC@p is 1.

The performance of our model according to these AUC metrics can be seen in Table 3. The high AUC indicates that our model can easily distinguish between the true response and negative responses. Furthermore, the AUC@p numbers show that the model has a relatively high true positive rate even under the difficult requirement of a low false positive rate.

Recall and Whitelist Size. In order to determine our model's ability to select the correct response from a whitelist, we use recall at k from n ($R_n@k$), which is the proportion of times that the true response is ranked as one of the top k responses in a whitelist containing n candidate responses.

Table 4 shows $R_n@k$ on the test set for dif-
ferent values of n and k when using a random whitelist, meaning a whitelist which contains the true response and $n-1$ randomly sampled responses[5]. As discussed in the introduction, most prior work evaluate their models using a random whitelist with $n = 10$ candidates. However, a production whitelist needs to contain hundreds or thousands of response candidates in order to provide relevant responses in a variety of contexts. Therefore, a more meaningful metric for production purposes is $R_n@k$ for $n \geq 100$. Table 4 shows that recall drops significantly as n grows, meaning that the $R_{10}@k$ evaluation performed by prior work may significantly overstate model performance in a production setting.

Comparison Between Whitelists. An interesting question we would like to address is whether

---

[5]To be precise, we sampled responses without replacement weighted according to the frequency with which the response was sent by agents.

Whitelist	R@1	R@3	R@5	R@10	BLEU
Random 10K+	0.252	0.400	0.472	0.560	37.71
Frequency 10K+	0.257	0.389	0.455	0.544	41.34
Clustering 10K+	0.230	0.376	0.447	0.541	37.59
Random 1K+	0.496	0.663	0.728	0.805	59.28
Frequency 1K+	0.513	0.666	0.726	0.794	67.05
Clustering 1K+	0.481	0.667	0.745	0.835	61.88
Frequency 10K	0.136	0.261	0.327	0.420	30.46
Clustering 10K	0.164	0.292	0.360	0.457	31.47
Frequency 1K	0.273	0.465	0.550	0.658	47.13
Clustering 1K	0.331	0.542	0.650	0.782	49.26

Table 5: Recall@k for random, frequency, and clustering whitelists of different sizes. The "+" indicates that the true response is added to the whitelist.

Whitelist	R@1	Coverage
Frequency 10K	0.136	45.04%
Clustering 10K	0.164	38.38%
Frequency 1K	0.273	33.38%
Clustering 1K	0.331	23.28%

Table 6: Recall@1 versus coverage for frequency and clustering whitelists.

Whitelist	Great	Good	Bad	Accept
Freq. 1K	54%	26%	20%	80%
Cluster. 1K	55%	21%	23%	77%
Freq. 10K	56%	24%	21%	80%
Cluster. 10K	57%	23%	20%	80%
Real response	60%	24%	16%	84%

Table 7: Results of the human evaluation of the responses produced by our model. A response is acceptable if it is either good or great. Note: Numbers may not add up to 100% due to rounding.

a random whitelist serves as a good proxy for whitelists generated using other methods. To this end, we also evaluate recall on the frequency and clustering whitelists from Section 3.4.

First, we compute recall when the true response is added to the whitelist, as in the case of the random whitelists described above. Second, we compute recall only on the subset of examples for which the true response is already contained in the whitelist. The latter recall measure is more relevant to a production setting since the true response is not known at inference time and therefore cannot be artificially added to the whitelist.

The results in Table 5 show that the three types of whitelists perform comparably to each other when the true response is added. However, in the more realistic second case, when recall is only computed on examples with a response already in the whitelist, performance on the frequency and clustering whitelists drops significantly.

Additionally, we compute the BLEU (Papineni et al., 2002; Ward and Reeder, 2002) scores between the true responses and the best suggested responses. The BLEU score allows us to measure the semantic similarity when the true and suggested responses are not exactly matched. The BLEU scores computed with the frequency and clustering whitelists are slightly higher than those computed with random whitelists.

Recall versus Coverage. Although recall is a good measure of performance, recall alone is not a sufficient criterion for whitelist selection. The recall results in Table 5 seem to indicate that the clustering-based whitelists are strictly superior to the frequency-based whitelists in the realistic case when we only consider responses that are already contained in the whitelist, but this analysis fails to account for the frequency with which this is the case. For instance, a whitelist may have very high recall but may only include responses that were sent infrequently by agents, meaning the whitelist will perform well for a handful of conversations but will be irrelevant in most other cases.

To quantify this effect, we introduce the notion of *coverage*, which is the percent of all context-response pairs where the agent response appears in the whitelist, after accounting for minor deviations in capitalization, punctuation, and whitespace. A whitelist that contains responses that are sent more frequently by agents will therefore have a higher coverage.

Table 6 shows R@1 and coverage for the frequency and clustering whitelists. While the clustering whitelists have higher recall, the frequency whitelists have higher coverage. This is to be expected since the frequency whitelists were specifically chosen to maximize the frequency of the included responses. Since both recall and coverage are necessary to provide good responses for a wide range of conversations, these results indicate the importance of considering the trade-off between recall and coverage inherent in a given whitelist selection method.

It may be interesting in future work to further investigate these trade-offs in order to identify a whitelist selection method that can simultaneously optimize recall and coverage.

Human Evaluation. While offline metrics are indicative of model performance, the best measure of performance is a human evaluation of the model's predictions. Therefore, we performed a small-scale human evaluation of our model and whitelists. We selected 322 contexts from the test set and used our model to generate responses from the Frequency 10K, Frequency 1K, Clustering 10K, and Clustering 1K whitelists. Three human annotators were shown each context followed by five responses: one from each of the four whitelists and the true response sent by the agent. The annotators were blinded to the source of each response. The annotators were asked to rate each response according to the following categories:

Bad: The response is not relevant to the context.
Good: The response is relevant to the context but is vague or generic.
Great: The response is relevant to the context and directly addresses the issue at hand.

For example, three such responses for the context "My phone is broken" would be:

Bad response: Goodbye!
Good response: I'm sorry to hear that.
Great response: I'm sorry to hear that your phone is broken.

The results of the human evaluation are in Table 7. Our proposed system works well, selecting acceptable (i.e. good or great) responses about 80% of the time and selecting great responses more than 50% of the time.

Interestingly, the size and type of whitelist seem to have little effect on performance, indicating that all the whitelists contain responses appropriate to a variety of conversational contexts. Since the frequency whitelists are simpler to generate than the clustering whitelists and since the 1K whitelists contain fewer responses to manually review than the 10K whitelists, the Frequency 1K whitelist is the preferred whitelist for our production system.

Inference Speed. A major constraint in a production system is the speed with which the system can respond to users. To demonstrate the benefit of using an SRU encoder instead of an LSTM encoder in production, we compared the speed with which they encode a random conversation context at inference time, averaged over 1,000 samples. We used a single core of Intel Core i9 2.9 GHz

Encoder	Layer	Params	Time
SRU	2	3.7M	14.7
SRU	4	8.0M	21.9
LSTM	2	7.3M	90.9
LSTM	4	15.9M	174.8
+rank response	-	-	0.9

Table 8: Inference time (milliseconds) of our model to encode a context using an SRU or an LSTM encoder on a single CPU core. The last row shows the extra time needed to compare the response encoding to 10,000 cached candidate response encodings in order to find the best response.

CPU. As seen in Table 8, an SRU encoder is over 4x faster than an LSTM encoder with a similar number of parameters, making it more suitable for production use.

Table 8 also highlights the scalability of using a dual encoder architecture. Since the embeddings of the candidate responses are independent from the conversation context, the embeddings of the whitelist responses can be pre-computed and stored as a matrix. Retrieving the best candidate once the context is encoded takes a negligible amount of time compared to the time to encode the context.

Ablation analysis. Finally, we performed an ablation analysis to identify the effect of different aspects of the model architecture and training regime. The results are shown in Table 9, and details of the model variants are available in the Appendix.

As Table 9 shows, the training set size and the number of negative responses for each positive response are the most important factors in model performance. The model performs significantly worse when trained with hinge loss instead of cross-entropy loss, indicating the importance of the loss function. We also experimented with a hierarchical encoder, where two different recurrent neural networks are used to encode contexts, one at the word level and one at the utterance level. We observed no advantage to using a hierachical encoder, despite its complexity and popularity for encoding conversations (Serban et al., 2015; Zhou et al., 2016). Finally, we see that a 2 layer LSTM performs similarly to either a 4 layer or a 2 layer SRU with a comparable number of parameters. Since the SRU is more than 4x faster at inference time with the same level of performance, it is the

Model	Parameters	Validation AUC@0.05	Test AUC@0.05
Base	8.0M	**0.871**	0.816
4L SRU → 2L LSTM	7.3M	0.864	**0.829**
4L SRU → 2L SRU	7.8M	0.856	**0.829**
Flat → hierarchical	12.4M	0.825	0.559
Cross entropy → hinge loss	8.0M	0.765	0.693
6.6M → 1M examples	8.0M	0.835	0.694
6.6M → 100K examples	8.0M	0.565	0.417
200 → 100 negatives	8.0M	0.864	0.647
200 → 10 negatives	8.0M	0.720	0.412

Table 9: An ablation study showing the effect of different model architectures and training regimes on performance on the proprietary help desk dataset.

preferred encoder architecture.

5 Conclusion

In this paper, we present a fast dual encoder neural model for retrieval-based human-computer conversations. We address technical considerations specific to the production setting, and we evaluate our model and two whitelist generation methods on a large help desk chat dataset. We observe that traditional offline evaluation metrics significantly overestimate model performance, indicating the importance of using evaluation metrics more relevant to a production setting. Furthermore, we find that our proposed model performs well, both on offline metrics and on a human evaluation. Due to its strong performance and its speed at inference time, we conclude that our proposed model is suitable for use in a production conversational system.

One important direction for future work is a deeper analysis of the whitelist selection process. Although our analysis found similar performance across whitelists according to a human evaluation, our offline metrics indicate underlying trade-offs between different charactcristics of the whitelists such as recall and coverage. A better understanding the implications of these trade-offs may lead to improved whitelist generation methods, thereby further improving the performance of retrieval-based models.

Acknowledgments

We would like to thank Howard Chen for the invaluable conversations we had with him during the development of our model. We would also like to thank Anna Folinsky and the ASAPP annotation team for their help performing the human evaluation, and Hugh Perkins for his support on the experimental environment setup. Thank you as well to Ethan Elenberg, Kevin Yang, and Adam Yala for reviewing early drafts of this paper and providing valuable feedback. Finally, thank you to the anonymous reviewers for their constructive feedback.

References

Rami Al-Rfou, Marc Pickett, Javier Snaider, Yun hsuan Sung, Brian Strope, and Ray Kurzweil. 2016. Conversational contextual cues: The case of personalization and history for response ranking. *arXiv preprint arXiv:1606.00372*.

Piotr Bojanowski, Edouard Grave, Armand Joulin, and Tomas Mikolov. 2016. Enriching word vectors with subword information. *arXiv preprint arXiv:1607.04606*.

Budhaditya Deb, Peter Bailey, and Milad Shokouhi. 2019. Diversifying reply suggestions using a matching-conditional variational autoencoder. *arXiv preprint arXiv:1903.10630*.

Sepp Hochreiter and Jürgen Schmidhuber. 1997. Long short-term memory. *Neural computation*, 9(8):1735–1780.

Zongcheng Ji, Zhengdong Lu, and Hang Li. 2014. An information retrieval approach to short text conversation. *arXiv preprint arXiv:1408.6988*.

Diederik P. Kingma and Jimmy Ba. 2014. Adam: A method for stochastic optimization. *arXiv preprint arXiv:1412.6980*.

Tao Lei, Yu Zhang, Sida I. Wang, Hui Dai, and Yoav Artzi. 2018. Simple recurrent units for highly parallelizable recurrence. *arXiv preprint arXiv:1709.02755*.

Jiwei Li, Michel Galley, Chris Brockett, Georgios P. Spithourakis, Jianfeng Gao, and Bill Dolan. 2016. A persona-based neural conversation model. *arXiv preprint arXiv:1603.06155*.

Zhouhan Lin, Minwei Feng, Cicero Nogueira dos Santos, Mo Yu, Bing Xiang, Bowen Zhou, and Yoshua Bengio. 2017. A structured self-attentive sentence embedding. *arXiv preprint arXiv:1703.03130*.

Lajanugen Logeswaran and Honglak Lee. 2018. An efficient framework for learning sentence representations. *arXiv preprint arXiv:1803.02893*.

Ryan Lowe, Nissan Pow, Iulian Serban, and Joelle Pineau. 2015. The ubuntu dialogue corpus: A large dataset for research in unstructured multi-turn dialogue systems.

Yichao Lu, Phillip Keung, Shaonan Zhang, Jason Sun, and Vikas Bhardwaj. 2017. A practical approach to dialogue response generation in closed domains. *arXiv preprint arXiv:1703.09439*.

Kishore Papineni, Salim Roukos, Todd Ward, and Wei-Jing Zhu. 2002. Bleu: a method for automatic evaluation of machine translation. In *Proceedings of the 40th annual meeting on association for computational linguistics*, pages 311–318. Association for Computational Linguistics.

Adam Paszke, Sam Gross, Soumith Chintala, Gregory Chanan, Edward Yang, Zachary DeVito, Zeming Lin, Alban Desmaison, Luca Antiga, and Adam Lerer. 2017. Automatic differentiation in pytorch. In *NIPS-W*.

Iulian V. Serban, Alessandro Sordoni, Yoshua Bengio, Aaron Courville, and Joelle Pineau. 2015. Building end-to-end dialogue systems using generative hierarchical neural network models. *arXiv preprint arXiv:1507.04808*.

Igor Shalyminov, Ondej Duek, and Oliver Lemon. 2018. Neural response ranking for social conversation: A data-efficient approach. *arXiv preprint arXiv:1811.00967*.

Ashish Vaswani, Noam Shazeer, Niki Parmar, Jakob Uszkoreit, Llion Jones, Aidan N. Gomez, Lukasz Kaiser, and Illia Polosukhin. 2017. Attention is all you need. *arXiv preprint arXiv:1706.03762*.

Oriol Vinyals and Quoc Le. 2015. A neural conversational model. *arXiv preprint arXiv:1506.05869*.

Hao Wang, Zhengdong Lu, Hang Li, and Enhong Chen. 2013. A dataset for research on short-text conversation. *Proceedings of the 2013 Conference on Empirical Methods in Natural Language Processing*, pages 935–945.

Kishore Papineni Salim Roukos Todd Ward and John Henderson Florence Reeder. 2002. Corpus-based comprehensive and diagnostic mt evaluation: Initial arabic, chinese, french, and spanish results.

Bowen Wu, Baoxun Wang, and Hui Xue. 2016. Ranking responses oriented to conversational relevance in chat-bots. *COLING16*.

Yu Wu, Wei Wu, Chen Xing, Ming Zhou, and Zhoujun Li. 2017. Sequential matching network: A new architecture for multi-turn response selection in retrieval-based chatbots. *Proceedings of the 55th Annual Meeting of the Association for Computational Linguistics*.

Chen Xing, Wei Wu, Yu Wu, Jie Liu, Yalou Huang, Ming Zhou, and Wei-Ying Ma. 2016. Topic aware neural response generation. *arXiv preprint arXiv:1606.08340*.

Rui Yan, Yiping Song, and Hua Wu. 2016. Learning to respond with deep neural networks for retrieval-based human-computer conversation system. *SIGIR*, pages 55–64.

Liu Yang, Junjie Hu, Minghui Qiu, Chen Qu, Jianfeng Gao, W. Bruce Croft, Xiaodong Liu, Yelong Shen, and Jingjing Liu. 2019. A hybrid retrieval-generation neural conversation model. *arXiv preprint arXiv:1904.09068*.

Zhuosheng Zhang, Jiangtong Li, Pengfei Zhu, Hai Zhao, and Gongshen Liu. 2018. Modeling multi-turn conversation with deep utterance aggregation. *arXiv preprint arXiv:1806.09102*.

Xiangyang Zhou, Daxiang Dong, Hua Wu, Shiqi Zhao, Dianhai Yu, Hao Tian, Xuan Liu, and Rui Yan. 2016. Multi-view response selection for human-computer conversation. *Proceedings of the 2016 Conference on Empirical Methods in Natural Language Processing*, pages 372–381.

Xiangyang Zhou, Lu Li, Daxiang Dong, Yi Liu, Ying Chen, Wayne Xin Zhao, Dianhai Yu, and Hua Wu. 2018. Multi-turn response selection for chatbots with deep attention matching network. *Proceedings of the 56th Annual Meeting of the Association for Computational Linguistics*, pages 1118–1127.

A Appendix

A.1 Ablation Study

Table 9 shows the results of an ablation study we performed to identify the most important components of our model architecture and training regime. Each variant is described below.

Base. This is the model architecture described in Section 3.

4L SRU $\rightarrow$ 2L LSTM. We replace the 4 layer SRU encoder with a 2 layer LSTM encoder, which has a comparable number of parameters when using the same hidden sizes.

4L SRU $\rightarrow$ 2L SRU. We use an SRU with 2 layers instead of 4 layers. In order to match parameters, we use a hidden size of $d_h = 475$ instead of $d_h = 300$ in the model with 2 layers.

Flat $\rightarrow$ hierarchical. We replace the SRU encoder with two SRU encoders, one which operates at the word level and one which operates at the utterance level, following the architectures of Serban et al. (2015); Wu et al. (2017).

Cross entropy $\rightarrow$ hinge loss. Instead of using the cross-entropy loss defined in Equation 6, we use the hinge loss, which is defined as:

$$\mathcal{L} = \sum_{i=1}^{k} |s(c, r^+) - s(c, r_i^-) + m| \qquad (7)$$

where the margin $m = 0.25$ encourages separation between the score of the correct response and the score of each negative response.

6.6M $\rightarrow$ 1M examples. We train on a dataset with 1 million examples instead of the full 6.6 million training examples.

6.6M $\rightarrow$ 100K examples. We trained on a dataset with 100 thousand examples instead of the full 6.6 million training examples.

200 $\rightarrow$ 100 negatives. During training, we sample 100 negatives for each context-response pair instead of 200 negatives.

200 $\rightarrow$ 10 negatives. During training, we sample 10 negatives for each context-response pair instead of 200 negatives.

Co-Operation as an Asymmetric Form of Human-Computer Creativity. Case: Peace Machine

Mika Hämäläinen
Department of Digital Humanities
University of Helsinki
mika.hamalainen@helsinki.fi

Timo Honkela
Department of Digital Humanities
University of Helsinki
timo.honkela@helsinki.fi

Abstract

This theoretical paper identifies a need for a definition of asymmetric co-creativity where creativity is expected from the computational agent but not from the human user. Our co-operative creativity framework takes into account that the computational agent has a message to convey in a co-operative fashion, which introduces a trade-off on how creative the computer can be. The requirements of co-operation are identified from an interdisciplinary point of view. We divide co-operative creativity in *message creativity, contextual creativity* and *communicative creativity*. Finally these notions are applied in the context of the Peace Machine system concept.

1 Introduction

When we say something in a language, we say it to communicate something. Every utterance we say has a meaning behind it, a *message* we want to convey to others. This is true not only in everyday conversation, but in any act of language use, no matter the medium, whether it was spoken, written, signed etc.

For computationally creative systems, exhibiting linguistic creativity, expressing a message is not a requirement. In fact, just generating a linguistic realization, a surface form, is challenging enough and is considered of a merit.

The situation becomes more difficult when *mere surface generation*, i.e. producing natural language without a message, is not enough. When a system has to generate a creative poem that expresses a complete message or has to make a meaning conveying contribution to a conversation. It is often the case that a computationally creative system is not fully aware of the meaning its creations convey, but rather rely on people to pour their understanding of the world into the creative artifact and perceive creativity in it.

In this paper, we focus on co-operative creativity with the focus on dialog systems. We are not greatly interested in purely generative dialog systems that serve more for chitchat. Instead, we focus on goal-oriented dialog systems that have a clear message they need to convey, such as a price or available times, and the role of computational creativity in encapsulating their message in a creative form.

Creative behavior consisting of a human and a computer is called co-creativity. In the following section, we start by discussing this notion and why it is insufficient for modelling our task. In the following sections, we take an interdisciplinary view on what co-operation means and formulate a creative framework based on these notions. Finally we show a more concrete way of using our framework by applying it on the Peace Machine concept.

In the field of computational creativity, working with a definition for creativity plays a crucial role in evaluation of a creative system (Jordanous, 2012; Alnajjar and Hämäläinen, 2018). While a myriad of more abstract level theories on computational creativity have been elaborated in the past (Colton, 2008; Wiggins, 2006; Colton et al., 2011), our work aims to develop a theoretical framework to a more concrete problem of creative dialog generation.

2 Co-Creativity

In this section, we describe some of the existing definitions of human computer co-creativity as the co-creativity paradigm is closest to our case.

Co-creativity can be divided into four categories as identified by Lubart (2005). The computer can act as a *nanny* to a person guiding and motivating him in the creative task, where as if the computer acts as a *coach*, it will more actively help the

Proceedings of the 1st Workshop on NLP for Conversational AI, pages 42–50
Florence, Italy, August 1, 2019. ©2019 Association for Computational Linguistics

creative person to explore new ways of thinking by educating them about different creativity techniques. In a *pen-pal* scenario, the computer helps a creative individual in communicating ideas with others. Finally, the computer can be a *colleague* in which case humans and computers are in a creative dialogue taking turns in forming a creative artefact.

Davis (2013) identifies a gap between the AI research focusing on computational creativity and HCI (human-computer interaction) research focusing on creativity support tools. He argues that co-creativity can narrow this gap. Creativity is seen as an emergent phenomenon from the interactions of a human and a computer. The interactions are collaborative and both parties influence on each other.

In mixed initiative co-creativity (Yannakakis et al., 2014), both the computer and a human user take an active role in contributing to solving a creative problem, although, not necessarily to the same extent. This differs from turn-based collaboration between the two parties and from the computer being merely a supportive tool, as the both parties are actively creative.

In a recent study outlining evaluation of co-creativity (Karimi et al., 2018), the concept of co-creativity is defined as an interaction involving at least one AI agent and one human. They act based on the creative response of the other party and their own understanding of creativity.

The current definitions of co-creativity always expect the presence of human creativity in addition to computational creativity or computer assisted creativity. However, a co-operation setting does not require creativity at all, and if the computational agent is creative, it does not mean that there has to be human creativity present at the same time.

3 Co-Operation

Co-operative creativity requires the computer to exhibit creativity in its way of communication. However, creativity is not a requirement for the human user. Even though dialogue itself can be seen as an interplay between two or more parties forming an ephemeral creative artefact of its own, we want to clearly distinguish co-operative creativity from co-creativity. Therefore, we are not looking at dialogue as a creative artefact but rather how creativity can take place one-sidedly on the level of utterances.

3.1 Communicative-Creative Trade off

The purpose of a dialogue system, whether it is made for chitchat or to answer queries, is always to co-operate with a human. Co-operation can thus, in its simplest form, be contributing to the conversation in a meaningful way to keep the conversation on going.

The rules of conversation are governed by linguistic, cognitive and social mechanisms that have to be followed, and they set limitations for creativity. For instance, a dialogue system for booking movie tickets can deliver a very uncreative communicative answer stating just the name of the movie and its showtime or on the other extreme of creativity, answering by a riddle.

We argue that the co-operative nature of conversation, where creativity is only expected from the computer, not from the human, and where a certain communicative function has to be filled in accordance to higher level rules of conversation, has to balance in between creativity and predictability.

3.2 Communication in Pragmatics

The field of pragmatics has been studying meaning in its context for multiple decades. In this section, we will explain the key pragmatic theories in understanding conversation and meaning of utterances.

Grice (1975) famously defined four maxims for co-operative principle of communication: manner, quality, quantity and relevance. Through these maxims, we can identify linguistic rules that a machine should follow in order to be converse in a co-operative fashion.

The maxim of manner means that the communication is conducted in an orderly and unambiguous fashion. The maxim of quality refers to the truthfulness of the utterance. The speaker shall not say anything he believes to be false.

If there is just enough information communicated in an utterance, the maxim of quantity is followed. This means that both communicating too little or too much is against this maxim. The last maxim, namely that of relevance, requires the utterance to be contextually related and not off topic.

When it comes to the function of utterances, i.e. their relation to the surrounding world, we can use Searle's speech acts (Searle, 1969) (cf. Nonaka, 1994; Rus et al., 2012). According to this theory, all utterances are either representative, expressive, declarative, commissive or directive.

Representative and expressive are close to each other in a communicative function. The former states something factual about the surrounding reality outside of the speaker, where as the latter is a statement about the internal state, such as the emotion, of the speaker.

Directive speech acts are commands, i.e. their intention is to make someone else perform an action. Commissive speech acts have a similar function as they are promises, in their case the speaker is the one who is going to perform the action. Declarative speech acts are, by their definition, supposed to change the surrounding world. An example of such a speech act is sentencing someone guilty of a crime.

It is important to note that the surface form of an utterance does not dictate the speech act it is used to perform, but rather its contextualization plays an important role. For instance, a prayer is an expressive speech act even though on the surface it might seem as a directive speech act. This interplay between the context and the words themselves opens up a great potential for creativity.

3.3 Socio-Cognitive Views

In cognitive science, the concept of scripts (cf. Bower et al., 1979) can be used in a higher level to explain communication. In day-to-day life, our brains rely on heuristics when processing information. This helps us perform tasks in a cognitively less intensive fashion. Scripts store learned patterns of behaviour and outcome of different situations. For instance, paying for groceries follows a well defined script: stand in a line waiting for your turn, place the items on the belt, pay and go packing. By following this script, we do not have to figure out how to pay for our groceries every time we need to buy food. It is to be noted, though, that the scripts vary according to geographical and cultural areas. The script for visiting a grocery store or bank is different, e.g., in the USA, different parts of Europe or China.

A higher level theory of the same phenomenon is the one presented by Goffman (1959). According to his view, social life is assimilated to a theater play, where every participant is supposed to play their own role. In the level of interaction, the focus of his interest is in maintaining face. The common goal of the interlocutors in a conversation is to maintain their own social face and those of the other participants.

3.4 Usability and Design

When we are dealing with dialogue systems, we cannot overlook the fact that we are inherently dealing with a user interface. In the fields of usability and design, the problem of communication has been dealt with from the human-computer interaction point of view.

A simple heuristic in usability for assessing a user interface is to look at the mental and physical effort (cf. Komogortsev et al., 2009) required to perform a task. For dialogue systems, physical effort can be calculated by how many queries the user has to perform to complete a given task. Mental effort refers to all cognitively demanding tasks such as how much information the user has to gather and memorize from different parts of the interface. Thus a dialogue system listing all the possible flights with all the details when requested would have low requirement for physical effort, but would be cognitively intensive as the user would have to memorize every flight he finds suitable.

Maybe a more intriguing concept in design is that of elegance (cf. White 2011). An elegant design communicates the intended message fully with as little as possible. The communication in a message can be divided in two: in denotation and connotation. Where denotation is the pure information content of the message, connotation is more in the way the message is communicated - in the emotional response it evokes.

3.5 Synthesis

In the previous sections, we have dedicated much room for describing the theories from different disciplines that in their core, are dealing with the very same phenomenon - communication. This section is dedicated into putting the theories together to form an interdisciplinary framework for a dialog system that is independent of the technical realization or creativity at this point.

We take elegance and script as higher level concepts as they are on the highest level of abstraction. Reflecting these in terms of the co-operative principle, i.e. the maxims, we can notice that elegance is closely related to the maxims of quantity and quality. As the requirement of elegance is to express the message as fully as possible (quality) with as little as possible (quantity), an elegant utterance needs to fulfill these two maxims.

Scripts are most strongly related to the maxims of manner and relevance. As scripts give us behavioral patterns to follow in different situations, they govern the manner in which we are expected to express ourselves. The behavioral patterns also entail what is relevant to say in which situation.

We place the usability terms on the lowest level in our synthesized model of co-operation, as they are meant to assess a concrete human-computer interaction scenario. Physical effort is linked mostly to the maxims of quantity and relevance. A dialogue system providing too little information will force the user to ask for more details, which increases the amount of physical effort. This is true also in the case of non-relevant information, which provokes more queries by the user to reach to a relevant answer.

The maxim of quantity relates to mental effort as well. Too much information will force the user to store it in his memory, which increases the mental effort. Another maxim affecting on mental effort is that of manner. If the information is not presented in an orderly manner, it makes it more difficult for the user to gather the important bits of information into a cohesive whole.

Coming back to the highest level concepts, elegance and script, a bridge needs to be built to connect them. We argue that they are connected through the context in which the conversation takes place. The context triggers a script, but it also changes the meaning of what is elegant. Talking with a person who knows a great deal about the topic of the conversation requires less words to communicate the message whereas more explaining is in order for a person new to the topic.

The context is also dictated by the *role* one is expected to *play* in the social situation. Therefore Goffman's theory is a part of the contextual bridge linking the two highest level concepts. We also introduce a mental model of the interlocutor as a part of the context as it has been proven evident by the previous discussion, that the maxims depend on the interlocutor as well. Furthermore, the conversation develops in time, which means that the prior utterances are also building the current context.

Now that we have synthesized what co-operative conversation requires, it is time to add the remaining notions into the model. No conversation can take place meaningfully if there is no

message to be conveyed by the words of an utterance. This message can be divided into its denotative and connotative function. How the message can be conveyed is limited by the speech acts, and they function as a gate to the conversation.

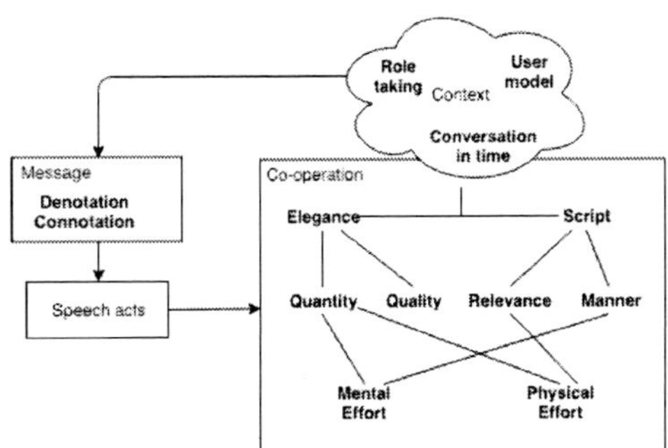

Figure 1: Model of co-operation

Figure 1 depicts the model described in this section. This model does not take creativity into account, but rather describes the requirements of co-operation and their inter-dependencies. The context is connected back into the message component as it affects on the next utterance of the conversation.

4 Co-Operative Creativity

In the previous section, we identified three main components of a co-operative dialogue system: message (including speech acts), context and co-operation , which correspond to *message, contextual* and *communicative creativity* respectively. In this section, we shed light into how computational creativity can manifest itself without jeopardizing the strict requirement of co-operation.

4.1 Message Creativity

In a co-operative setting, there is a limitation to what can be communicated so that it is still relevant for the conversation. The limitation can be very strict like in the case of a dialogue system selling tickets or lenient as in the case of chitchat.

4.1.1 Creativity in Denotation

Even if the set of possible denotations was limited, there is room for creativity in finding something else to communicate that is still co-operative. For example, *glass is half full* and *glass is half empty* communicate about the same phenomenon, yet their denotations are different. Thus, finding a creative point of view to communicate about the same phenomenon is a way of altering the denotation of the message without making it non-co-operative.

In a more lenient setting, the context of the message can be explored to find a way to communicate a denotation that still contributes to the co-operativity. This could, for instance, be a change of topic or a message provoking an emotional change such as a joke.

4.1.2 Creativity in Connotation

Even if the denotation of a message was fully fixed, for example, if the system has to communicate the price of a movie ticket and cannot communicate any other denotation to avoid risking co-operativity, connotation opens up more room for creativity.

Connotation can be altered as easily as by the choice of words or by a structural change. Consider for example the following sentences *An appointment for vaccination has been reserved for Monday* and *You will get your shot on Monday*. Both of them communicate the same denotation, but their connotation is different. The first sentence sounds more official and establishes social distance where as the latter is more casual in style.

4.1.3 Exploiting Speech Acts

Speech acts are more abstract in nature than any linguistic form, and thus speech acts themselves do not offer much room for creativity. However, understanding that certain surface realizations are most closely attached to certain speech acts, opens up a window for creativity.

I like strawberries is seemingly an expressive speech act; the person tries to communicate about his liking of strawberries. However, the actual speech act might be directive *give me strawberries* or commissive *I will buy strawberries*, depending on the context. Therefore mixing and matching speech acts with non-typical surface forms that still communicate the message is an exploitable possibility of computational creativity.

4.2 Contextual Creativity

The context has a huge effect on how communicated messages are understood. As we have seen throughout this paper, words can mean different things in different contexts. A context also sets limits to what can be said and how it should be said.

4.2.1 User Adaptation

Knowing the user and establishing trust with him gives more freedom for creative behavior. Even in tightly scripted situations, if the user is known well, the communication can deviate more from the script without it damaging the co-operation.

A semantic model that has been learned from the user in question could be used to creatively adapt a message to the user's own vocabulary. If for example the user hates *frozen yogurt* a flight connection with tediously long layovers could be communicated as *a frozen yogurt route*.

A creatively expressed message has a higher risk to not being understood. A good user model can then provide a way of assessing whether a creative communication solution will be understood as intended or not.

4.2.2 Role Identification

If we look at communication from the perspective of role-taking, a great source of creativity can come from identifying the possible roles supported by the context and picking the one that gives the greatest freedom in expression.

Role identification from user perspective, especially if there are many human users, can contribute to the creative freedom. If there are more than one possible roles the users can take, changing their role to one that offers more freedom of creativity can be of a benefit. The roles can be changed by communicative means.

4.2.3 Time Perspective

Planning the flow of the conversation ahead doing constant predictions is a potential way of shifting the context towards one that has more room for creativity. The planning itself can also be a creative process where the conversation will take unexpected turns that still contribute to co-operation.

Just as much as predicting the future can be a creative process, knowing the past can be used creatively as well. This is not limited to creative comebacks to what the user has said, but also can mean re-interpretation of what has been said before. Language is ambiguous and this fact can be celebrated by reusing bits of the conversation form the past in the new current context.

4.3 Communicative Creativity

The co-operation section in Figure 1 is probably the part that limits creativity the most. Maxims and the other components they relate to set rules to how one is supposed to communicate in order to do it in a co-operative fashion. However, there is room for creativity even with these tight rules.

4.3.1 Script Selection

In a conversation situation, there might be multiple social scripts to choose from. Picking a non-typical, but yet contextually fitting script can make it possible to find new creative solutions in the conversation.

As scripts are not predefined hand-written rules, but rather learned behavioral patterns, scripts offer flexibility in changing them. Identifying how to change a script, or how to go outside of one, in a way that it does not startle the interlocutor, is a task requiring creativity.

4.3.2 Adjustment of Elegance

Optimizing for elegance is probably too limiting for creativity and not an interesting way to go about creativity in conversation. The question should be what is elegant enough, and what is expected to be communicated. A longer message might be seen inelegant as it uses too many words to communicate a message, if we are only interested in the denotation. However, the additional length might contribute to connotation.

Making justified statements about elegance requires a definition of what is communicated, the message itself. This tells what is expected to be communicated, which then in its turn, makes it possible to assess the elegance of the utterance.

4.3.3 Informed Deviation from Maxims

Maxims are a part of co-operative principle and thus by definition they are tailored towards co-operative conversation. However, they are highly contextual and therefore what is enough, relevant and so on is a matter of the context in which an utterance occurs.

A system seeking to deviate from the maxims and still maintain co-operativity in the communication needs to be able to assess the effect of such a deviation in a reasoned way. For example, if the goal is to make the user think and ask questions, communicating a bit too little or increasing ambiguity might be useful.

A seemingly irrelevant communication can be useful if the communication is later contextualized and made relevant for the initial conversation topic. Sometimes telling anecdotes or giving analogous examples might seem irrelevant to the in-terlocutor, but later in the conversation they can prove to be helpful in understanding the problem from another perspective.

The maxim of quality relates to truthfulness of the utterance. Expressing something that is clearly untrue can be a way of expressing the opposite meaning in a sarcastic fashion (cf. Hämäläinen, 2016). If the sarcasm is understood correctly by the user, the communication can still be co-operative, even though on the surface it appears to be insincere.

5 The Context of Peace Machine

Peace Machine (Honkela, 2017) is a concept on how to use different parts of Artificial Intelligence (AI) to promote peaceful conditions in the world. This highly ambitious objective may sound unrealistic at first. It is to be remembered, though, that the range of AI technologies that have considerable impact in various domains is wide and increasing.

The Peace Machine concept consists of three main areas. The question is not about one system but a number of different applications and systems. The three main areas considered are (1) Improved communication, (2) Understanding emotions, and (3) Improving societal conditions.

5.1 Co-Operative Creativity in Peace Machine

In the following, the Peace Machine concept is considered from the point of view of Co-Operative Creativity defined and described in this paper. Peace Machine serves as a general application context for the theoretical work presented in this paper and its components can be studies in the communicative framework presented in this paper.

5.2 Message Creativity

The objective of Peace Machine is to help the user of a component of the system use and learn communicative acts that help him navigate in the conversational space in a peaceful and constructive manner or understand one's own or others' emotions in a constructive way. To be successful in this task, the system must be able to express itself in a creative manner when necessary. The user may need help in seeing matters from a novel point of view or in understanding the current situation beyond the limits of the conceptual system that he may have available. This help may be reached, for instance, with the use of metaphor.

5.2.1 Creativity in Denotation

The topic of conversation may be guided into areas in which, for instance, the risk of emotional outbursts are lowered. The creativity of the system would lie in the ability to guide the topics of the conversation even when the overall communicative goal remains the same. One opportunity is to find a path in the conversation that minimizes unintended choice of topics or expressions that might endanger the overall goal. It is known from practical experience in peace negotiations that the use of a poorly chosen single word or theme may jeopardize the whole process. Here it is to be remembered that Peace Machine is not focusing on peace negotiations between nations or other such organizations but between any two or more people.

5.2.2 Creativity in Connotation

In Peace Machine, consideration of the connotation is very important. When the aim is to reach peaceful and constructive communication, expressions that have negative connotations should be avoided. In a conversation between two people, the system may help the persons to avoid expressions that hurt other's emotions or the ground of his identity. In many cultures it is important to take social aspects into account. Depending on the relationship between the people, their status and cultural background, the expressions that are appropriate in one situation may be quite the opposite in another. For instance, the same content can be expressed in two quite different ways regarding the style: *Let's have a meeting tomorrow!* or *May I have the honor to ask your presence in meeting in the near future, potentially already tomorrow?*.

5.2.3 Exploiting Speech Acts

Useful computational creativity that helps people through potentially problematic communication can take place through suitable choices regarding speech acts. In a homely context, there is a clear difference between the expressions *Take out the trash bin* and *The trash bin is quite smelly*. The intention can be considered to be the same in both cases but the emotional outcome may be quite different. Whether illocutionary, perlocutionary, propositional or utterance act should be chosen depends on multiple factors that concern the persons involved, their background, history of the communication and the broader context. At

the present moment, it is still difficult to take into account the non-linguistic context in human-like manner. It is, however, good to keep in mind that persons may interpret the non-linguist or implicit context in a different way especially if they, for instance, have different education or cultural background (cf. Anderson and Shifrin, 2017).

5.3 Contextual Creativity

In Peace Machine, as in any general purpose system, the challenge of world knowledge and the huge complexity of the contexts that a system may encounter is a great challenge as well as an opportunity. This could be an indirect or direct access to the context. Here indirect refers to the use of language and the direct refers to use of perceptual senses. The underlying matters have been a subject to philosophical debates for very long time (cf. Gärdenfors, 2000; Von Foerster, 2007; Bundgaard, 2010) and it is not possible to cover this theme here. From the point of view of Peace Machine, the room for computational creativity is extensive and given broad range of opportunities. In building peace one possible approach is to choose the topics and dimensions suitably. For instance, the choice can help the discussants feel safe and secure. A useful notion is the division into foreground and background that is used in cognitive linguistics (Langacker, 2008). Sometimes it may be useful and constructive to start conversational from the background and gradually proceed into the foreground. The creative system may help humans in finding such conversational routes.

5.3.1 User Adaptation

In the above discussion referring to context, the aspect of subjectivity was briefly brought up. In addition to their experiences, values, preferences and identity, people are also different regarding their linguistic and conceptual systems. We do not know the same set of words and their meanings and we even have different interpretations of words and expressions. The words "fair" or "beautiful" refer to different things, which should be obvious, but more difficult to measure than comparing the limits or distributions of interpretation of color "orange" or whether some product is "expensive". In Peace Machine, this theme is very important as it has been pointed out that misunderstanding is a very common phenomenon that has wide practical consequences. Creative user adaptation on language and conceptual systems is presented as a potentially important means to serve a basis for highly improved communication. This is a hypotheses that needs to be tested in various kinds of settings.

5.3.2 Role Identification

A machine, the purpose of which is to help people understand one another, can take up different roles in a communicative setting. In a situation of conflict, a suitable role might be that of a mediator while some situations require a more active leader-like role from the machine. This gives the machine a spectrum of roles from the passive to active to choose from.

5.3.3 Time Perspective

Helping people understand one another is a task with a persuasive goal. This persuasion requires planning, and the creative outcomes of the flow of the conversation have to be taken into account by the system.

With an aim for peace, Peace Machine should be able to take turns in the conversation that get the interlocutor off guard. In an extremely polarized setting, the two opposing parties are biased towards not being open towards the other party's opinions. A persuasion technique such as this one requires creative planning.

5.4 Communicative Creativity for Peace Machine

In the following, we consider how to communicate in a co-operative fashion while using the Peace Machine system.

5.4.1 Script Selection

Useful scripts to promote mutual understanding and respect can be learned based on large corpora of conversations. The real world variety of contexts makes its useful to apply creative solutions when the corpus-based solution does not provide close enough solution. Two or more solutions may be merged.

5.4.2 Adjustment of Elegance

Elegance is seemingly an important criterion regarding Peace Machine. The system should communicate in such a manner that it matches with the user's linguistic expectations and situation-specific needs. Too short and ambiguous message may be considered impolite or rude. Equally well, a message too long may be considered uninteresting or impolite. The Peace Machine system component can be used to train a person to handle potentially troublesome situations, during the conversation with someone else, or to help by analyzing an earlier conversation.

5.4.3 Informed Deviation from Maxims

From the point of view of the Peace Machine concept and system use, among the Grice's (1975) four maxims for co-operative principle of communication, manner, quality, quantity and relevance, can be used to judge potential usefulness of breaking these rules in a creative way. Regarding manner, the system may guide a person to be unclear or ambiguous in order to give room for alternative helpful interpretations or ideas, or to point out that the terminology and conceptual space may be such that meaning negotiation would be useful regarding the conversational situation at hand. The initial problem may help in understanding that the basis is not the same regarding the meaning of some key term in the conversation.

Changing the topic in the middle of a conversation and not being relevant may be a means to create a possibility to escape a problematic conversational situation. This approach should be used with care because it may lead into unintended consequences. For instance, the expression may be interpreted as an insult rather than as, for instance, humorous break to a heated discussion.

6 Conclusions

This paper has identified a need for theoretical framework for asymmetric human-computer creativity, where, for the first time, the computer is the only party with a requirement for creativity. Thus our initial framework fills a theoretical void in the field.

In this paper we have outlined from an interdisciplinary point of view what the requirements are for a co-operative conversation. Based on this definition, we have identified three different kinds of creativity in a co-operative setting: message, contextual and conversational creativity.

Furthermore, we have highlighted the importance of having a message to convey creatively. This makes a clear distinction with the creative systems that generate language without a need to communicate a certain idea, a message. Due to the nature of dialogue systems that are meant to aid users reach their goal, this need for a message cannot be ignored.

References

Khalid Alnajjar and Mika Hämäläinen. 2018. A Master-Apprentice Approach to Automatic Creation of Culturally Satirical Movie Titles. In *Proceedings of the 11th International Conference on Natural Language Generation (INLG)*, pages 274—283.

Richard C Anderson and Zohara Shifrin. 2017. The meaning of words in context. In *Theoretical issues in reading comprehension*, pages 331–348. Routledge.

Gordon H Bower, John B Black, and Terrence J Turner. 1979. Scripts in memory for text. *Cognitive Psychology*, 11(2):177 – 220.

Peer F Bundgaard. 2010. Husserl and language. In *Handbook of phenomenology and cognitive science*, pages 368–399. Springer.

Simon Colton. 2008. Creativity Versus the Perception of Creativity in Computational Systems. In *AAAI Spring Symposium: Creative Intelligent Systems*, Technical Report SS-08-03, pages 14—-20, Stanford, California, USA.

Simon Colton, John William Charnley, and Alison Pease. 2011. Computational creativity theory: The face and idea descriptive models. In *ICCC*, pages 90–95.

Nicholas Davis. 2013. Human-computer co-creativity: Blending human and computational creativity. In *Ninth Artificial Intelligence and Interactive Digital Entertainment Conference*.

Erving Goffman. 1959. *The Presentation of Self in Everyday Life*. University of Edinburgh Social Sciences Research Centre.

H Paul Grice. 1975. Logic and conversation. *1975*, pages 41–58.

Peter Gärdenfors. 2000. *Conceptual Spaces: The Geometry of Thought*. MIT Press, Cambridge, MA, USA.

Mika Hämäläinen. 2016. Reconocimiento automático del sarcasmo - ¡Esto va a funcionar bien! Master's thesis, University of Helsinki, Finland. URN:NBN:fi:hulib-201606011945.

Timo Honkela. 2017. *Rauhankone. Tekoälytutkijan testamentti*. Gaudeamus.

Anna Jordanous. 2012. A standardised procedure for evaluating creative systems: Computational creativity evaluation based on what it is to be creative. *Cognitive Computation*, 4(3):246–279.

Pegah Karimi, Kazjon Grace, Mary Lou Maher, and Nicholas Davis. 2018. Evaluating creativity in computational co-creative systems. In *The Proceedings of the Ninth International Conference on Computational Creativity, ICCC*.

O Komogortsev, Carl J Mueller, Dan Tamir, and Liam Feldman. 2009. An effort based model of software usability. In *2009 International Conference on Software Engineering Theory and Practice (SETP-09)*.

Ronald Langacker. 2008. *Cognitive grammar: A basic introduction*. OUP USA.

Todd Lubart. 2005. How can computers be partners in the creative process: Classification and commentary on the special issue. *International Journal of Human-Computer Studies*, 63(4):365 – 369. Computer support for creativity.

Ikujiro Nonaka. 1994. A dynamic theory of organizational knowledge creation. *Organization science*, 5(1):14–37.

Vasile Rus, Cristian Moldovan, Nobal Niraula, and Arthur C Graesser. 2012. Automated discovery of speech act categories in educational games. *International Educational Data Mining Society*.

John Rogers Searle. 1969. *Speech acts: An essay in the philosophy of language*. Cambridge university press.

Heinz Von Foerster. 2007. *Understanding understanding: Essays on cybernetics and cognition*. Springer Science & Business Media.

Alex W White. 2011. *The Elements of Graphic Design*. Allworth Press.

Geraint A Wiggins. 2006. A preliminary framework for description, analysis and comparison of creative systems. *Knowledge-Based Systems*, 19(7):449–458.

Georgios N Yannakakis, Antonios Liapis, and Constantine Alexopoulos. 2014. Mixed-initiative co-creativity. In *Proceedings of the 9th Conference on the Foundations of Digital Games*.

Conversational Response Re-ranking Based on Event Causality and Role Factored Tensor Event Embedding

Shohei Tanaka[1], Koichiro Yoshino[1,2], Katsuhito Sudoh[1], Satoshi Nakamura[1]

[1] Nara Institute of Science and Technology
[2] PRESTO, Japan Science and Technology Agency
{takana.shohei.tj7, koichiro, sudoh, s-nakamura}@is.naist.jp

Abstract

We propose a novel method for selecting coherent and diverse responses for a given dialogue context. The proposed method re-ranks response candidates generated from conversational models by using event causality relations between events in a dialogue history and response candidates (e.g., "be stressed out" precedes "relieve stress"). We use distributed event representation based on the Role Factored Tensor Model for a robust matching of event causality relations due to limited event causality knowledge of the system. Experimental results showed that the proposed method improved coherency and dialogue continuity of system responses.

1 Introduction

While a variety of dialogue models such as the neural conversational model (NCM) (Vinyals and Le, 2015) have been researched widely, such dialogue models often generate simple and dull responses due to the limitation of their ability to take dialogue context into account. It is very difficult for these models to generate coherent responses to a dialogue history. We tackle this problem with a new architecture by incorporating event causality relations between response candidates and a dialogue history. Typical event causality relations are cause-effect relations between two events, such as "be stressed out" precedes "relieve stress." In this paper, event causality relations are defined that an effect event is likely to happen after a corresponding cause event happens (Shibata and Kurohashi, 2011; Shibata et al., 2014). Event causality relations have been used in why-question answering systems to focus on causalities between questions and answers (Oh et al., 2013, 2016, 2017). It is also reported that a conversational model using event causality relations can generate diverse and coherent responses (Fujita et al., 2011). However,

the relation between dialogue continuity and the coherency of system responses is still an underlying problem.

In this paper, we propose a novel method to select an appropriate response from response candidates generated by NCMs. We define a score for re-ranking to select a response that has an event causality relation to a dialogue history. Re-ranking effectively improves response reliability in language generation tasks such as why-question answering and dialogue systems (Oh et al., 2013; Jansen et al., 2014; Bogdanova and Foster, 2016; Ohmura and Eskenazi, 2018). We used event causality pairs extracted from a large-scale corpus (Shibata and Kurohashi, 2011; Shibata et al., 2014). We also use distributed event representation based on the Role Factored Tensor Model (RFTM) (Weber et al., 2018) to realize a robust matching of event causality relations, even if these causalities are not included in the extracted event causality pairs. In human and automatic evaluations, the proposed method outperformed conventional methods in selecting coherent and diverse responses.

2 Response Re-ranking Using Event Causality Relations

Figure 1 shows an overview of the proposed method. The process consists of four parts. First, N-best response candidates are generated from an NCM given a dialogue history (Figure 1 ①; Section 2.1). Then, events (predicate-argument structures) are extracted by an event parser from both the dialogue history and the response candidates (Figure 1 ②). We used Kurohashi Nagao Parser (KNP)[1] (Kawahara and Kurohashi, 2006; Sasano and Kurohashi, 2011) as the event parser. Next, the extracted events are converted to dis-

---

[1] http://nlp.ist.i.kyoto-u.ac.jp/?KNP

Proceedings of the 1st Workshop on NLP for Conversational AI, pages 51–59
Florence, Italy, August 1, 2019. ©2019 Association for Computational Linguistics

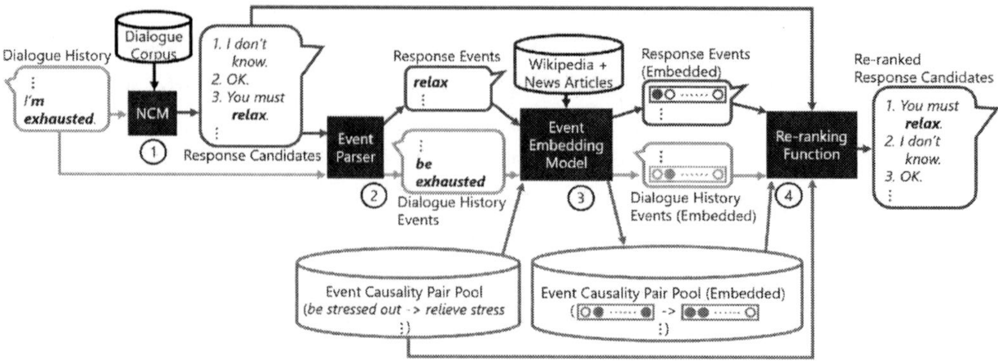

Figure 1: Neural conversational model+re-ranking using event causality; a response that has an event causality relation ("*be exhausted*" → "*relax*") to the dialogue history is selected by the re-ranking.

predicate 1	argument 1	predicate 2	argument 2	$lift$
be stressed out	-	relieve	stress	10.02

Table 1: Example of event causality relations included in event causality pairs

tributed event representations by an event embedding model (Figure 1 ③; Section 2.3). Events in event causality pairs are also converted to distributed representations to calculate similarities. The RFTM is used for the embedding. Finally, response candidates are re-ranked (Figure 1 ④; Section 2.2, 2.4). We describe these components in more detail below.

2.1 Neural Conversational Model (NCM)

NCM learns a mapping between input and output word sequences by using recurrent neural networks (RNNs). NCMs can generate N-best response candidates by using beam search or sampling (Macherey et al., 2016).

2.2 Event Causality Pairs

The proposed method uses event causality pairs. Events in a pair, which have cause-effect relations, are extracted from a large-scale corpus on the basis of co-occurring statistics and case frames (Shibata and Kurohashi, 2011; Shibata et al., 2014). 420,000 entries are extracted from 1.6 billion texts: each entry consists of information denoted in Table 1. "predicate 1" and "argument 1" are components of a cause event, and "predicate 2" and "argument 2" are components of an effect event. Each event consists of a predicate and arguments. The predicate is required, and the argument is optional. We used arguments that have the following roles: nominative, accusative, dative, instrumental, and locative cases. $lift$ is the mutual

information score between two events, which indicates the strength of the causality relation. Using $lift$, we propose a score for re-ranking as,

$$score = \max_{<e_h, e_r>} \frac{\log_2 p}{\left(\log_2 lift(e_h, e_r)\right)^\lambda}. \quad (1)$$

p is the posterior probability of the response candidate provided by NCM. λ is a hyper parameter to decide the weight of event causality relations. $lift(e_h, e_r)$ is the $lift$ score between an event e_h in the dialogue history, and an event e_r in the response candidate, which is equal to 2 if the pair does not appear in the extracted event causality pair pool. Note that $lift(e_h, e_r)$ is log-scaled because it has a wide range of values ($10 < lift(e_h, e_r) < 10,000$). In the case where more than one event causality relations are recognized between the dialogue history and the response candidate, the score of the candidate is determined by the relation with the highest $lift(e_h, e_r)$. We call this model "Re-ranking."

2.3 Distributed Event Representation Based on Role Factored Tensor Model (RFTM)

It is difficult to determine event causality relations by using only the pairs observed in an actual corpus. Therefore, we introduce a distributed event representation to improve the robustness of matching events in a dialogue with those in the event causality pair pool. Any events are embedded into fixed length vectors to calculate their similarities.

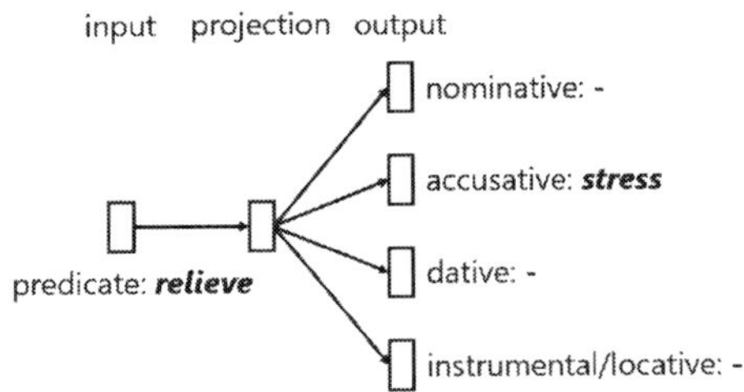

Figure 2: Model architecture of predicate embedding

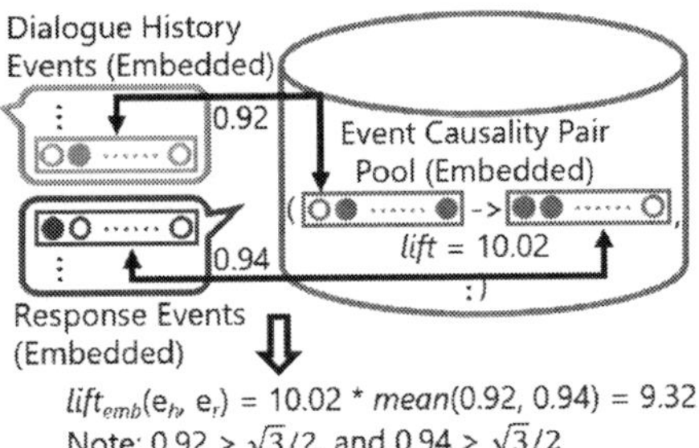

$lift_{emb}(e_h, e_r) = 10.02 * mean(0.92, 0.94) = 9.32$
Note: $0.92 > \sqrt{3}/2$, and $0.94 > \sqrt{3}/2$

Figure 3: Event causality relation matching; the $lift$ of the event causality relation in which "*be exhausted*" precedes "*relax*," is calculated from the $lift$ of the most similar event causality relation where "*be stressed out*" precedes "*relieve stress*."

	Ave.dist-1	Ave.dist-2
EncDec	0.44	0.56
HRED	0.33	0.42

Table 2: Diversity of N-best Response Candidates

We define an event with a single predicate or a pair of a predicate and arguments. Argument a of an event is embedded into vector as v_a by using Skip-gram (Mikolov et al., 2013c,a,b). Predicate p of an event is embedded into vector as v_p by using predicate embedding which is based on case-unit Skip-gram. Figure 2 shows the model architecture of predicate embedding. The model learns predicate vector representations which are good at predicting its arguments. To get an event embedding for the pair of v_p and v_a, we propose to use RFTM, which was proposed by Weber et al. (2018). The RFTM embeds a predicate and its arguments into vector e as,

$$e = \sum_a W_a T(v_p, v_a). \qquad (2)$$

The relation of a predicate and its arguments is computed using a 3D tensor T and matrices W_a. If the event has no arguments, e is substituted by v_p. The RFTM is trained to predict an event sequence; thus it can represent the meaning of the event in a particular context.

2.4 Event Causality Relation Matching Based on Distributed Event Representation

Figure 3 illustrates the process of matching events on the basis of distributed event representation. Given an event pair from a response candidate and a dialogue history, the proposed method finds an event causality pair that has the highest cosine similarity from the pool. $lift$ score, strength of the event causality relation, is extended as,

$$lift_{emb}(e_h, e_r) =$$
$$lift(e_c, e_e) * mean\big(sim(e_h, e_c), sim(e_r, e_e)\big). \qquad (3)$$

e_h is an event in the dialogue history, e_r is an event in the response candidate. e_c and e_e are respectively a cause and an effect event of an event causality pair. We also calculate the score for the case in which the cause and effect events are exchanged to deal with the inverse case. Note that both sim values have a threshold to prevent overgeneralization. The threshold was empirically decided as $\sqrt{3}/2$. Replacing $lift(e_h, e_r)$ in Eq. (1) with $lift_{emb}(e_h, e_r)$, the score using distributed event representation is defined as,

$$score = \max_{<e_h, e_r>} \frac{\log_2 p}{\left(\log_2 lift_{emb}(e_h, e_r)\right)^\lambda}. \qquad (4)$$

We call this model "Re-ranking (emb)."

3 Experiments

We conducted automatic and human evaluations to compare responses with and without the re-ranking. We evaluated our proposed re-ranking method on a conventional Encoder-Decoder with Attention (EncDec) model (Bahdanau et al., 2015, Luong et al., 2015) and a Hierarchical Recurrent Encoder-Decoder (HRED) model (Sordoni et al., 2015; Serban et al., 2016). While HRED tries to generate more coherent responses to dialogue context than a simple Encoder-Decoder, the diversity of responses is small due to context constraints.

We used the Japanese data from a Wikipedia dump for training Skip-gram and predicate word embeddings of RFTM, and the *Maichichi* newspaper dataset 2017[2] for training RFTM. We col-

---

[2] http://www.nichigai.co.jp/sales/mainichi/mainichi-data.html

Method			Evaluation							
NCM	history	re-ranking	re-ranked (%)	BLEU	NIST	extrema	dist-1	dist-2	PMI	length
reference	-	-	-	-	-	-	0.06	0.40	1.86	21.43
EncDec	-	1-best	-	1.12	1.19	**0.42**	0.06	0.18	1.77	15.55
EncDec	1	Re-ranking	4,016 (7.90)	1.10	1.18	**0.42**	0.06	0.19	1.78	15.52
EncDec	1	Re-ranking (emb)	29,343 (57.71)	1.02	1.07	0.40	0.06	0.20	1.77	15.64
EncDec	5	Re-ranking	6,469 (12.72)	1.09	1.17	**0.42**	0.06	0.19	1.78	15.50
EncDec	5	Re-ranking (emb)	35,284 (69.39)	1.00	1.04	0.39	**0.07**	**0.21**	1.77	15.66
HRED	-	1-best	-	**1.34**	**2.74**	**0.42**	**0.07**	0.20	1.84	35.05
HRED	1	Re-ranking	3,671 (7.22)	1.33	**2.74**	**0.42**	0.06	0.20	1.84	35.20
HRED	1	Re-ranking (emb)	30,992 (60.95)	1.28	**2.74**	0.41	0.06	0.20	**1.86**	34.80
HRED	5	Re-ranking	6,231 (12.25)	1.33	2.73	**0.42**	0.06	0.20	1.84	**35.30**
HRED	5	Re-ranking (emb)	**36, 373(71.53)**	1.28	**2.74**	0.41	0.06	0.20	**1.86**	34.60

Table 3: Comparison results before and after re-ranking

lected 2,632,114 dialogues from Japanese micro blogs (Twitter) to train and test the dialogue models. The average dialogue turn was 21.99, and the average utterance length was 22.08 words. We removed emoticons from utterances to reduce vocabulary size and accelerate the training. The dialogue corpus was split into 2,509,836, 63,308, and 58,970 dialogues as training, validation, and testing data, respectively.

3.1 Model Settings

The hidden unit size of Skip-gram (Mikolov et al., 2013c,a,b), predicate embedding, and RFTM (Weber et al., 2018) was 100. We used gated recurrent units (GRUs) (Cho et al., 2014; Chung et al., 2014) whose number of layers was 2 and hidden unit size was 256, for the encoder and decoder of the NCMs. The batch size was 100, the dropout probability was 0.1, and the teacher forcing rate was 1.0. We used Adam (Kingma and Ba, 2015) as the optimizer. The gradient clipping was 50, the learning rate for the encoder and the context RNN of HRED was $1e^{-4}$, and the learning rate for the decoder was $5e^{-4}$. The loss function was inverse token frequency (ITF) loss (Nakamura et al., 2019). We used sentencepiece (Kudo and Richardson, 2018) as the tokenizer, and the vocabulary size was 32,000. These settings were the same in all models.

Repetitive suppression (Nakamura et al., 2019) and length normalization (Macherey et al., 2016) were used at the decoding step. Finally, λ of Eq. (1) and Eq. (4) was set to 1.0.

3.2 Diversity of Beam Search

We investigated internal diversity of N-best response candidates generated from each dialogue model. It is expected that the higher diversity is, the more effective re-ranking is. Hence, we evaluated diversity on the test data by dist-1, 2 (Li et al., 2016). Beam width was set to 20; it is same in the following experiments.

The result is shown in Table 2: Ave.dists are averages of dist computed internal N-best response candidates. The diversity of EncDec is higher than that of HRED.

3.3 Comparison in Automatic Metrics

Table 3 shows the results of our evaluation using automatic metrics. We compared the results by referring to the ratio of responses different from the without re-ranking method ("re-ranked"), bilingual evaluation understudy (BLEU) (Papineni et al., 2002), NIST (Doddington, 2002), and vector extrema (Gabriel et al., 2014) ("extrema") score. NIST is based on BLEU, but heavily weights less frequent N-grams to focus on content words. Vector extrema computes cosine similarity between sentence vectors of a reference and a generated response from a model. Each sentence vector e_s is computed by taking extrema of Skip-gram word vectors e_w in each dimension d as,

$$e_{sd} = \begin{cases} \max_{w \in s} e_{wd} & \text{if } e_{wd} > |\min_{w' \in s} e_{w'd}| \\ \min_{w \in s} e_{wd} & \text{otherwise} \end{cases}.$$

(5)

e_{sd} and e_{wd} are the dth dimensions of e_s and e_w respectively. Additionally, we evaluated dist (Li et al., 2016), Pointwise Mutual Information (PMI) (Newman et al., 2010), and average response length ("length"). Dist and PMI are used to evaluate diversity and coherency respectively. PMI between a response and a dialogue history is defined as,

$$\text{PMI} = \frac{1}{|response|} \sum_{wr}^{|response|} \max_{wh} \text{PMI}(wr, wh).$$

(6)

wr and wh are words in the response and the dialogue history respectively. Each method used a

	word coherency	dialogue continuity
1-best	28.62	**40.84**
Re-ranking	**33.91**	38.53
neither	37.47	20.62

Table 4: 1-best v.s. Re-ranking; # dialogues is 100.

	word coherency	dialogue continuity
1-best	**30.10**	35.50
Re-ranking (emb)	25.40	**38.20**
neither	44.50	26.30

Table 5: 1-best v.s. Re-ranking (emb); # dialogues is 100.

	word coherency	dialogue continuity
Re-ranking	**23.70**	35.53
Re-ranking (emb)	22.91	**35.65**
neither	55.39	28.83

Table 6: Re-ranking v.s. Re-ranking (emb); # dialogues is 100.

specific NCM, a range of dialogue history used for re-ranking, and re-ranking method. Methods with "1-best" used neither re-ranking and event embedding. Those with "Re-ranking" used re-ranking but did not use event embedding. Those with "Re-ranking (emb)" used both the re-ranking and the proposed event embedding method.

Re-ranking lowered scores of the similarity to reference: BLEU, NIST, and extrema, because normal NCM models were trained to generate similar responses to the references, generated top 1 response before re-ranking should have the highest scores in those similarity metrics. Dist-2 and PMI were improved by re-ranking. This indicates that words in re-ranked responses are diverse and coherent to dialogue histories. However, ratios of re-ranked responses were around 10%; hence, the effect of re-ranking was limited. By introducing the proposed event embedding method, the ratios of re-ranked responses improved drastically (Re-ranking vs. Re-ranking (emb)). Moreover, the re-ranking models with event embedding have highest dist-1, dist-2, and PMI. As the HRED models had higher BLEU, NIST, and PMI values than those of EncDec models in all re-ranking methods, we conducted a human evaluation by comparing HRED model-based systems.

3.4 Human Evaluation

It is difficult to evaluate system performances only with automatic metrics (Liu et al., 2016). Hence, we compared a baseline model and our models in a human evaluation to confirm coherency and dialogue continuity of responses selected by our proposed methods. We compared baseline HRED model with our proposed models, re-ranked without embedding and with embedding using the last five histories. To reduce evaluators' workload, we used test data whose the number of user utterances is less than three, and removed dialogues which need external knowledge to evaluate. We used crowdsourcing for the human evaluation. Ten crowd-workers compared responses selected by two of three models in the following two subjective criteria. The first one is "which words in a response are more related to a dialogue history" (word coherency), which indicates system response coherency to dialogue histories. The second criterion is "which response is easier to respond to" (dialogue continuity), which indicates how much dialogue continuity system responses have. We were inspired to make these criteria by those of the Alexa Prize (Ram et al., 2018).

The results are shown in Table 4, 5, and 6. Word coherency was improved by our model without embedding, but lowered by the model with embedding. This is because workers acknowledged causality relations included in the event causality pair pool, but did not acknowledge generalized causalities with event embedding. However, dialogue continuity was improved by the proposed re-ranking model with embedding, it is probably because the proposed model reduced the number of dull responses. We need to investigate the better threshold in the event embedding to balance out the coherency and the continuity as the future work.

4 Discussion

We analyzed an adequacy of re-ranking using event causality relations. Here are system response examples of our proposed method. "()" indicates original Japanese sentences, "[]" indicates event causality relations used for re-ranking, and "<>" indicates responses before re-ranking. All examples are translated from Japanese to English.

Conversation 1:

User 1: Because of my fears, I have **been stressed out**.

(*Mou fuan-na koto ga oosugite **sutoresu ga tama**tteku.*)
User 2 (System): Are you OK? Don't **work too hard**.
ß (*Daijobu desuka **muri shin**aide kuda-saine*)
[work too hard → be stressed out
(*muri wo suru → sutoresu ga tamaru*)]
<Are you OK? (*Daijobu desuka*)>

Conversation 2:

User 1: Someone, let's **go** to eat lunch around *Yayoi-ga-oka* tomorrow. Everyone is welcome.
(*Dareka, ashita, yayoi-ga-oka shuhen de hiru-gohan tabe ni **iko** daredemo iiken onegai*)
User 2 : Let's go. (*Ikimasuka*)
User 1: Where will we go?
(*Doko kui iku*)
User 2 (System): Anywhere **near** *Shinjuku* station
(*Shinjuku-eki no **chikaku***)
[be near → go (*chiaku → ikeru*)]
<Where are you? (*doko inno*)>

In above examples, appropriate event causality relations are used to select logical, coherent, and diverse responses. However, we found that these cases are not majority. Our method used inadequate event causality relations even if coherent responses were selected as a result ("Conversation 3"). Responses selected by our method are sometimes unnatural and incoherent than those before re-ranking as "Conversation 4", "Conversation 5", or "Conversation 6".

Conversation 3:

User 1: I can't **stop coughing**:_(
(*Hen na **seki ga tomara**nai...namida*)
User 2 (System): Don't **catch a cold**.
(*kaze hika**nai dene*)
[catch cold → stop coughing
(*kaze wo hiku → seki ga tomaru*)]
<Are you OK? (*daijobu-ka*)>

Conversation 4:

User 1: Our president who **cannot drink alcohol** gives me beer...

(*Osake wo nome**nai shacho ga biru wo kureru...*)
User 2 (System): I will **drink alcohol**.
(*Osake nomu*.)
[drink alcohol → can drink alcohol
(*osake wo nomu → osake wo nomeru*)]
<I see. (*wakaru*)>

Conversation 5:

User 1: Despite of **morning**, ambulances and police cars were noisy... I was wondered what happened?
(*Asa nanoni, kyu-kyu-sha to patoka no oto ga sugoi...doshitandaro*)
User 2 (System): **Good morning**.
(*Ohayogozaimasu*)
[morning → good morning
(*asa → ohayo*)]
<Are you OK? (*Daijobu desuka*)>

Conversation 6:

User 1: I, I can't get up... I'm gonna **take a day off**... I have a fever...
(*O, okiagarenai... kaisha **yasumu**... netsu...*)
User 2 (System): You must **be tired**.
(*Otsukaresama desu*)
[be tired → take a day off
(*tsukare → yasumu*)]
<Take care of yourself. (*Odaiji-ni*)>

Considering the result of human evaluation and above examples, we hypothesized that our method have two problems in slecting appropriate event causality relations. The first problem is that the event embedding over-generalized events ("Conversation 4"). The causality in Conversation 4 ("drink alcohol" precedes "can drink alcohol") is obtained by generalizing a causality that "enter restaurant" precedes "order beer", which is included in the event causality pair pool. It is necessary to prevent over-generalization by improving the embedding architecture. The second problem is that our method focuses on only word coherency, not response naturalness ("Conversation 5" and "Conversation 6"). To solve the problem, our method has to maintain response naturalness while improving coherency of word choices.

5 Conclusion

We proposed a selection of response candidates generated from a neural conversational model (NCM) utilizing event causality relations. The method had a robust matching of event causality relations attributed to distributed event representation. Experimental results showed that the proposed method selects a coherent and diverse response. The proposed method can be applied to any languages that have a semantic parser, because it uses predicate-argument structure based event expressions. However, unnatural responses were sometimes selected due to inadequate event causality relations. Future work will focus on solving the problem by preventing overgeneralization of events, and maintaining response naturalness.

Acknowledgments

We would like to thank Sadao Kurohashi, Ph.D. and Tomohide Shibata, Ph.D. of Kurohashi Laboratory in Kyoto University who provided us the event causality pairs.

This work is supported by JST PRESTO (JP-MJPR165B).

References

Dzmitry Bahdanau, Kyunghyunand Cho, and Yoshua Bengio. 2015. Neural Machine Translation by Jointly Learning to Align and Translate. In *Proceedings of the 3rd International Conference on Learning Representations (ICLR)*.

Dasha Bogdanova and Jennifer Foster. 2016. This is how we do it: Answer Reranking for Open-Domain How Questions with Paragraph Vectors and Minimal Feature Engineering. In *Proceedings of the 15th Annual Conference of the North American Chapter of the Association for Computational Linguistics: Human Language Technologies (NAACL-HLT)*, pages 1290–1295.

Kyunghyun Cho, Bart van Merrienboer, Caglar Gulcehre, Dzmitry Bahdanau, Fethi Bougares, Holger Schwenk, and Yoshua Bengio. 2014. Learning Phrase Representations Using RNN Encoder-Decoder for Statistical Machine Translation. In *Proceedings of the 2014 Conference on Empirical Methods in Natural Language Processing (EMNLP)*.

Junyoung Chung, Caglar Gulcehre, KyungHyun Cho, and Yoshua Bengio. 2014. Empirical Evaluation of Gated Recurrent Neural Networks on Sequence Modeling. In *Proceedings of the 28th Conference Neural Information Processing Systems, Deep Learning and Representation Learning Workshop (NIPS)*.

George Doddington. 2002. Automatic Evaluation of Machine Translation Quality Using N-gram Co-occurrence Statistics. In *Proceedings of the 2nd International Conference on Human Language Technology Research (HLT)*, pages 138–145.

Motoyasu Fujita, Rafal Rzepka, and Kenji Araki. 2011. Evaluation of Utterances Based on Causal Knowledge Retrieved from Blogs. In *Proceedings of the 14th IASTED International Conference Artificial Intelligence and Soft Computing (ASC)*, pages 294–299.

Forgues Gabriel, Joelle Pineau, Jean-Marie Larchevêque, and Réal Tremblay. 2014. Bootstrapping Dialog Systems with Word Embeddings.

Peter Jansen, Mihai Surdeanu, and Peter Clark. 2014. Discourse Complements Lexical Semantics for Non-factoid Answer Reranking. In *Proceedings of the 52nd Annual Meeting of the Association for Computational Linguistics (ACL)*, pages 977–986.

Daisuke Kawahara and Sadao Kurohashi. 2006. A Fully-Lexicalized Probabilistic Model for Japanese Syntactic and Case Structure Analysis. In *Proceedings of Human Language Technology Conference - North American Chapter of the Association for Computational Linguistics Annual Meeting (HLT-NAACL)*, pages 176–183.

Diederik P. Kingma and Jimmy Ba. 2015. Adam: A Method for Stochastic Optimization. In *Proceedings of the 3rd International Conference on Learning Representations (ICLR)*.

Taku Kudo and John Richardson. 2018. SentencePiece: A Simple and Language Independent Subword Tokenizer and Detokenizer for Neural Text Processing. In *Proceedings of the 2018 Conference on Empirical Methods in Natural Language Processing (EMNLP)*.

Jiwei Li, Michel Galley, Chris Brockett, Jianfeng Gao, and Bill Dolan. 2016. A Diversity-Promoting Objective Function for Neural Conversation Models. In *Proceedings of the 15th Annual Conference of the North American Chapter of the Association for Computational Linguistics: Human Language Technologies (NAACL-HLT)*, pages 110–119.

Chia-Wei Liu, Ryan Lowe, Iulian V. Serban, Michael Noseworthy, Laurent Charlin, and Joelle Pineau. 2016. How NOT to Evaluate Your Dialogue System: An Empirical Study of Unsupervised Evaluation Metrics for Dialogue Response Generation. In *Proceedings of the 2016 Conference on Empirical Methods in Natural Language Processing (EMNLP)*.

Minh-Thang Luong, Hieu Pham, and Christopher D. Manning. 2015. Effective Approaches to Attention-Based Neural Machine Translation. In *Proceedings of the 2015 Conference on Empirical Methods in Natural Language Processing (EMNLP)*.

Wolfgang Macherey, Maxim Krikun, Yuan Cao, Qin Gao, Klaus Macherey, Jeff Klingner, Apurva Shah, Melvin Johnson, Xiaobing Liu, Łukasz Kaiser, Stephan Gouws, Yoshikiyo Kato, Taku Kudo, Hideto Kazawa, Keith Stevens, George Kurian, Nishant Patil, Wei Wang, Cliff Young, Jason Smith, Jason Riesa, Alex Rudnick, Oriol Vinyals, Greg Corrado, Macduff Hughes, and Jeffrey Dean. 2016. Google's Neural Machine Translation System: Bridging the Gap Between Human and Machine Translation. In *arXiv:1609.08144*.

Tomas Mikolov, Kai Chen, Greg Corrado, and Jeffrey Deany. 2013a. Efficient Estimation of Word Representations in Vector Space. In *Proceedings of the 1st International Conference on Learning Representations (ICLR)*.

Tomas Mikolov, Ilya Sutskever, Kai Chen, Greg Corrado, and Jeffrey Dean. 2013b. Distributed Representations of Words and Phrases and Their Compositionality. In *Proceedings of the 26th International Conference on Neural Information Processing Systems (NIPS)*, volume 2, pages 3111–3119.

Tomas Mikolov, Wen-tau Yih, and Geoffrey Zweig. 2013c. Linguistic Regularities in Continuous Space Word Representations. In *Proceedings of the 12th Annual Conference of the North American Chapter of the Association for Computational Linguistics: Human Language Technologies (NAACL-HLT)*, pages 746–751.

Ryo Nakamura, Katsuhito Sudoh, Koichiro Yoshino, and Satoshi Nakamura. 2019. Another Diversity-Promoting Objective Function for Neural Dialogue Generation. In *Proceedings of the 33rd Association for the Advancement of Artificial Intelligence Conference on Artificial Intelligence, Workshop on Reasoning and Learning for Human-Machine Dialogues (DEEP-DIAL 2019) (AAAI)*.

David Newman, Jey Han Lau, Karl Grieser, and Timothy Baldwin. 2010. Automatic Evaluation of Topic Coherence. In *Proceedings of the 11th Annual Conference of the North American Chapter of the Association for Computational Linguistics: Human Language Technologies (NAACL-HLT)*, pages 100–108.

Jong-Hoon Oh, Kentaro Torisawa, Chikara Hashimoto, Ryu Iida, Masahiro Tanaka, and Julien Kloetzer. 2016. A Semi-supervised Learning Approach to Why-Question Answering. In *Proceedings of the 30th Association for the Advancement of Artificial Intelligence Conference on Artificial Intelligence (AAAI)*, pages 3022–3029.

Jong-Hoon Oh, Kentaro Torisawa, Chikara Hashimoto, Motoki Sano, Stijn De Saeger, and Kiyonori Ohtake. 2013. Why-Question Answering Using Intra- and Inter-Sentential Causal Relations. In *Proceedings of the 51st Annual Meeting of the Association for Computational Linguistics (ACL)*, pages 1733–1743.

Jong-Hoon Oh, Kentaro Torisawa, Canasai Kruengkrai, Ryu Iida, and Julien Kloetzer. 2017.

Multi-Column Convolutional Neural Networks with Causality-Attention for Why-Question Answering. In *Proceedings of the 10th Association for Computing Machinery International Conference on Web Search and Data Mining (WSDM)*, pages 415–424.

Junki Ohmura and Maxine Eskenazi. 2018. Context-Aware Dialog Re-ranking for Task-Oriented Dialog Systems. In *Proceedings of IEEE Spoken Language Technology Workshop (SLT)*.

Kishore Papineni, Salim Roukos, Todd Ward, and Wei-Jing Zhu. 2002. BLEU: a Method for Automatic Evaluation of Machine Translation. In *Proceedings of the 40th Annual Meeting of the Association for Computational Linguistics (ACL)*, pages 311–318.

Ashwin Ram, Rohit Prasad, Chandra Khatri, Anu Venkatesh, Raefer Gabriel, Qing Liu, Jeff Nunn, Behnam Hedayatnia, Ming Cheng, Ashish Nagar, Eric King, Kate Bland, Amanda Wartick, Yi Pan, Han Song, Sk Jayadevan, Gene Hwang, and Art Pettigrue. 2018. Conversational AI: The Science Behind the Alexa Prize. In *arXiv:1801.03604*.

Ryohei Sasano and Sadao Kurohashi. 2011. A Discriminative Approach to Japanese Zero Anaphora Resolution with Large-Scale Lexicalized Case Frames. In *Proceedings of the 5th International Joint Conference on Natural Language Processing (IJCNLP)*, pages 758–766.

Iulian V. Serban, Alessandro Sordoni, Yoshua Bengio, Aaron Courville, and Joelle Pineau. 2016. Building End-To-End Dialogue Systems Using Generative Hierarchical Neural Network Models. In *Proceedings of the 30th Association for the Advancement of Artificial Intelligence Conference on Artificial Intelligence (AAAI)*.

Tomohide Shibata, Shotaro Kohama, and Sadao Kurohashi. 2014. A Large Scale Database of Strongly-Related Events in Japanese. In *Proceedings of the 9th International Conference on Language Resources and Evalu ation (LREC)*.

Tomohide Shibata and Sadao Kurohashi. 2011. Acquiring Strongly-Related Events Using Predicate-Argument Co-occurring Statist ics and Case Frames. In *Proceedings of the 5th International Joint Conference on Natural Language Proce ssing (IJCNLP)*, pages 1028–1036.

Alessandro Sordoni, Yoshua Bengio, Hossein Vahabi, Christina Lioma, Jakob G. Simonsen, and Jian-Yun Nie. 2015. A Hierarchical Recurrent Encoder-Decoder For Generative Context-Aware Query Suggestion. In *Proceedings of the 24th Association for Computing Machinery International Conference on Information Knowledge and Management (ACM)*.

Oriol Vinyals and Quoc V. Le. 2015. A Neural Conversational Model. In *Proceedings of the 32nd International Conference on Machine Learning, Deep Learning Workshop (ICML)*.

Noah Weber, Niranjan Balasubramanian, and Nathanael Chambers. 2018. Event Representations with Tensor-Based Compositions. In *Proceedings of the 32nd Association for the Advancement of Artificial Intelligence Conference on Artificial Intelligence (AAAI)*.

DSTC7 Task 1: Noetic End-to-End Response Selection

Chulaka Gunasekara[1]
Lazaros Polymenakos[1]
T.J. Watson Research Center[1]
IBM Research AI
chulaka.gunasekara@ibm.com

Jonathan K. Kummerfeld[2]
Walter S. Lasecki[2]
Computer Science & Engineering[2]
University of Michigan
{jkummerf,wlasecki}@umich.edu

Abstract

Goal-oriented dialogue in complex domains is an extremely challenging problem and there are relatively few datasets. This task provided two new resources that presented different challenges: one was focused but small, while the other was large but diverse. We also considered several new variations on the next utterance selection problem: (1) increasing the number of candidates, (2) including paraphrases, and (3) not including a correct option in the candidate set. Twenty teams participated, developing a range of neural network models, including some that successfully incorporated external data to boost performance. Both datasets have been publicly released, enabling future work to build on these results, working towards robust goal-oriented dialogue systems.

1 Introduction

Automatic dialogue systems have great potential as a new form of user interface between people and computers. Unfortunately, there are relatively few large resources of human-human dialogues (Serban et al., 2018), which are crucial for the development of robust statistical models. Evaluation also poses a challenge, as the output of an end-to-end dialogue system could be entirely reasonable, but not match the reference, either because it is a paraphrase, or it takes the conversation in a different, but still coherent, direction.

In this shared task, we introduced two new datasets and explored variations in task structure for research on goal-oriented dialogue. One of our datasets was carefully constructed with real people acting in a university student advising scenario. The other dataset was formed by applying a new disentanglement method (Kummerfeld et al., 2019) to extract conversations from an IRC channel of technical help for the Ubuntu operating system. We structured the dialogue problem as next utterance selection, in which participants receive partial dialogues and must select the next utterance from a set of options. Going beyond prior work, we considered larger sets of options, and variations with either additional incorrect options, paraphrases of the correct option, or no correct option at all. These changes push the next utterance selection task towards real-world dialogue.

This task is not a continuation of prior DSTC tasks, but it is related to tasks 1 and 2 from DSTC6 (Perez et al., 2017; Hori and Hori, 2017). Like DSTC6 task 1, our task considers goal-oriented dialogue and next utterance selection, but our data is from human-human conversations, whereas theirs was simulated. Like DSTC6 task 2, we use online resources to build a large collection of dialogues, but their dialogues were shorter (2 - 2.5 utterances per conversation) and came from a more diverse set of sources (1,242 twitter customer service accounts, and a range of films).

This paper provides an overview of (1) the task structure, (2) the datasets, (3) the evaluation metrics, and (4) system results. Twenty teams participated, with one clear winner, scoring the highest on all but one sub-task. The data and other resources associated with the task have been released[1] to enable future work on this topic and to make accurate comparisons possible.

2 Task

This task pushed the state-of-the-art in goal-oriented dialogue systems in four directions deemed necessary for practical automated agents, using two new datasets. We sidestepped the challenge of evaluating generated utterances by formulating the problem as next utterance selection, as proposed by Lowe et al. (2015). At test time, participants were provided with partial conversations, each paired with a set of utterances that could be

---

[1]https://ibm.github.io/dstc7-noesis/public/index.html

Proceedings of the 1st Workshop on NLP for Conversational AI, pages 60–67
Florence, Italy, August 1, 2019. ©2019 Association for Computational Linguistics

the next utterance in the conversation. Systems needed to rank these options, with the goal of placing the true utterance first. Prior work used sets of 2 or 10 utterances. We make the task harder by expanding the size of the sets, and considered several advanced variations:

Subtask 1 100 candidates, including 1 correct option.

Subtask 2 120,000 candidates, including 1 correct option (Ubuntu data only).

Subtask 3 100 candidates, including 1-5 correct options that are paraphrases (Advising data only).

Subtask 4 100 candidates, including 0-1 correct options.

Subtask 5 The same as subtask 1, but with access to external information.

These subtasks push the capabilities of systems. In particular, when the number of candidates is small (2-10) and diverse, it is possible that systems are learning to differentiate topics rather than learning dialogue. Our variations move towards a task that is more representative of the challenges involved in dialogue modeling.

As part of the challenge, we provided a baseline system that implemented the Dual-Encoder model from Lowe et al. (2015). This lowered the barrier to entry, encouraging broader participation in the task.

3 Data

We used two datasets containing goal-oriented dialogues between two participants, but from very different domains. This challenge introduced the two datasets, and we kept the test set answers secret until after the challenge.[2] To construct the partial conversations we randomly split each conversation. Incorrect candidate utterances are selected by randomly sampling utterances from the dataset. For subtask 3 (paraphrases), the incorrect candidates are sampled with paraphrases as well. For subtask 4 (no correct option sometimes), twenty percent of examples were randomly sampled and the correct utterance was replaced with an additional incorrect one.

---

^[2]The entire datasets are now publicly available at https://ibm.github.io/dstc7-noesis/public/datasets.html

10:30	<elmaya>	is there a way to setup grub to not press the esc button for the menu choices?
10:31	<scaroo>	elmaya, edit /boot/grub/menu.lst and comment the "hidemenu" line
10:32	<scaroo>	elmaya, then run grub -install
10:32	<scaroo>	grub-install
10:32	<elmaya>	thanls scaroo
10:32	<elmaya>	thanks

Figure 1: Example Ubuntu dialogue before our preprocessing.

Along with the datasets we provided additional sources of information. Participants were able to use the provided knowledge sources as is, or automatically transform them to appropriate representations (e.g. knowledge graphs, continuous embeddings, etc.) that were integrated with end-to-end dialogue systems so as to increase response accuracy.

3.1 Ubuntu

We constructed one dataset from the Ubuntu Internet Relay Chat (IRC) support channel, in which users help each other resolve technical problems related to the Ubuntu operating system. We consider only conversations in which one user asks a question and another helps them resolve their problem. We extracted conversations from the channel using the conversational disentanglement method described by Kummerfeld et al. (2019), trained with manually annotated data using Slate (Kummerfeld, 2019).[34] This approach is not perfect, but we inspected one hundred dialogues and found seventy-five looked like reasonable conversations. See Kummerfeld et al. (2019) for detailed analysis of the extraction process. We further applied several filters to increase the quality of the extracted dialogues: (1) the first message is not directed, (2) there are exactly two participants (a questioner and a helper), not counting the channel bot, (3) no more than 80% of the messages are by a single participant, and (4) there are at least three turns. This approach produced 135,000 conversations, and each was cut off at different points to create the necessary conversations for all the sub-

---

^[3] Previously, Lowe et al. (2015) extracted conversations from the same IRC logs, but with a heuristic method. Kummerfeld et al. (2019) showed that the heuristic was far less effective than a trained statistical model.

^[4] The specific model used in DSTC 7 track 1 is from an earlier version of Kummerfeld et al. (2019), as described in the ArXiv preprint and released as the C++ version.

Student	Hi professor, I am looking for courses to take. Do you have any suggestions?
Advisor	What topic do you prefer, computer science or electrical engineering?
Student	I prefer electrical engineering.
Advisor	Based on your background, I would like to suggest you take one of the two courses: EECS 550 Information Theory and EECS 551: Matrix Methods for Signal Processing, Data Analysis and Machine Learning FA 2012
Student	Can you describe a little bit about EECS 550?
Advisor	This course contains a lot of concepts about source, channel, rate of transformation of information, etc.
Student	Sounds interesting. Do you know the class size of this course?
Advisor	This is a relatively small class and the average size of it is around 12.
Student	I would prefer class with larger class size. What is EECS 551 about?
Advisor	This course is about theory and application of matrix methods to signal processing, data analysis and machine learning
Student	What is the course size of EECS 551?
Advisor	It is around 71
Student	I would take EECS 551. Thanks professor!
Advisor	You are welcome!

Figure 2: Example Advising dialogue.

tasks. For this setting, manual pages were provided as a form of knowledge grounding.

Figure 1 shows an example dialogue from the dataset. For the actual challenge we identify the users as 'speaker_1' (the person asking the question) and 'speaker_2' (the person answering), and removed usernames from the messages (such as 'elmaya' in the example). We also combined consecutive messages from a single user, and always cut conversations off so that the last speaker was the person asking the question. This meant systems were learning to behave like the helpers, which fits the goal of developing a dialogue system to provide help.

3.2 Advising

Our second dataset is based on an entirely new collection of dialogues in which university students are being advised which classes to take. These were collected at the University of Michigan with IRB approval. Pairs of Michigan students play-acted the roles of a student and an advisor. We provided a persona for the student, describing the classes they had taken already, what year of their degree they were in, and several types of class preferences (workloads, class sizes, topic areas, time of day, etc.). Advisors did not know the student's preferences, but did know what classes they

Property	Advising	Ubuntu
Dialogues	500	135,078
Utterances / Dialogue	18.6	10.0
Tokens / Utterance	9.6	9.9
Utterances / Unique utt.	4.4	1.1
Tokens / Unique tokens	10.5	22.9

Table 1: Comparison of the diversity of the underlying datasets. Advising is smaller and has longer conversations, but less diversity in utterances. Tokens are based on splitting on whitespace.

had taken, what classes were available, and which were suggested (based on aggregate statistics from real student records). The data was collected over a year, with some data collected as part of courses in NLP and social computing, and some collected with paid participants.

In the shared task, we provide all of this information - student preferences, and course information - to participants. 815 conversations were collected, and then the data was expanded by collecting 82,094 paraphrases using the crowdsourcing approach described by Jiang et al. (2017). Of this data, 500 conversations were used for training, 100 for development, and 100 for testing. The remaining 115 conversations were used as a source of negative candidates in the candidate sets. For the test data, 500 conversations were constructed by cutting the conversations off at 5 points and using paraphrases to make 5 distinct conversations. The training data was provided in two forms. First, the 500 training conversations with a list of paraphrases for each utterance, which participants could use in any way. Second, 100,000 partial conversations generated by randomly selecting paraphrases for every message in each conversation and selecting a random cutoff point.

Two versions of the test data were provided to participants. The first had some overlap with the training set in terms of source dialogues, while the second did not. We include results on both in this paper for completeness, but encourage all future work to only consider the second test set.

3.3 Comparison

Table 1 provides statistics about the two raw datasets. The Ubuntu dataset is based on several orders of magnitude more conversations, but they are automatically extracted, which means there are errors (conversations that are missing utterances or contain utterances from other conversations). Both have similar length utterances, but these values are on the original Ubuntu dialogues, before we merge consecutive messages from the same user. The Advising dialogues contain more messages on average, but the Ubuntu dialogues cover a wider range of lengths (up to 118 messages). Interestingly, there is less diversity in tokens for Ubuntu, but more diversity in utterances.

4 Results

Twenty teams submitted entries for at least one subtask.[5] Teams had 14 weeks to develop their systems with access to the training and validation data, plus the external resources we provided. Additional external resources were not permitted, with the exception of pre-trained embeddings that were publicly available prior to the release of the data.

4.1 Participants

Table 5 presents a summary of approaches teams used. One clear trend was the use of the Enhanced LSTM model (ESIM, Chen et al., 2017), though each team modified it differently as they worked to improve performance on the task. Other approaches covered a wide range of neural model components: Convolutional Neural Networks, Memory Networks, the Transformer, Attention, and Recurrent Neural Network variants. Two teams used ELMo word representations (Peters et al., 2018), while three constructed ensembles. Several teams also incorporated more classical approaches, such as TF-IDF based ranking, as part of their system.

We provided a range of data sources in the task, with the goal of enabling innovation in training methods. Six teams used the external data, while four teams used the raw form of the Advising data. The rules did not state whether the validation data could be used as additional training data at test time, and so we asked each team what they used. As Table 5 shows, only four teams trained their systems with the validation data.

4.2 Metrics

We considered a range of metrics when comparing models. Following Lowe et al. (2015), we use Recall@N, where we count how often the correct

answer is within the top N specified by a system. In prior work, there were either 2 or 10 candidates (including the correct one), and N was set at 1, 2, or 5. Our sets are larger, with 100 candidates, and so we considered larger values of N: 1, 10, and 50. 10 and 50 were chosen to correspond to 1 and 5 in prior work (the expanded candidate set means they correspond to the same fraction of the space of options). We also considered a widely used metric from the ranking literature: Mean Reciprocal Rank (MRR). Finally, for subtask 3 we measured Mean Average Precision (MAP) since there are multiple correct utterances in the set.

To determine a single winner for each subtask, we used the mean of Recall@10 and MRR, as presented in Table 2.

4.3 Discussion

Table 2 presents the overall scores for each team on each subtask, ordered by teams' average rank. Table 4 presents the full set of results, including all metrics for all subtasks.

Overall Results Team 3 consistently scored highest, winning all but one subtask. Looking at individual metrics, they had the best score 75% of the time on Ubuntu and all of the time on the final Advising test set. The subtask they were beaten on was Ubuntu-2, in which the set of candidates was drastically expanded. Team 10 did best on that task, indicating that their extra filtering step provided a key advantage. They filtered the 120,000 sentence set down to 100 options using a TF-IDF based method, then applied their standard approach to that set.

Subtasks

1. The first subtask drew the most interest, with every team participating in it for one of the datasets. Performance varied substantially, covering a wide range for both datasets, particularly on Ubuntu.

2. As expected, subtask 2 was more difficult than task 1, with consistently lower results. However, while the number of candidates was increased from 100 to 120,000, performance reached as high as half the level of task 1, which suggests systems could handle the large set effectively.

3. Also as expected, results on subtask 3 were slightly higher than on subtask 1. Comparing

---

[5] Note that in the DSTC shared tasks participants remain anonymous, and so we refer to them using numbers.

| | Ubuntu, Subtask | | | | Advising, Subtask | | | |
Team	1	2	4	5	1	3	4	5
3	**0.819**	0.145	**0.842**	**0.822**	**0.485**	0.592	**0.537**	**0.485**
4	0.772	-	-	-	0.451	-	-	-
17	0.705	-	-	0.722	0.434	-	-	0.461
13	0.729	-	0.736	0.635	0.458	0.461	0.474	0.390
2	0.672	0.033	0.713	0.672	0.430	0.540	0.479	0.430
10	0.651	**0.307**	0.696	0.693	0.361	0.434	0.262	0.361
18	0.690	0.000	0.721	0.710	0.287	0.380	0.398	0.326
8	0.641	-	0.527	-	0.310	0.433	0.233	-
16	0.629	0.000	0.683	-	0.280	-	0.370	-
15	0.473	-	-	0.478	0.300	-	-	0.236
7	0.525	-	0.411	-	-	-	-	-
11	-	-	-	-	0.075	0.232	-	-
12	0.077	-	0.000	0.077	0.075	0.232	0.000	0.075
1	0.580	-	-	-	0.239	-	-	-
6	-	-	-	-	0.245	-	-	-
9	0.482	-	-	-	-	-	-	-
14	0.008	-	0.072	-	-	-	-	-
19	0.265	-	-	-	0.180	-	-	-
5	0.076	-	-	-	-	-	-	-
20	0.002	-	-	-	0.004	-	-	-

Table 2: Results, ordered by the average rank of each team across the subtasks they participated in. The top result in each column is in bold. For these results the metric is the average of MRR and Recall@10.

| | Recall @ | | | |
Team	1	10	50	MRR
1	0.402	0.662	0.916	0.497
2	0.478	0.765	0.952	0.578
3	**0.645**	**0.902**	**0.994**	**0.735**
4	0.608	0.853	0.984	0.691
5	0.010	0.101	0.514	0.510
7	0.309	0.635	0.889	0.414
8	0.446	0.732	0.937	0.551
9	0.251	0.601	0.881	0.362
10	0.469	0.739	0.946	0.564
12	0.014	0.098	0.504	0.055
13	0.565	0.810	0.977	0.649
14	0.008	0.008	0.008	0.008
15	0.236	0.592	0.858	0.355
16	0.471	0.700	0.926	0.557
17	0.475	0.814	0.978	0.595
18	0.503	0.783	0.962	0.598
19	0.098	0.346	0.730	0.184
20	0.001	0.003	0.012	0.200

| | Recall @ | | | |
Team	1	10	50	MRR
1	0.170	0.482	0.850	0.274
2	0.242	0.676	0.954	0.384
3	0.398	0.844	**0.986**	0.541
4	0.420	0.768	0.972	0.538
6	0.206	0.548	0.824	0.322
8	0.114	0.398	0.782	0.205
10	0.234	0.600	0.952	0.358
11	0.000	0.000	0.000	0.000
12	0.010	0.102	0.490	0.520
13	0.348	0.804	0.978	0.491
14	0.064	0.064	0.064	0.064
15	0.252	0.620	0.894	0.375
16	0.122	0.474	0.868	0.234
17	**0.494**	**0.850**	0.980	**0.608**
18	0.240	0.630	0.906	0.365
19	0.068	0.322	0.778	0.150
20	0.000	0.000	0.012	0.100

| | Recall @ | | | |
Team	1	10	50	MRR
1	0.078	0.320	0.760	0.158
2	0.152	0.574	0.930	0.286
3	**0.214**	**0.630**	**0.948**	**0.339**
4	0.194	0.582	0.908	0.320
6	0.088	0.320	0.728	0.169
8	0.100	0.420	0.802	0.200
10	0.116	0.492	0.882	0.230
11	0.012	0.096	0.512	0.053
12	0.012	0.096	0.512	0.053
13	0.170	0.610	0.952	0.306
15	0.074	0.420	0.834	0.180
16	0.064	0.398	0.800	0.161
17	0.180	0.562	0.940	0.307
18	0.086	0.390	0.836	0.184
19	0.038	0.250	0.730	0.111
20	0.000	0.006	0.014	0.001

Table 3: Subtask 1 results. The left table is for Ubuntu, the middle table is for the initial Advising test set, and the right table is for the final Advising test set. The best results are bolded.

MRR and MAP it is interesting to see that while the ranking of systems is the same, in some cases MAP was higher than MRR and in others it was lower.

4. For both datasets, results on subtask 4, where the correct answer was to choose no option 20% of the time, are generally similar. On average, no metric shifted by more than 0.016, and some went up while others went down. This suggests that teams were able to effectively handle the added challenge.

5. Finally, on subtask 5 we see some slight gains in performance, but mostly similar results, indicating that effectively using external resources remains a challenge.

Advising Test Sets Table 4 provides a comparison of the two versions of the Advising test set. The middle column of tables is for the first test set, which had overlap with the source dialogues from training (the actual utterances are different due to paraphrasing), while the right column is from entirely distinct dialogues. Removing overlap made

Subtask 2 - Ubuntu Only

Team	Recall @ 1	10	50	MRR
2	0.016	0.041	0.068	0.024
3	0.067	0.185	0.266	0.106
10	**0.196**	**0.361**	**0.429**	**0.253**
16	0.000	0.000	0.005	0.000
18	0.000	0.000	0.000	0.000

Subtask 3 - Advising Only

Team	Recall @ 1	10	50	MRR	MAP
2	0.328	0.772	0.978	0.472	0.591
3	**0.476**	**0.906**	**0.996**	**0.624**	**0.779**
8	0.212	0.586	0.906	0.338	0.370
10	0.340	0.776	0.972	0.482	0.581
11	0.038	0.314	0.852	0.130	0.079
12	0.038	0.314	0.852	0.130	0.079
13	0.250	0.684	0.978	0.393	0.482
14	0.048	0.334	0.848	0.138	0.129
18	0.250	0.740	0.966	0.404	0.487

Team	Recall @ 1	10	50	MRR	MAP
2	0.244	0.692	0.954	0.388	0.478
3	**0.290**	**0.750**	**0.978**	**0.434**	**0.533**
8	0.176	0.570	0.926	0.297	0.342
10	0.186	0.602	0.926	0.316	0.379
11	0.040	0.334	0.854	0.131	0.118
12	0.040	0.334	0.854	0.131	0.118
13	0.182	0.604	0.938	0.317	0.395
18	0.118	0.512	0.916	0.249	0.303

Subtask 4

Team	Recall @ 1	10	50	MRR
2	0.478	0.826	0.959	0.601
3	**0.624**	**0.941**	**0.997**	**0.742**
7	0.255	0.484	0.706	0.338
8	0.388	0.592	0.751	0.463
10	0.446	0.810	0.956	0.581
12	0.000	0.000	0.000	0.000
13	0.516	0.841	0.978	0.632
14	0.072	0.072	0.072	0.072
16	0.487	0.772	0.936	0.593
18	0.493	0.825	0.960	0.617

Team	Recall @ 1	10	50	MRR
2	0.250	0.726	0.974	0.408
3	**0.372**	**0.886**	**0.990**	**0.541**
8	0.088	0.310	0.618	0.162
10	0.274	0.712	0.942	0.419
12	0.000	0.000	0.000	0.000
13	0.272	0.842	0.988	0.453
14	0.006	0.062	0.352	0.035
16	0.224	0.552	0.896	0.328
18	0.270	0.716	0.948	0.426

Team	Recall @ 1	10	50	MRR
2	0.194	0.620	**0.938**	0.339
3	**0.232**	**0.692**	**0.938**	**0.383**
8	0.066	0.316	0.686	0.150
10	0.170	0.566	0.912	0.301
12	0.000	0.000	0.000	0.000
13	0.164	0.640	0.954	0.307
16	0.178	0.470	0.856	0.270
18	0.178	0.510	0.882	0.287

Subtask 5

Team	Recall @ 1	10	50	MRR
2	0.478	0.765	0.952	0.578
3	**0.653**	**0.905**	**0.995**	**0.740**
10	0.501	0.783	0.963	0.602
12	0.014	0.098	0.504	0.055
13	0.448	0.729	0.957	0.542
15	0.221	0.606	0.882	0.349
17	0.504	0.827	0.980	0.617
18	0.517	0.803	0.965	0.617

Team	Recall @ 1	10	50	MRR
2	0.242	0.676	0.954	0.384
3	0.398	0.844	**0.986**	0.541
10	0.234	0.600	0.952	0.358
12	0.010	0.102	0.490	0.520
13	0.238	0.716	0.972	0.392
15	0.346	0.660	0.894	0.454
17	**0.538**	**0.864**	**0.986**	**0.645**
18	0.204	0.634	0.920	0.341

Team	Recall @ 1	10	50	MRR
2	0.152	0.574	0.930	0.286
3	**0.214**	**0.630**	**0.948**	**0.339**
10	0.116	0.492	0.882	0.230
12	0.012	0.096	0.512	0.053
13	0.138	0.518	0.914	0.261
15	0.068	0.316	0.786	0.156
17	0.178	0.608	0.944	0.315
18	0.106	0.436	0.870	0.215

Table 4: Subtask 5 results. The left column of tables is for Ubuntu, the middle column is for the initial Advising test set, and the right column is for the final Advising test set. The best results are bolded.

the task considerably harder, though more realistic. In general, system rankings were not substantially impacted, with the exception of team 17, which did better on the original dataset. This may relate to their use of a memory network over the raw advising data, which may have led the model to match test dialogues with their corresponding training dialogues.

Metrics Finally, we can use Table 4 to compare the metrics. In 39% of cases a team's ranking is identical across all metrics, and in 34% there is a difference of only one place. The maximum difference is 5, which occurred once, between team 6's results in the final Advising results shown in Table 3, where their Recall@1 result was 8th, their Recall@10 result was 11th and their Recall@50 result was 13th. Comparing MRR and Recall@N, the MRR rank is outside the range of ranks given by the recall measures 9% of the time (on Ubuntu and the final Advising evaluation).

5 Future Work

This task provides the basis for a range of interesting new directions. We randomly selected negative options, but other strategies could raise the difficulty, for example by selecting very similar candidates according to a simple model. For evaluation, it would be interesting to explore human judgements, since by expanding the candidate sets we are introducing options that are potentially reasonable.

6 Conclusion

This task introduced two new datasets and three new variants of the next utterance selection task. Twenty teams attempted the challenge, with one clear winner. The datasets are being publicly released, along with a baseline approach, in order to facilitate further work on this task. This resource will support the development of novel dialogue systems, pushing research towards more realistic and challenging settings.

7 Acknowledgements

This material is based in part upon work supported by IBM under contract 4915012629. Any opinions, findings, conclusions or recommendations expressed above are those of the authors and do not necessarily reflect the views of IBM.

References

Qian Chen, Xiaodan Zhu, Zhen-Hua Ling, Si Wei, Hui Jiang, and Diana Inkpen. 2017. Enhanced LSTM for natural language inference. In *Proceedings of the 55th Annual Meeting of the Association for Computational Linguistics (Volume 1: Long Papers)*, volume 1, pages 1657–1668.

Chiori Hori and Takaaki Hori. 2017. End-to-end conversation modeling track in DSTC6. In *Dialog System Technology Challenges 6*.

Youxuan Jiang, Jonathan K. Kummerfeld, and Walter S. Lasecki. 2017. Understanding task design trade-offs in crowdsourced paraphrase collection. In *Proceedings of the 55th Annual Meeting of the Association for Computational Linguistics (Volume 2: Short Papers)*.

Jonathan K. Kummerfeld. 2019. Slate: A super-lightweight annotation tool for experts. In *Proceedings of ACL 2019, System Demonstrations*.

Jonathan K. Kummerfeld, Sai R. Gouravajhala, Joseph Peper, Chulaka Gunasekara, Vignesh Athreya, Siva Sankalp Patel, Lazaros Polymenakos, and Walter S. Lasecki. 2019. A large-scale corpus for conversation disentanglement.

Ryan Lowe, Nissan Pow, Iulian Serban, and Joelle Pineau. 2015. The ubuntu dialogue corpus: A large dataset for research in unstructured multi-turn dialogue systems. In *Proceedings of the 16th Annual Meeting of the Special Interest Group on Discourse and Dialogue*, pages 285–294.

Julien Perez, Y-Lan Boureau, and Antoine Bordes. 2017. Dialog system technology challenge 6 overview of track 1 - end-to-end goal-oriented dialog learning. In *Dialog System Technology Challenges 6*.

Matthew Peters, Mark Neumann, Mohit Iyyer, Matt Gardner, Christopher Clark, Kenton Lee, and Luke Zettlemoyer. 2018. Deep contextualized word representations. In *Proceedings of the 2018 Conference of the North American Chapter of the Association for Computational Linguistics: Human Language Technologies, Volume 1 (Long Papers)*, pages 2227–2237.

Iulian Vlad Serban, Ryan Lowe, Peter Henderson, Laurent Charlin, and Joelle Pineau. 2018. A survey of available corpora for building data-driven dialogue systems: The journal version. *Dialogue & Discourse*, 9(1):1–49.

Team	Model Type	External Data Use	Used Raw Advising	Val in No	Model Details
1	CNN	-	No	Yes	Combination of CNN for utterance representation and GRU for modeling the dialogue.
2	LSTM	-	Yes	No	ESIM with an aggregation scheme that captures the dialog-specific aspects of the data + ELMo.
3	LSTM	Embeddings	Yes	No	ESIM plus a filtering stage for subtask 2.
4	LSTM	-	No	No	ESIM with (1) enhanced word embeddings to address OOV issues, (2) an attentive hierarchical recurrent encoder, and (3) an additional layer before the softmax.
6	Ensemble	-	No	No	An ensemble of CNNs.
7	LSTM	-	No	Yes	LSTM representation of utterances followed by a convolutional layer.
8	Other	-	Yes	No	A multi-level retrieval-based approach that aggregates similarity measures between the context and the candidate response on the sequence and word levels.
10	LSTM	TF-IDF Extraction	No	No	ESIM with matching against similar dialogues in training, and an extra filtering step for subtask 2.
12	RNN	TF-IDF Extraction	No	No	BoW over ELMo with context as an RNN.
13	Ensemble	Embeddings	No	No	Ensemble approach, combining a Dynamic-Pooling LSTM, a Recurrent Transformer and a Hierarchical LSTM.
14	Ensemble	-	No	No	An ensemble using voting, combining the baseline LSTM, a GRU variant, Doc2Vec, TF-IDF, and LSI.
15	Memory	Memory	No	No	Memory network with an LSTM cell.
16	LSTM	-	No	No	ESIM with utterance-level attention, plus additional features.
17	Memory	Memory & Embeddings	Yes	No	Self-attentive memory network, with external advising data in memory and external ubuntu data for embedding training.
18	GRU		No	No	Stacked Bi-GRU network with attention, aggreagting attention across the temporal dimension followed by a CNN and softmax.
19	LSTM	-	No	Yes	Bidirectional LSTM memory network.
20	CNN	-	No	Yes	CNN with attention and a pointer network, plus a novel top-k attention mechanism.

Table 5: Summary of approaches used by participants. All teams applied neural approaches, with ESIM being a particularly popular basis for system development. External data refers to the man pages for Ubuntu, and course information for Advising. Raw advising refers to the variant of the training data in which the complete dialogues and paraphrase sets are provided. Three teams (5, 9 and 11) did not provide descriptions of their approaches. For full details of systems, see the system description papers presented at the DSTC workshop.

End-to-End Neural Context Reconstruction in Chinese Dialogue

Wei Yang,[1,2] Qiao Rui,[2] Haocheng Qin,[2]
Amy Sun,[3] Luchen Tan,[2] Kun Xiong,[2] Ming Li[1,2]
[1] David R. Cheriton School of Computer Science, University of Waterloo
[2] RSVP.ai   [3] Huawei Inc

Abstract

We tackle the problem of context reconstruction in Chinese dialogue, where the task is to replace pronouns, zero pronouns, and other referring expressions with their referent nouns so that sentences can be processed in isolation without context. Following a standard decomposition of the context reconstruction task into referring expression detection and coreference resolution, we propose a novel end-to-end architecture for separately and jointly accomplishing this task. Key features of this model include POS and position encoding using CNNs and a novel pronoun masking mechanism. One perennial problem in building such models is the paucity of training data, which we address by augmenting previously-proposed methods to generate a large amount of realistic training data. The combination of more data and better models yields accuracy higher than the state-of-the-art method in coreference resolution and end-to-end context reconstruction.

1 Introduction

The chatbot is claimed to become a platform for the next generation of the human-computer interface. Recent researches on open-domain chatting systems (Lowe et al., 2017; Mei et al., 2015), open-domain question answering systems (Minaee and Liu, 2017; Chen et al., 2017) have shown promising results on single-round conversations. Meanwhile, most of these systems require the input question to be syntactically and semantically complete sentences. However, due to the language nature of humans, facing more than one round of conversation, we need to tackle the problem of contextual relationship where coreference and ellipsis occur frequently in dialogues leaving the sentence incomplete. The goal of context reconstruction in dialogues is to load context information from a multi-round dialogue, and remove the dependency on the previous contexts in the sentences, so that each sentence have complete and independent semantic meanings, so are answerable and processible by down-stream dialogue or question answering systems.

In this paper, we addressed the context reconstruction problem, which includes referring expression detection and coreference resolution in the dialogue domain. We present our part-of-speech (POS) tagging based deep neural network, including both the step-by-step models and the end-to-end model, for the detections and resolutions of coreference and ellipsis. Our coreference and ellipsis detection model reasons over the input sequence to detect the positions of coreference and ellipsis in the sentence. Our resolution model ranks the candidate entities with the input sentence where coreference and/or ellipsis are annotated. We also present an end-to-end detection-resolution network which consumes only the non-annotated input sentence and candidate entities. Our models utilize both the syntactic and semantic information by employing word embedding, convolution layers, and Long-short-term-memory (LSTM) units. Due to the lack of large well-annotated data, in this paper, we proposed a novel approach to construct annotated data in dialogue domain.

We summarize our contribution in this paper with three points: 1) We formulate the problem definition of context reconstruction in dialogue into one detection problem and one ranking problem and present the difference between it and traditional tasks such as pronoun and zero pronoun detection and mention candidate selection; 2) We present the analysis of the application of deep neural work for contextual resolution in dialogue, including both step-by-step and end-to-end approaches; 3) We propose a way to effectively construct a huge amount of silver data for the con-

Proceedings of the 1st Workshop on NLP for Conversational AI, pages 68–76
Florence, Italy, August 1, 2019. ©2019 Association for Computational Linguistics

text reconstruction task.

2 Related Work

There has been much classical or linguistic theoretical work on coreference resolution in texts. Coreference resolution is mainly concerned with two tasks, referring expressions detection, and mention candidate ranking. Referring expressions detection can be further divided into two subtasks: 1). find all words that do not have real meaning and refer to other mentions (他/he，她/she，它/it，这/this，那/that,...). We use the term 'pronoun' to represent these words without losing preciseness of linguistic definition in this paper. 2). find all zero pronouns. A close task to the first subtask of referring expressions detection is coreference detection, which is to identify noun phrases and pronouns that are referring to the same entities. Haghighi and Klein (2010) proposed an unsupervised generative approach for text coreference detections. Uryupina and Moschitti (2013) proposed a rule-based approach which employed parse trees and SVM. Peng et al. (2015) improved the performance of mention detections by applying a binary classifier on the feature set.

Similarly, there has been much previous work in mention candidate ranking using deep neural network. In recent years, applying deep neural networks on the task has reached great success. Clark and Manning (2016) applied reinforcement learning on mention-ranking coreference resolution. Lee et al. (2017) presented an end-to-end coreference resolution model which reasons over all the anteceding spans. Lee et al. (2018) presented a high-order coreference resolution. These approaches do not generalize to dialogue for the reason that 1) these approaches require a rich amount of well-annotated contextual data, 2) dialogue is short and has ambiguous syntactic structures which are difficult to handcraft rules, and 3) the resolution module should distinguish wrong detection results so that the systems have a higher fault tolerance on the detection module. However, most existed work simply assumes a golden detection label and perform lots of feature engineering based on that.

Although there is a series of related work that can contribute to coreference resolution in Chinese dialogue, there are many common restrictions when transferring them into a practical product: 1). the limited data source in a general domain;

Context (**c**): 打雷 了 怎么 发 短信 安慰 女朋友？
(How to send texts to comfort girlfriend when it thunders?)

Text (**q**): 打雷 时 还给 她 发？
(Send to her even when it thunders?)

Text (**q**) after detection: 打雷 时 还给 她 发 ϕ？
Text (**q**) after resolution: 打雷 时 还给 女朋友 发 短信？
(Send **texts** to **your girlfriend** even when it thunders?)

Figure 1: Example of context reconstruction

2). most work concentrates on general coreference. Few of them focus on pronoun or zero pronoun resolution, which is the vital step for dialogue NLU; 3). no work known to us compares traditional feature-based methods and neural network based models on an end-to-end system for coreference resolution in Chinese dialogue.

3 Our Approach

Figure 1 provides a running example of our context reconstruction approach. We assume an input utterance **q** whose context we are trying to reconstruct with respect to some other context utterance **c**. In the chat context, **c** would come from previous utterances in the dialogue. In a benchmark dataset, we locate the context using the first sentence where the co-referred mention appears. We assume that **q** and **c** have already been tokenized. Our approach breaks the context reconstruction problem into two subtasks: detection and resolution.

Detection is formulated as a sequence labeling task that tries to identify referring expressions that need to be resolved and to recover zero pronouns. In our running example, 她 (her) is identified as such, as well as a zero pronoun ϕ (an elided object). Resolution is formulated as a ranking task. For each "slot" that needs to be resolved (她 and ϕ in the example above), our model provides a ranking of $(\mathbf{c}, \mathbf{q}, m)$ triplets, where $m \in \{m_1, \ldots, m_k\}$, the candidates for resolution. Candidates are selected from noun phrases in the context **c**. At inference time, the candidate m with the highest score is selected as the replacement. If there are multiple slots to be resolved, our model proceeds from left to right incrementally. The final output of the model is shown in the last line of Figure 1. In this paper, we call our POS tagging based model as POSNet. The detection and ranking part is named POSNet-D and POSNet-R accordingly.

3.1 Detection

The detection subtask attempts to identify referring expressions that need to be resolved and to recover the position of zero pronouns. Note that not all referring expressions require resolution. For example, '这' (this) in '这个理由很有说服力' (This reason is convincing) requires no resolution, while '这' (this) in '这个不是我想要的' (this is not what I want) does. Detection is formulated as a sequence labeling task where the output labels $y \in [0, 1, 2]$. The label '1' indicates the boundary of a "slot" while the label '2' is assigned to expressions requiring resolution. Thus, in our running example, the input [PAD 打雷时还给她发 PAD] would be tagged with [0 0 0 1 2 1 0]. That is, the pronoun '她' is explicitly tagged, together with its left and right boundaries; consecutive '1' tags indicates a zero pronoun.

In our detection model, the (padded) sentence and POS tagging encoding layer consists of the following components: First, we apply 200-dimensional embedding layer (Mikolov et al., 2013) to s and a 20-dimensional embedding layer to t. Let $\mathbf{s} = \{s_1, \ldots, s_m\}$ and $\mathbf{t} = \{t_1, \ldots, t_m\}$ be the embedded representations. To leverage to position information which is important in this task, we also include the position embeddings suggested by Gehring et al. (2017) in the model with the same size as the word embedding, denoted as $\mathbf{p} = (p_1, \ldots, p_m)$. The word embeddings and POS embeddings are incorporated together by summing and then concatenated with the position embedding as the combined input: $\mathbf{w} = \{w_1, \ldots, w_m\}, w_i = [s_i + p_i, t_i]$.

Inspired by the recent success of convolutional models for various NLP tasks (Kim, 2014), we apply a stack of 5 convolution layers followed by a global max pooling layer on top of the word and POS tagging encodings to extract underlying patterns in the sentence. We use gated linear units (GLU) (Dauphin et al., 2016) as the activation function, and we included residual connections to reduce training difficulty (He et al., 2016). After the encoding the input using convolutional layers with residual connections, we apply LSTM as the decoder to generate the sequential predictions for the location of referring expressions as $\{d_1, \ldots, d_n\}$. To train this model, we apply categorical cross entropy loss $\mathcal{L}_{seq}$ over a text sequence:

$$\mathcal{L}_{seq} = -\frac{1}{n} \sum_{i=1}^{m} \sum_{j=1}^{n_{\text{class}}} y_{ij} \log(d_{ij})$$

3.2 Resolution

The output of the detection model is a list of "slots" that require resolution, which could either be a referring expression or a zero pronoun. In the resolution task, for each slot, the model finds the most appropriate replacement to best reconstruct the context. This is formulated as a ranking problem over $(\mathbf{c}, \mathbf{q}, m)$ triplets, where $m \in \{m_1, \ldots, m_k\}$ are the candidate mentions for resolution. In our running example, there are two slots to be resolved (她 and ϕ); at inference time, our model selects the highest scoring m for each slot, proceeding from left to right.

The input to the model comprises a sentence, its corresponding POS tags, a known pronoun or zero pronoun slot, and a candidate mention. Then, we concatenate word embeddings and POS tagging embedding as the input of mentions and encode it using multilayer perceptron. To enrich the semantic information of the mention candidate, we find the context sentence that contains this mention as another input. Usually this context is the sentence exactly before the query sentence in dialogues. Then we encode the query and context in the same way described in Section 3.1. We did not add attention mechanism, as the interaction method as described by Yin et al. (2018b) to our model because we did not see significant improvement with preliminary experiments. To train the mention candidate ranking model, we apply hinge loss to maximize the margin between a positive sample and a negative sample as below:

$$\mathcal{L}_{\text{hinge}} = \max\{0,$$
$$\delta + \mathcal{F}(\mathbf{w}_q, \mathbf{w}_c, \mathbf{m}^-) - \mathcal{F}(\mathbf{w}_q, \mathbf{w}_c, \mathbf{m}^+)\}$$

where $\mathcal{F}(\cdot)$ is the ranking model. $\mathbf{w}_q$ and $\mathbf{w}_c$ are the input with words, POS tagging and position embeddings of query and context. $\mathbf{m}^-$ and $\mathbf{m}^+$ are the positive and negative mention embedding including the POS tagging embedding. δ is a hyper-parameter and we set $\delta = 1$ in our experiments.

3.3 End-to-End Reconstruction

When combining the detection and ranking modules, we propose a masking structure to add a

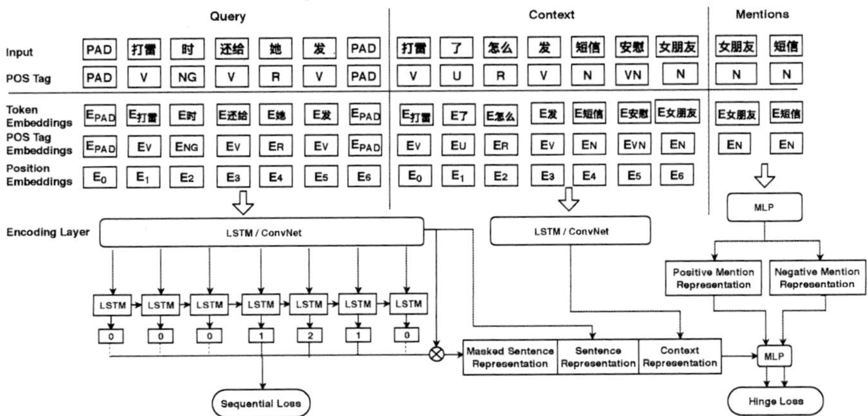

Figure 2: Architecture of the neural end-to-end model for coreference resolution in Chinese dialogue

masked sentence representation layer in the joint model. The mask vector is from the sequential prediction of the detection module, and we apply it back to encoded sentence matrix to highlight the words near the pronoun or zero pronoun slot to get the masked sentence representation $\mathbf{v_{ms}}$:

$$\mathbf{v_{ms}} = \text{Pooling}(M_s\mathbf{v_m})$$

where $\mathbf{v_m}$ is the binary mask vector and M_s is the encoded sentence representation matrix. A max pooling function is applied to project the masked sentence matrix into a vector. Through this way we try to force the model to selection mention candidate that is mostly likely to co-occur near a pronoun or zero pronoun. These words are usually verbs (e.g. love, publish) but seldom prepositions (e.g. through) or adjectives (e.g. wonderful). Based on the above two individual models, we combine the learnt (masked) sentence representation and the mention representation and build the end-to-end context reconstruction model (or joint model), where the detection and resolution models are trained jointly. The overall framework is shown in Figure 2.

To train this model, we combine the hinge loss $\mathcal{L}_{\text{hinge}}$ and the sequential loss $\mathcal{L}_{\text{seq}}$ mentioned above. The two losses are aggregated by a hyper-parameter λ for the trade-off. Finally, we add a regularization term to the target function to reduce overfitting. The final loss can be written as follows:

$$\mathcal{L} = \mathcal{L}_{\text{hinge}} + \lambda \cdot \mathcal{L}_{\text{seq}} + \mu \cdot ||W||$$

where λ and μ are hyper-parameters, and $||W||$ is the regularization term over all weights in the

Data	Docs	Sents	ZP
CONLL2012$_{Train}$	1,394	36,487	12,111
CONLL2012$_{Test}$	172	6,083	1,713
OntoNote$_{BC}$	-	2,800	1,400
OntoNot$_{TC}$	-	1,628	814

Table 1: Statistics of the CONLL2012 and the OntoNote datasets

model. When integrating the POSNet-R with POSNet-D, we find that sometimes POSNet-D predicts a word in a sentence to be a reference when it is not. This requires our POSNet-R to have the ability to predict that nothing fits for a wrong slot detection. To achieve this, we create a special mention candidate UNK, representing the null string. At inference time we can input UNK along with other candidates NPs to POSNet-R. If UNK token has the highest score, that means nothing should be fit into the reference slot. We trained POSNet-R again with the aforementioned modifications on the same training data set. Thus, we modify the hinge loss as below:

$$\mathcal{L}_{\text{hinge}} = \max\{0, \delta + \mathcal{F}(\mathbf{w}_c, \mathbf{w}_q, \mathbf{m}^-) \\ - \mathcal{F}(\mathbf{w}_c, \mathbf{w}_q, \mathbf{m}_0)\} \\ + \max\{0, \delta + \mathcal{F}(\mathbf{w}_c, \mathbf{w}_q, \mathbf{m}_0) \\ - \mathcal{F}(\mathbf{w}_c, \mathbf{w}_q, \mathbf{m}^+)\}$$

Where $\mathbf{m}_0$ represents the embedding for UNK.

4 Experimental Setup

4.1 Dataset

We conduct all of our experiments on Chinese datasets. Note all of our models used in this pa-

Type	Neg	ZP	Pronoun	Total
NP	1M	800 000	1 200 000	3 000 000
Location	1M	200 000	750 000	1 950 000
Person	1M	200 000	750 000	1 950 000
Time	1M	990 000	601 000	1 700 000

Table 2: Statistics of the generated CQA dataset

per are language-independent. We have evaluated our models on three datasets. The statistics of all datasets is shown in Table 1 and Table 2.

- CONLL2012: To get a fair comparison with the previous methods, we applied POSNet-R to the zero pronoun resolution task on the CONLL2012 benchmark dataset following Yin et al. (2018a) and Yin et al. (2018b)'s processing methods. Note this is the dataset annotated with the coreference of zero pronouns in a general domain and this task assumes the pre-known location of zero pronouns so we apply POSNet-R as a comparison.

- OntoNote (BC/TC): Since there is no known end-to-end evaluation benchmark for Chinese context reconstruction, we extracted data from the BC (broadcast conversation) and TC (telephone conversation) subsets from OnotoNote 5.0 corpus (which is the same source of CONLL2012) and build the end-to-end training and evaluation dataset for zero pronoun resolution. We apply basic cleaning on the corpus such as removing the cataphoric reference and filling multiple coreferences in one sentence. For each sentence with a zero pronoun, we sample one negative candidate from the last sentence and use this sentence as a context sentence.

- CQA: Since CONLL2012 and OntoNote are either too small to evaluate the performance of neural network or too domain-specific to provide a satiated training and evaluation on a general domain, we collected and built new training and testing set from Chinese CQA (community question answering website) websites including BaiduZhidao[1], SosoWenwen[2], which contains over 300,000,000 QA pairs. We generated *time*,

location, *people* and *noun phrase* examples. Each subset is divided into the training data and the testing data at the ratio of 9:1. We use this generated data to mimic the coreference in the real data and we will show this generated data contributes to both general evaluation and external assistance to a specific domain.

4.2 Dataset Generation

Contextual resolution on dialogue corpus requires large-scale and annotated training data. Obtaining such a data set is the key to this problem. We introduce our three-phases data generation method as follows: data collection, keywords detection, and data splitting.

Data Collection: Sentences in dialogues have the features of being short and containing only one or two entities. Corpus from CQA websites fit our purpose perfectly since 1). these questions and answers tend to be short and precise; 2). large user groups provide a huge corpus of data; 3). these single round question-answering dialogues share some language features with chatting dialogues. Initially, QA pairs from the internet are collected. These are our *raw data*. These raw data are mostly precise, complete, short, and independent sentences and contain no coreferences to the context.

Keyword Detection: First of all, we detect and label words that refer to *time*, *location*, *people* or *noun phrases*. We parse questions using the Parser (Roger Levy, 2003) to generate syntax trees annotated with POS taggings. The POS taggings provide syntactic information that helps guide the data generation rules. Then, we use the Stanford named entity recognizer (Finkel et al., 2005) to tag tokens that refer to *time*, *location* or *people* entities, named *marked words*.

Data Splitting: Our goal is to transform short sentences from dialogues into positive examples of coreference and ellipsis. The main challenge in generating those is to identify segments that can be omitted or replaced with a pronoun so that the resulting sentence is both grammatical and natural. Our method splits complete sentences into sentences that contain pronoun or zero pronoun according to the self-defined syntactic pattern: 1) Pronoun samples: Since pronouns actually refer to an entity from the context, we can reverse the process and create coreference cases by replacing entities with pronouns in sentences. It is feasible also because for a certain entity type (e.g. time), the corresponding pronouns are limited. 2) Zero pronoun samples: For the same reason as above, the process of understanding zero pronouns could be reversed. We can create ellipsis cases by omitting entities in sentences. Therefore, we create ellipsis cases by deleting the marked words in the sentence directly. 3) Negative samples: There are two types of negative samples in this problem. The first type is a sentence without generated pronoun or zero pronoun. In order to provide competitive samples for training, negative examples are randomly sampled out of the whole CQA corpus. In addition, a number of complete sentences that contain pronouns and zero pronouns already are added. It could enhance our model's ability to distinguish real coreference and "fake" coreference. The second negative samples are the mention candidates that are not referred to. We randomly sample mentions from the same session or document to make the negative samples challenging.

4.3 Model Training

We use Jieba[3], a Chinese word segmentation tool to segment a sentence into a sequence of words. The Chinese word embeddings are pre-trained using skip-gram model (Mikolov et al., 2013) on the raw CQA corpus. The LSTM-encoder and LSTM-decoder in all of our models have a state size of 512. The convolution layers have 512 filters with width 3. The models are trained by the Adam optimization algorithm (Kingma and Ba, 2014) with a learning rate of 3×10^{-4}. Vocabulary size is truncated by selecting the most frequent 200,000 tokens. λ is set to 20 and μ is set to 0.01 in all of our experiments.

5 Results

5.1 Detection

Although we model referring expression detection as a sequence labeling task, we assume there is at most one pronoun or zero pronoun in a sentence. So we report sentence-level precision, recall, and F_1 scores for evaluation in coreference resolution task in dialogue. Note we can run this detection algorithm iteratively after one round of context reconstruction if the sentence contains multiple pronouns or zero pronouns in practical application. The experimental results on CQA dataset are shown in Table 3.

[3] https://github.com/fxsjy/jieba

Data	Pre.	Rec.	F_1
Name phrase	92.7	96.9	94.8
Location	95.3	95.7	95.5
Person	92.9	97.5	95.1
Time	91.1	95.7	93.3
Average	93.0	96.5	94.7

Table 3: Results of POSNet-D for referring expression detection on CQA dataset

Model	P@1	P@2	P@3
Bigram	22.8	37.1	48.2
Yin et al. (2018b)	68.1	87.3	89.5
Yin et al. (2018a)	68.3	**87.7**	89.7
POSNet-R	**69.1**	85.2	**91.2**

Table 4: Results of mention candidate ranking on the CQA dataset

According to Table 3, the high F1 scores indicate the strong ability of POSNet-D to distinguish positive examples and negative examples. The slightly higher recall rate than precision indicates the model tends to treat potentially words as positive and retrieve more potentially positive candidates, which meets our requirement to provide more candidates for ranking in this detection step properly. Note that from Table 3, we can also find the accuracy on location and people subsets is higher than NP and time. This is because there are more ellipse detection cases in NP and time subsets, which bring a challenge to our model and baseline method by causing more false negatives.

5.2 Resolution

We test mention candidate ranking on two datasets: CQA and CONLL2012. For each sentence in the test set, we feed it into the model together with the correct mentions and nine randomly sampled mentions. The model outputs the ranking scores for all 10 mentions and we choose the one with the highest score as the model's prediction. Under this setting, a naive model that outputs random scores should result in an overall top 1 accuracy close to 10%. The overall performance is shown in Table 4. Bigram in Table 4 is the baseline method that we select the candidate with the largest co-occurrence frequency with the preceding and the following word as the prediction. Additionally, POSNet-R pretrained on the CQA dataset outperforms al baselines, which demonstrates the effectiveness of our generated data.

Model	F_1	P@1
POSNet-D+Yin et al. (2018a)	92.9	69.7
POSNet-D+Yin et al. (2018b)	92.9	69.9
POSNet	**95.4**	**71.7**

Table 5: Results of the end-to-end evaluation for coreference resolution on the CQA dataset

Model	F_1
Zhao and Ng (2007)	41.5
Chen and Ng (2016)	52.2
Yin et al. (2017)	54.9
Liu et al. (2016)	55.3
Yin et al. (2018b)	57.3
Yin et al. (2018a)	57.2
POSNet-R (raw)	52.1
POSNet-R (pretrained on CQA)	**58.1**

Table 6: Results of mention candidate ranking for zero pronouns on the CONLL2012 dataset

Test	Pretrain	Train	F_1	Accuracy
TC	CQA	BC	45.3	92.5
		-	10.4	66.8
	-	BC	18.3	72.5
BC	CQA	TC	36.1	84.5
		-	11.8	65.0
	-	TC	16.2	69.2

Table 7: Results of end-to-end zero pronoun resolution on OntoNote dataset

For the CONLL2012 dataset, the result is shown in Table 6. Following Yin et al. (2018b), we add the features from existing work on zero anaphora resolution into the fully connection layer. We try POSNet-R and find it performs close to the previous nerual network methods but cannot beat the Yin et al. (2018b)'s model. We think this is because our model needs more training data to learn an effective representation of the text and POS tagging so we pretrain our model on the whole CQA dataset. The result shows we can achieve the best performance on this benchmark.

5.3 End-to-end Evaluation

End-to-end model is tested on two datasets: the generated CQA and the extracted OntoNote. This model is trained with the original sentence as well as the correct NP and 9 sampled negative NPs. The output consists of two parts, the coreference and ellipsis detection of the sentence, and the ranking score of the mention candidate. The experiment results of the end-to-end evaluation on CQA and OntoNote datasets are shown in Table 5 and Table 7. Comparing the results of the joint model (Table 5) with the Table 3, we found that the end-to-end model has improvements on the F1 score. We find that it is because the precision score increases while the recall score drops a little. This result shows that involving candidate phrase information, the ability to detect the correct coreference and ellipsis is improved. Comparing to the joint model with the POSNet-R, we found that the top 1 accuracy is slightly improved, while top 2 and top 3 accuracies are dropped. The drops are expected as the position information of coreference and ellipsis are not given.

Since there is no known end-to-end Chinese context reconstruction model for the dialogue corpus, we compare POSNet with two step-by-step baselines: POSNet-D for the detection first, Yin et al. (2018a) and Yin et al. (2018b)'s methods for the ranking next. Comparing to the joint model with the baselines, we can see that step-by-step approach will cause serious cascade error if one step cannot perform well. In contrast, our model joint performs reasonably well considering the returned top 3 candidates. However, to better help the down-stream natural language understanding task, we should mainly aim at transforming a sentence extracted from the dialogue corpus to an independent sentence. So accuracy at top 1 is the most important evaluation metric.

We shows the results on OntoNote dataset in Table 7. From the result of these two small data sets we can see it is important to 1). learn a general knowledge by pretraining on a large corpus; 2). fine tune on a domain-specific dataset to get the downstream information such as common terms, common grammar, etc. In addition, by looking at Table 5 and 7 together, we can see that coreference detection, especially zero pronoun detection, is the bottleneck of the end-to-end context reconstruction system.

5.4 Ablation Study

We compare our model to the following ablated models: replacing the encoding layer with the BiLSTM layer, removing the UNK token candidate, removing word position embedding, and removing POS tagging from the input. The results are shown in Table 8. From Table 8 we find that

Model	P@1	P@2	P@3
POSNet	70.1	82.9	89.0
POSNet-LSTM	68.1	82.2	90.2
POSNet w/o UNK	67.4	81.2	86.2
POSNet w/o pos-embed	67.2	81.0	88.1
POSNet w/o POS input	61.8	71.4	73.7

Table 8: Alation study of the end-to-end contexual resolution on the CQA dataset

POSNet achieves better performance than the base POSNet model without UNK augmentation. We believe it is because 1) the UNK token helps enlarges the distance between the relevance of positive samples and negative samples. 2). it allows the mention candidate ranking model to identify the false positive of the detection model and replace it with a rejection token.

In addition, we try BiLSTM as the encoder as the comparison to the CNN based encoder in the experiments and we name it POSNet-LSTM. From the result, we can see BiLSTM gives weaker performance than ConvNet layers. We argue that this is because ConvNets layers are more sensitive to the distant and global dependency information in coreference while LSTM cares more about adjacent words. From the result of removing position embedding and the POS input, we can see that this task heavily relies on the understanding of the sentence syntactic structure. We believe there will be better ways to leverage this kind of information in a sentence.

6 Conclusion

In this paper, we systematically define the context reconstruction problem in dialogue domain and initiated a comprehensive study of this problem. We have demonstrated how to create training data to train both two step-by-step neural networks and an end-to-end deep neural network to tackle this problem. This study leads to many open research directions. Our work could be extended to wider contextual domains, including more conjunctive relations and more careful linguistic studies of conjunctive relations in conversations. Studies could go beyond context reconstruction and include semantics from conversation history. At the application level, neural context reconstruction can be easily integrated with an end-to-end question answering system (Yang et al., 2019) for a extrinsic evaluation.

References

Chen Chen and Vincent Ng. 2016. Chinese zero pronoun resolution with deep neural networks. In *Proceedings of the 54th Annual Meeting of the Association for Computational Linguistics (Volume 1: Long Papers)*, volume 1, pages 778–788.

Danqi Chen, Adam Fisch, Jason Weston, and Antoine Bordes. 2017. Reading wikipedia to answer open-domain questions. *arXiv preprint arXiv:1704.00051*.

Kevin Clark and Christopher D Manning. 2016. Deep reinforcement learning for mention-ranking coreference models. *arXiv preprint arXiv:1609.08667*.

Yann N Dauphin, Angela Fan, Michael Auli, and David Grangier. 2016. Language modeling with gated convolutional networks. *arXiv preprint arXiv:1612.08083*.

Jenny Rose Finkel, Trond Grenager, and Christopher Manning. 2005. Incorporating non-local information into information extraction systems by gibbs sampling. In *Proceedings of the 43rd annual meeting on association for computational linguistics*, pages 363–370. Association for Computational Linguistics.

Jonas Gehring, Michael Auli, David Grangier, Denis Yarats, and Yann N Dauphin. 2017. Convolutional sequence to sequence learning. *arXiv preprint arXiv:1705.03122*.

Aria Haghighi and Dan Klein. 2010. Coreference resolution in a modular, entity-centered model. In *Human Language Technologies: The 2010 Annual Conference of the North American Chapter of the Association for Computational Linguistics*, pages 385–393. Association for Computational Linguistics.

Kaiming He, Xiangyu Zhang, Shaoqing Ren, and Jian Sun. 2016. Deep residual learning for image recognition. In *Proceedings of the IEEE conference on computer vision and pattern recognition*, pages 770–778.

Yoon Kim. 2014. Convolutional neural networks for sentence classification. *arXiv preprint arXiv:1408.5882*.

Diederik Kingma and Jimmy Ba. 2014. Adam: A method for stochastic optimization. *arXiv preprint arXiv:1412.6980*.

Kenton Lee, Luheng He, Mike Lewis, and Luke Zettlemoyer. 2017. End-to-end neural coreference resolution. *arXiv preprint arXiv:1707.07045*.

Kenton Lee, Luheng He, and Luke Zettlemoyer. 2018. Higher-order coreference resolution with coarse-to-fine inference. *arXiv preprint arXiv:1804.05392*.

Ting Liu, Yiming Cui, Qingyu Yin, Weinan Zhang, Shijin Wang, and Guoping Hu. 2016. Generating and exploiting large-scale pseudo training data for zero pronoun resolution. *arXiv preprint arXiv:1606.01603*.

Ryan Thomas Lowe, Nissan Pow, Iulian Vlad Serban, Laurent Charlin, Chia-Wei Liu, and Joelle Pineau. 2017. Training end-to-end dialogue systems with the ubuntu dialogue corpus. *Dialogue & Discourse*, 8(1):31–65.

Hongyuan Mei, Mohit Bansal, and Matthew R Walter. 2015. What to talk about and how? selective generation using lstms with coarse-to-fine alignment. *arXiv preprint arXiv:1509.00838*.

Tomas Mikolov, Kai Chen, Greg Corrado, and Jeffrey Dean. 2013. Efficient estimation of word representations in vector space. *arXiv preprint arXiv:1301.3781*.

Shervin Minaee and Zhu Liu. 2017. Automatic question-answering using a deep similarity neural network. *arXiv preprint arXiv:1708.01713*.

Haoruo Peng, Kai-Wei Chang, and Dan Roth. 2015. A joint framework for coreference resolution and mention head detection. In *Proceedings of the Nineteenth Conference on Computational Natural Language Learning*, pages 12–21.

Christopher D. Manning Roger Levy. 2003. Is it harder to parse chinese, or the chinese treebank? pages 439–446. Association for Computational Linguistics.

Olga Uryupina and Alessandro Moschitti. 2013. Multilingual mention detection for coreference resolution. In *Proceedings of the Sixth International Joint Conference on Natural Language Processing*, pages 100–108.

Wei Yang, Yuqing Xie, Aileen Lin, Xingyu Li, Luchen Tan, Kun Xiong, Ming Li, and Jimmy Lin. 2019. End-to-end open-domain question answering with bertserini. *arXiv preprint arXiv:1902.01718*.

Qingyu Yin, Yu Zhang, Weinan Zhang, and Ting Liu. 2017. Chinese zero pronoun resolution with deep memory network. In *Proceedings of the 2017 Conference on Empirical Methods in Natural Language Processing*, pages 1309–1318.

Qingyu Yin, Yu Zhang, Weinan Zhang, Ting Liu, and William Yang Wang. 2018a. Deep reinforcement learning for chinese zero pronoun resolution. *arXiv preprint arXiv:1806.03711*.

Qingyu Yin, Yu Zhang, Weinan Zhang, Ting Liu, and William Yang Wang. 2018b. Zero pronoun resolution with attention-based neural network. In *Proceedings of the 27th International Conference on Computational Linguistics*, pages 13–23.

Shanheng Zhao and Hwee Tou Ng. 2007. Identification and resolution of chinese zero pronouns: A machine learning approach. In *Proceedings of the 2007 Joint Conference on Empirical Methods in Natural Language Processing and Computational Natural Language Learning (EMNLP-CoNLL)*.

Energy-Based Modelling for Dialogue State Tracking

Anh Duong Trinh [†]**, Robert J. Ross** [†]**, John D. Kelleher** [‡]
[†] School of Computer Science
[‡] Information, Communications & Entertainment Institute
Technological University Dublin, Ireland
`anhduong.trinh@mydit.ie, {robert.ross, john.d.kelleher}@dit.ie`

Abstract

The uncertainties of language and the complexity of dialogue contexts make accurate dialogue state tracking one of the more challenging aspects of dialogue processing. To improve state tracking quality, we argue that relationships between different aspects of dialogue state must be taken into account as they can often guide a more accurate interpretation process. To this end, we present an energy-based approach to dialogue state tracking as a structured classification task. The novelty of our approach lies in the use of an energy network on top of a deep learning architecture to explore more signal correlations between network variables including input features and output labels. We demonstrate that the energy-based approach improves the performance of a deep learning dialogue state tracker towards state-of-the-art results without the need for many of the other steps required by current state-of-the-art methods.

1 Introduction

Dialogue processing is a challenging task due to the nature of human conversations. Currently most Spoken Dialogue Systems (SDS) have a core component called the Dialogue Manager that is responsible for: (a) handling dialogue context and understanding user utterances by tracking dialogue states; and (b) generating useful contributions through the use of an appropriate dialogue policy. The dialogue manager component can be developed independently (Budzianowski et al., 2017; Su et al., 2017; Zhao and Eskenazi, 2016) or in an end-to-end dialogue fashion (Williams et al., 2017; Li et al., 2017; Serban et al., 2016). Between the two dialogue manager components, the dialogue state tracker is arguably the more challenging to perfect, as its performance depends on the quality of the speech recognition component, the complexity of natural language used by users,

and even the situational context (Ross and Bateman, 2009).

Generally task-oriented dialogue systems with predefined ontologies represent dialogue states as a set of slot-value pairs, and define dialogue state tracking as a multi-task classification problem. The common deep learning approach to dialogue state tracking therefore is to develop different subsystems for the tracking of each slot – though early layers in the network will often be shared to varying degrees. While this approach has provided reasonable results, we argue that this method does not reflect the natural way that humans process information; specifically that the inter-relationships between slots are not properly taken into account.

In order to account for such relationships in the dialogue context, it is appropriate to consider the problem not as a multi-task classification problem, as is currently common, but as a structured prediction problem. This insight is not in itself novel, as there have been several attempts in the research community to investigate the variable dependencies in dialogue state tracking such as in the multi-task learning model (Trinh et al., 2018), the language modelling tracker (Platek et al., 2016), work building on Conditional Random Fields (Kim and Banchs, 2014), work on Attention-based Sequence to Sequence models (Hori et al., 2016) and the work by Williams (2010). Although these architectures are good attempts to engage variable dependencies at different levels of abstraction into the dialogue state tracking process, they have not yet achieved state-of-the-art results and do not provide a clear analysis of the relationships between variables.

Performing prediction of dialogue states where we acknowledge the relationship between slot values casts the problem into a structured prediction task; this is similar to how both image segmentation and part-of-speech tagging are struc-

Proceedings of the 1st Workshop on NLP for Conversational AI, pages 77–86
Florence, Italy, August 1, 2019. ©2019 Association for Computational Linguistics

tured prediction problems in that that output labels are not assumed to be independent. One efficient approach to structured prediction that has been applied widely in recent years are energy-based methods (LeCun et al., 2006). A key intuition of energy-based structured learning approaches is that it can be easier to learn a function to critique a potential solution Y than to learn to predict Y directly from an input signal X. Given this intuition, energy-based approaches essentially attempt to learn a function that estimates the goodness of fit between some input feature variable X and an output hypothesis Y. Given such a trained function, a gradient descent-based inference process then searches for an appropriate Y at run-time that demonstrates the best fit to a new input vector X.

To investigate the appropriateness of this method, in this paper we apply a variant of the Structured Prediction Energy Network (SPEN) (Belanger and McCallum, 2016) to the Dialogue State Tracking Challenge (DSTC) 2 dataset (Henderson et al., 2014a). To our knowledge, this is the first attempt to apply this formulation of modelling to the DST task. We benchmark our work by comparing it against a number of other dialogue state trackers including the state-of-the-art hybrid dialogue state tracker (Vodolan et al., 2015, 2017).

2 Analysis of Variable Dependencies

The goal of applying a structured learning approach to dialgoue state tracking is predicated on the assumption that there are indeed dependencies between slots in the dialogue state. In this section we recap some of the features of the dataset that we have applied and investigate whether such dependencies exist for this dataset.

2.1 DSTC2 Dataset

The Dialogue State Tracking Challenge 2 (Henderson et al., 2014a) is a popular dataset for spoken dialogue state tracking in the Cambridge restaurant information domain. The main task of this challenge, called *Joint Goals*, requires the models to classify slot-value pairs for four Informable slots; namely *food*, *price range*, *area*, and *name*. At every turn of the dialogue, each slot must be assigned a value from its set of possible values detailed in the task ontology. However, the analysis shows that the slot *name* rarely appears in the dataset (see Appendix A.1). Therefore following the approach of a number of other researchers,

we focus on the remaining three slots only.

The DSTC2 dataset contains 1612 dialogues in a training set, 506 in a development (validation) set, and 1117 in a test set.

2.2 Data Analysis

We conducted a data analysis on the DSTC2 data using the chi-square test to examine the dependencies between target variables. The chi-square test;is an important statistical test to detect associations between variables; however, this test can only give the answer to the question of whether there exist dependencies between variables. Therefore, it is also important to measure the strength of detected dependencies. For this purpose, we perform a chi-square test on the three informable slots in a pairwise fashion and use the chi-square test's ϕ coefficient to measure the strength of their dependencies (see Appendix A.2). The chi-square test result confirms the existence of pairwise dependencies among DSTC2 data informable slots with the statistical significance $p < 0.05$. The dependencies are reported in Table 1 with the ϕ coefficient.

	food	price	area
food	-		
price	0.608	-	
area	0.707	0.393	-

Table 1: Data analysis of variable dependencies on DSTC2 data. The result is reported with ϕ coefficient values.

The statistical test shows that there are associations of different levels among informable slots in the DSTC2 data. We observe that two pairs *food – price range* and *food – area* have strong dependencies, while the relationship *price range – area* is weaker. We argue that this observation indicates the validity of the motivation for our work in that there are dependencies between target labels and hence the dialogue state tracking task can be cast as a structured prediction problem.

3 Energy-Based Learning

Energy-Based Learning is a branch of machine learning that is notable for its usefulness in structured prediction tasks. Energy-based structured prediction methods have been applied in tasks ranging from Part-of-Speech (POS) tagging (Voutilainen, 1995; Ma and Hovy, 2016) through to instance segmentation tasks in computer vision (Corso et al., 2004; Li and Zhao, 2009; Ngiam et al., 2011). In all of these tasks the output is not a highly structured object, but is rather a set of labels that are not assumed to be independent of each other.

The main intuition behind energy-based methods is that it is too challenging to learn a structured output Y for a given input vector X, and that instead we should learn a function that essentially assesses the goodness of fit between a given structured output Y and the input vector X. In practice we often assume that the raw data is pre-processed in a domain appropriate way to give us a more useful representation of the data to evaluate against a given target. Thus the energy network actually calculates the goodness of fit between some representation of X, referenced from here on out as $F(X)$, and a candidate output Y. While in principle a wide range of methods could be used to generate a feature representation $F(X)$, in this work we assume the feature representation is generated by some form of deep network which we refer to as the feature network. For an image processing task such a network might be based on series of convolutions, while in a language processing task such a network might be based on a recurrent architecture. Given the above, we define that energy function itself simply as $E(F(X), Y)$ which returns some scalar value.

During training, an appropriate objective function $L(E, E^*)$, where $E^* = E((F)X, Y^*)$ is the ground truth energy calculated based on input feature representation $F(X)$ and target labels Y^*, is used to guide training such that the energy function is minimised for valid combinations of $F(X)$ and Y observed in the training data. During runtime we do not have gold standard values for Y, and instead we only have processed inputs $F(X)$. Thus at runtime we begin with an initial hypothesis for Y – usually that $Y = [0]^N$, and we then perform an inference process to update Y so as to find the best fit according to our learned differentiable energy function. This overall approach is illustrated by Figure 1.

The specific design of the energy function is important in achieving an appropriate estimator for goodness of fit between input vectors and candidate structured outputs. Belanger and McCallum (2016) propose an energy function based around the combination of a local and global en-

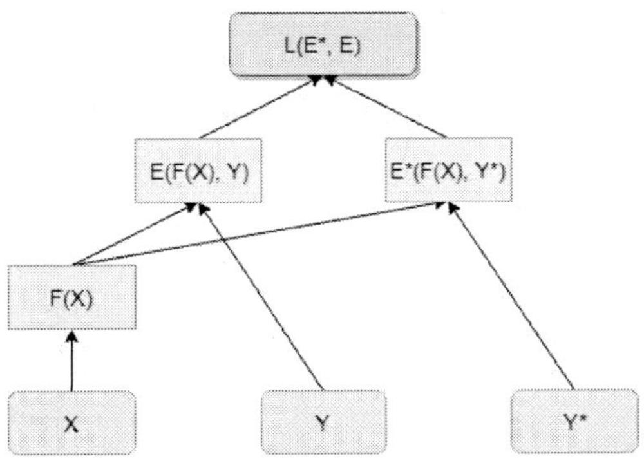

Figure 1: An example of Energy-Based Model, that consists of a feature network $F(X)$, an energy function $E(F(X), Y)$, and an objective function $L(E, E^*)$, where X is input variable, $F(X)$ is a feature representation generated by a feature network, Y is predicted output variable, and Y^* is a gold standard label output variable.

ergy where global energy gives a scalar that represents the cross correlations for the target vector Y only, and the local energy considers the relationship between the input vector X and individual elements of the total output structure variable, i.e., $y \in Y$. Both the local and global energy functions are approximated as layers in a neural network such that complex energy functions may be learned from the training data.

As indicated, the energy function beside being used to produce scalar energy values is also used to generate predicted output variables. This process is called the *Inference process*. Commonly a gradient-based technique is used to generate the output variable in a continuous space (Belanger and McCallum, 2016; Belanger et al., 2017). The inference process can be formulated as follow:

$$y_{t+1} \leftarrow y_t - \eta_t \nabla_y(E(X, Y)) \qquad (1)$$

where η_t is the learning rate at time step t, and $\nabla_y(E(X, Y))$ is the gradients of energy value with respect to the output variable.

The process to train the energy network parameters is called the *Learning process*, where an objective function is used to calculate how good the prediction is, and its gradients are used to backpropagate throughout the network. It is important to define a good objective function for the network (LeCun and Huang, 2005). This process is standard for deep learning models. The parameters are updated with the formula:

$$\theta \leftarrow \theta - \lambda \nabla_\theta(L(E, E^*)) \qquad (2)$$

where θ is the network parameters, λ is the learning rate, and $\nabla_\theta(L(E, E^*))$ is the gradients of the loss between predicted and ground truth energies with respect to trainable parameters of the network.

4 Energy-Based Dialogue State Tracker

Based on the general principles of energy based modelling, we propose a deep learning energy-based architecture for dialogue state tracking. Given the approach outlined in the previous section, the model consists of three main components:

- **Feature network** is a function implemented as a deep learning network to transform dialogue input into an appropriate representation which can be fed to the energy function.

- **Energy function** is a function implemented as a feed-forward network that is trained to assign scalar energy values to any given configuration of input and output variables.

- **Loss function** is a function that provides an measurement of the quality of the network predictions.

In the following we provide details of these components as we specifically designed them for the DSTC2 dataset.

4.1 Feature Network

DSTC2 dialogue data consists of a number of calls (conversations) which in turn are built out of a sequence of turn pairs. Each turn pair consists of the user utterance itself, and a system response – referred to as the machine act.

User utterances are sequences of words (tokens); thus we use a bidirectional LSTM architecture (Hochreiter and Schmidhuber, 1997) to generate an initial representation of the whole word sequence in a turn (see Figure 2). This utterance LSTM is fed using a word embedding layer that is trained directly on our data; empirically we found this to provide us with better results than using a public pre-trained word embedding component.

Machine acts are provided in a semantic representation format, therefore we first parse these into vector representations following the approach outlined in the Word-based Dialogue state tracker (Henderson et al., 2014b). These machine act vectors are high-dimensional one-hot encodings; therefore we find it useful to feed these through an

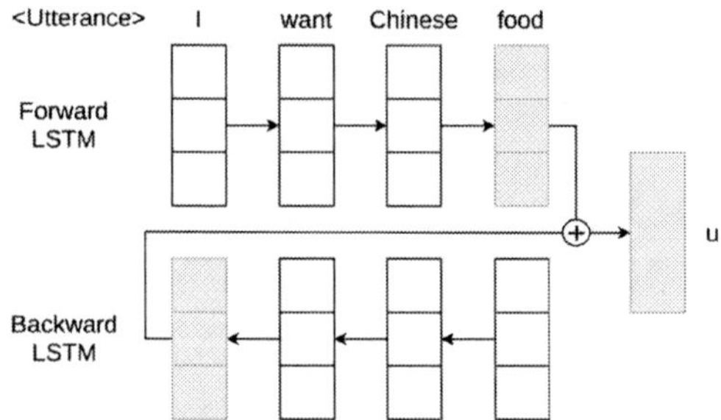

Figure 2: The bidirectional LSTM architecture to encode utterances. $\oplus$ denotes the concatenation operation.

encoder to produce a reduced distributed representation (see Figure 3).

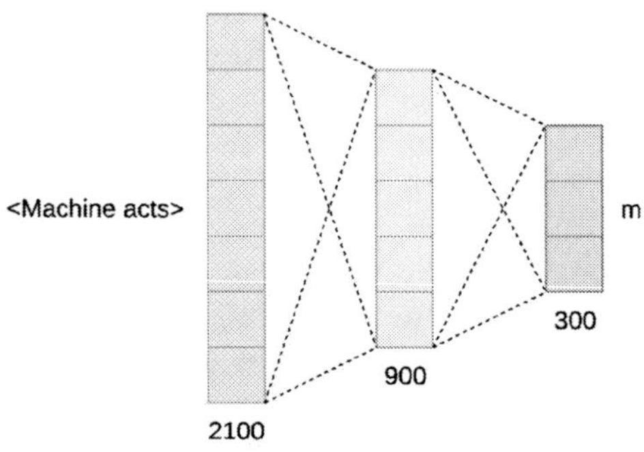

Figure 3: The encoder with two fully connected layers to reduce the dimensionality of machine act vectors.

We concatenate the encoded machine act vector with the output vector of the bi-directional utterance encoder to form a dialogue turn representation vector.

In order to handle dialogue input and dialogue history, it is necessary to use a second LSTM layer unrolling throughout individual turns to build up a complete representation of the dialogue (see Figure 4). Therefore, we feed the input vector produced for each turn into the second full-dialogue LSTM, and receive a fixed-size output vector – this is thus a representation of the whole dialogue up to the current turn. Hyper-parameters for the two LSTM layers plus the embeddings layers used to produce distributed representations of both user utterances and machine acts are presented later in Table 2.

While it is possible for us to feed the output of the second LSTM layer directly as input to an energy layer and perform training, this approach is sub-optimal. As noted by Belanger and McCallum

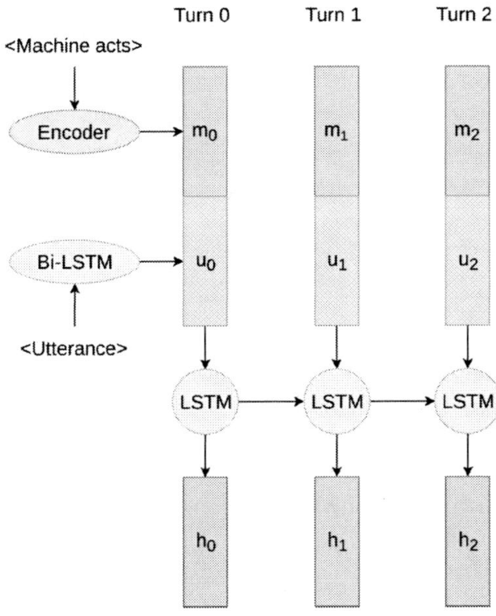

Figure 4: The deep LSTM architecture to transform dialogue input into fixed-size vector representations.

(2016), the feature network should ideally be pre-trained to improve the quality of features. Therefore we pre-train our feature network by plugging it into a multi-task style learning architecture for dialogue state tracking in the style of that proposed by Trinh et al. (2018). Specifically, to complete pre-training the outputs of the second LSTM are fed to a set of three softmax outputs that affect three independent multinomial targets. Optimisation with backpropagation is then used to train the network in the normal way. When used as input to the energy network, the final layer consisting of a set of three softmax operations are discarded and instead the LSTM outputs are taken to be the output of the feature network, i.e., $F(X)$.

The above approach has the advantage that the feature network's output vectors $F(X)$, i.e., the outputs of the turn based LSTM, are already well aligned to producing candidate target representations Y – although they are not actual candidate targets.

4.2 Energy Function

The energy function is implemented on top of the feature network to assign the scalar energy values to combinations of dialogue input and output variables. It should be noted though that the energy function in the literature is usually defined in terms of X and Y, but, for the sake of clarity, we will describe it in terms of Y and $F(X)$, our pre-trained feature representation.

We build our model based around that proposed for the Structured Prediction Energy Network (SPEN) model (Belanger and McCallum, 2016). In this approach the energy function is the summation of individual *Local energy* and *Global energy* terms:

$$\mathcal{E} = E_{local}(F(X), Y) + E_{global}(Y) \qquad (3)$$

Local energy is computed between input and output (label) variables.

$$E_{local}(F(X), Y) = \sum_{i=1}^{L} y_i W_i^\top F(X) \qquad (4)$$

where W_i is a vector for each label, and $y_i \in Y$ is the ith label in the label set.

Global energy meanwhile captures the relationship between labels in the set of output variables independently of the input features. It is also called Label energy and is given below:

$$E_{global}(Y) = W_{g2}^\top \tanh(W_{g1}^\top Y) \qquad (5)$$

where all weights W, W_{g1}, and W_{g2} are parameters that are learned during the training process.

4.3 Loss Function

There are several options for designing the loss function for use in energy-based modelling. In our architecture, we use a loss function based on that proposed for the end-to-end SPEN model (Belanger et al., 2017). This is given as follows:

$$\mathcal{L} = \frac{1}{T} \sum_{t=1}^{T} \frac{1}{T - t + 1} L(y_t, y^*) \qquad (6)$$

where T is the number of iterations in the inference process, t is an iterative variable running through the inference loop, and $L(y_t, y^*)$ is the loss function between the predicted output and the target labels.

The motivation for this loss function is that it measures the quality of every generated prediction $L(y_t, y^*)$ in the inference loop, and encourages the Energy function to produce good quality prediction by including the coefficient for each iteration $\frac{1}{T-t+1}$.

Although the end prediction y_T is our desired output, it is not advised to only calculate loss value of this output. If doing so, the model can possibly generate the output only at the last inference iteration rather than moving smoothly towards the output in the loop.

Since we define the dialogue state tracking task as a multilabel classification task, we use the cross entropy loss for the formula $L(y_t, y^*)$.

5 Experiments

In this section we provide details of the dataset, hyper-parameter selection, and validation results. Test results are presented in the next section.

We train our models with the training set and use the development set to select the best trained parameters. Following this, we run our models with the test set and report those results.

For the food type, price range, and area slots, we merge all three labels into a single multi-label classification task for the sake of the energy-based calculations. In other words we sacrifice the domain constraint that one and only variable can be active individually for each of our slots and instead look for complete global configurations. This is necessary to allow a more elegant integration with the energy-based mechanisms we introduced in the previous sections. In practice our model still (mostly) learns that we need one and only one slot for each of the *food*, *price range*, and *area* related subspace of our target variable.

The model performance is evaluated and reported with the *accuracy* metric, which is one of the feature metrics for the DSTC2.

5.1 Model hyper-parameters

As indicated earlier, we developed a multi-task deep learning state tracker to pre-train the feature network which is subsequently supplied to the energy-based network. This network in practice also serves as a valid benchmark against which we can compare the results of our energy-based model.

This multi-task learning network consists of our feature network (section 4.1) leading into three classifiers for the three informable slots. These three classifiers are implemented with *softmax* output activation function as tracking each slot by itself is a multinomial classification task. We train all parameters of this system end-to-end with a cross entropy loss function and use the Adam optimizer.

The energy-based system is trained with the best set of pre-trained parameters from the multi-task learning-based system having reviewed its performance on the DSTC2 development set. As we combine the labels of informable slots, the task then becomes a multilabel classification task. Therefore we use a *sigmoid* activation function for the output of the energy-based system to produce predictions rather than using three softmax functions as used in the multi-task network above.

The detail of the selected hyper parameters are presented in the Table 2. All hyper parameters are chosen through a strict selection based on the experiments on DSTC2 training and development sets. We developed our energy-based model in TensorFlow (TF) 1.13 (Abadi et al., 2015). As is the case with the multi-task system, we apply the cross entropy loss function and the Adam optimizer (Kingma and Ba, 2015) to train the energy-based network.

Hyper parameter	Value
Feature network	
Machine acts encoded size	300
Encoder output activation	tanh
Word embedding size	300
LSTM number of units	128
LSTM drop out	0.2
LSTM output activation	tanh
Inference process	
Number of iterations	50
Initial learning rates	0.001
Non-linearity function	tanh
Learning process	
Loss function	Cross entropy
Optimizer	Adam
Learning rate	0.001
Maximal global gradient norm	5.0

Table 2: Basic hyper parameters used in experiments constructing the energy-based dialogue state tracker.

5.2 Validation results

During the development phase we carry the evaluation of our multi-task learning-based and energy-based models against the DSTC2 development set in order to find the best set of parameters. We report on both a mean accuracy produced with Tensorflow directly from our data, and the Joint Goals accuracy produced by the toolset provided for the DSTC2 dataset (Henderson et al., 2013). We present the validation results in Table 3.

In the validation results we observe that ap-

Model	TF Acc.	DSTC2 Acc.
Multi-task	0.719	0.692
Energy-based	0.759	0.715
DSTC2 Baseline		0.623

Table 3: Model performances on the Joint Goals task of DSTC2 development set.

Model	Accuracy
Hybrid Tracker	0.796
Word-based Tracker	0.768
EncDec Framework	0.730
MTL Model	0.728
CRF Tracker	0.601
Our work	
Energy-based Tracker	0.749
Multi-task Tracker	0.720
DSTC2 Baseline	0.719

Table 4: The performances of Dialogue State Trackers on the Joint Goals task of DSTC2 test set.

plying the energy network on top of deep learning feature network improves the accuracy on the main tracking task by a margin up to 4%. We also see that there is a big gap between raw accuracy during the training process and external DSTC2 joint goal accuracy results when running evaluation on the output track file. This can be explained by a number of factors, including our exclusion of one of the informable slots from the DST task, that brings the accuracy on the DSTC2 development set down by nearly 1%, and the fact that the raw accuracy metric is carried on mini-batches while the DSTC2 metric evaluates the output of the whole dataset. Despite the differences, it is clear that the overall indicative result indicates a strong improvement with the application of the energy network.

6 Results & Discussions

We selected the best fitting set of hyper-parameters and the highest accuracy checkpoint from validation for use on the test set. We report our results against the DSTC2 baseline and other state-of-the-art trackers (see Table 4). We choose reference dialogue state trackers that are related to our work in different aspects such as their investigation of variable dependencies or because the network architecture is similar to or inspired that which we use. The evaluation metric used on test results is the accuracy provided by the DSTC2 reference evaluation system since this is the same metric used by the published solutions.

Similar to the development set, the energy-based model outperforms the multi-task deep learning tracker by a large margin. The observed improvement can only be achieved due to the energy function and inference process of the energy-based learning approach. Our multi-task learning-based tracker is developed with a straight-forward recurrent neural networks (RNN) architecture. The multi-task model is trained to track all three DSTC2 informable slots at the same time, but it does not really tackle the relationships between them. On the other hand, the energy-based network includes the possible dependencies of these slots by using an energy function over all slot labels and pre-trained features.

As mentioned above there exist Dialogue State Trackers that also tackle the relationships between variables such as EncDec Framework (Platek et al., 2016), MTL-based model (Trinh et al., 2018), and Conditional Random Field (CRF) tracker (Kim and Banchs, 2014). When comparing our energy-based model with those, we observe that our work achieves higher accuracy than those for the DSTC2 test set. Two out of three trackers, namely the MTL-based model and EncDec Framework, try to track Dialogue States within the incremental dialogue context, that limited their performances in general. Our work does not include the incrementality phenomenon. Kim and Banchs (2014) manually define input features in their work, that do not perform well. In our work we set up the model to learn these features automatically, and see improved results.

Among the state-of-the-art DSTC2 trackers, the Hybrid model (Vodolan et al., 2015, 2017) is the most similar in architecture to our work. Both approaches use a deep learning model as a feature network. The difference between their and our trackers lies in the algorithms applied on top of the feature network. For the hybrid tracker the authors apply a set of manual rule-based differentiable calculations to predict the dialogue states, while in our work we implement an energy network, that is also deep learning-based. The Word-based tracker (Henderson et al., 2014b) is a fully RNN-based model, that is notable for its high performance and the feature extraction technique. Vodolan et al. (2017) as well as our work adopts this technique to extract features from dialogue input.

6.1 Variable Associations Analysis

As observed above, the energy-based system performs better than the multi-task model in overall score of accuracy. However, the accuracy metric does not provide any extra information in terms of variable associations that the energy-based approach takes advantage of. Therefore, we performed further analysis on the results that our trackers produced for DSTC2 test set to compare our predictions to those of the DSTC2 baseline system. The analysis is conducted in a similar fashion to that presented in section 2.2, and is presented in Table 5.

	food-price	food-area	price-area
Testset	0.609	0.658	0.428
Our work			
Energy	0.577	0.659	0.428
MTL	0.523	0.687	0.447
Baseline	0.497	0.657	0.389

Table 5: Result analysis of variable dependencies on the DSTC2 test set. The analysis is reported using the ϕ coefficient values for each informable slot pair. In the table, the first block is variable dependencies in labels of the test set, while the second block is variable dependencies detected by our energy-based (*Energy*) and multi-task (*MTL*) trackers, and the last block is the result of the best DSTC2 baseline system.

The analysis result demonstrates that our energy-based system is capable of tackling the presence of variable dependencies in DSTC2 test set. The energy-based method reflects the relationships of two informable slot pairs, *food – area* and *price range – area*, and produces a very close relationship for the other pair, *food – price range*. On the other hand, the multi-task learning approach manages to capture some dependencies that is shown in the result with bigger margins for all variable pairs.

Overall both the deep learning-based methods outperform the best DSTC2 rule-based baseline system in comparing variable dependencies in the tracking process for at least two out of three informable slot pairs of the task.

7 Conclusion

In this paper we presented an energy-based approach to Dialogue State Tracking task that improves the overall performance of a basic deep learning-based model. Energy-based Learning is notably good at structured prediction that we argue applies to the DST task. The results of our work strengthen the hypothesis that dependencies between variables within the dialogue context have an impact on dialogue state tracking performance. To our knowledge this is the first attempt to apply energy-based learning in a dialogue processing task. Though our results do not in themselves improve on the state of the art, the difference relative to a multi-task deep learning model is significant enough to indicate that the method could lead to improvements on the state of the art if combined with the state of the art. Beyond that combination with hybrid state-of-the-art models, there is other room for improvement. Our current plans includes the investigation of multivariate dependencies in dialogue processing with a larger domain and cross domains. We also believe that it is good to conduct an extensive analysis on variable dependencies in data and performances of different architectures.

Acknowledgements

This research was supported by the ADAPT Centre for Digital Content Technology which is funded under the SFI Research Centres Programme (Grant 13/RC/2106) and is co-funded under the European Regional Development Fund.

References

Martín Abadi, Ashish Agarwal, Paul Barham, Eugene Brevdo, Zhifeng Chen, Craig Citro, Greg S. Corrado, Andy Davis, Jeffrey Dean, Matthieu Devin, Sanjay Ghemawat, Ian Goodfellow, Andrew Harp, Geoffrey Irving, Michael Isard, Yangqing Jia, Rafal Jozefowicz, Lukasz Kaiser, Manjunath Kudlur, Josh Levenberg, Dan Mane, Rajat Monga, Sherry Moore, Derek Murray, Chris Olah, Mike Schuster, Jonathon Shlens, Benoit Steiner, Ilya Sutskever, Kunal Talwar, Paul Tucker, Vincent Vanhoucke, Vijay Vasudevan, Fernanda Viegas, Oriol Vinyals, Pete Warden, Martin Wattenberg, Martin Wicke, Yuan Yu, and Xiaoqiang Zheng. 2015. TensorFlow: Large-Scale Machine Learning on Heterogeneous Distributed Systems.

David Belanger and Andrew McCallum. 2016. Structured Prediction Energy Networks. In *Proceedings of the 33rd International Conference on Machine Learning*, volume 48.

David Belanger, Bishan Yang, and Andrew McCallum. 2017. End-to-End Learning for Structured Prediction Energy Networks. In *Proceedings of the 34th International Conference on Machine Learning*.

Paweł Budzianowski, Stefan Ultes, Pei-Hao Su, Nikola Mrksic, Tsung-Hsien Wen, Inigo Casanueva, Lina Rojas-Barahona, and Milica Gasic. 2017. Subdomain Modelling for Dialogue Management with Hierarchical Reinforcement Learning. In *Proceedings of the SIGDIAL 2017 Conference*, pages 86–92.

Jason J. Corso, Maneesh Dewan, and Gregory D. Hager. 2004. Image Segmentation Through Energy Minimization Based Subspace Fusion. In *Proceedings of the 17th International Conference on Pattern Recognition ICPR 2004*, volume 2, pages 120–123. IEEE.

Matthew Henderson, Blaise Thomson, and Jason Williams. 2013. *Dialog State Tracking Challenge 2 & 3.*

Matthew Henderson, Blaise Thomson, and Jason D. Williams. 2014a. The Second Dialog State Tracking Challenge. In *Proceedings of the SIGDIAL 2014 Conference*, pages 263–272.

Matthew Henderson, Blaise Thomson, and Steve Young. 2014b. Word-Based Dialog State Tracking with Recurrent Neural Networks. In *Proceedings of the SIGDIAL 2014 Conference*, pages 292–299.

Sepp Hochreiter and Jurgen Schmidhuber. 1997. Long Short-Term Memory. *Neural Computation*, 9(8):1735–1780.

Takaaki Hori, Hai Wang, Chiori Hori, Shinji Watanabe, Bret Harsham, Jonathan Le Roux, John R. Hershey, Yusuke Koji, Yi Jing, Zhaocheng Zhu, and Takeyuki Aikawa. 2016. Dialog State Tracking With Attention-Based Sequence-To-Sequence Learning. In *Proceedings of 2016 IEEE Workshop on Spoken Language Technology*, pages 552–558.

Seokhwan Kim and Rafael E. Banchs. 2014. Sequential Labeling for Tracking Dynamic Dialog States. In *Proceedings of the SIGDIAL 2014 Conference*, pages 332–336.

Diederik P. Kingma and Jimmy Ba. 2015. Adam: A Method for Stochastic Optimization. In *Proceedings of the 3rd International Conference for Learning Representations*.

Yann LeCun, Sumit Chopra, Raia Hadsell, Marc'Aurelio Ranzato, and Fu Jie Huang. 2006. A Tutorial on Energy-Based Learning. *Predicting Structured Data*.

Yann LeCun and Fu Jie Huang. 2005. Loss Functions for Discriminative Training of Energy-Based Models. In *Proceedings of the 10th International Workshop on Artificial Intelligence and Statistics (AIStats'05)*, pages 206 – 213.

Qiuxu Li and Jieyu Zhao. 2009. MRF Energy Minimization for Unsupervised Image Segmentation. In *Proceedings of the 5th International Conference on Natural Computation, ICNC 2009*, volume 2, pages 67–73. IEEE.

Xiujun Li, Yun-Nung Chen, Lihong Li, Jianfeng Gao, and Asli Celikyilmaz. 2017. End-to-End Task-Completion Neural Dialogue Systems. In *Proceedings of the 8th International Joint Conference on Natural Language Processing*, pages 733–743. Asian Federation of Natural Language Processing.

Xuezhe Ma and Eduard Hovy. 2016. End-to-end Sequence Labeling via Bi-directional LSTM-CNNs-CRF. In *Proceedings of the 54th Annual Meeting of the Association for Computational Linguistics*, pages 1064–1074.

Jiquan Ngiam, Zhenghao Chen, Pang Wei Koh, and Andrew Y. Ng. 2011. Learning Deep Energy Models. In *Proceedings of the 28th International Conference on Machine Learning*.

Ondrej Platek, Petr Belohlavek, Vojtech Hudecek, and Filip Jurcicek. 2016. Recurrent Neural Networks for Dialogue State Tracking. In *Proceedings of CEUR Workshop, ITAT 2016 Conference*, volume 1649, pages 63–67.

Robert J. Ross and John Bateman. 2009. Daisie: Information State Dialogues for Situated Systems. In *Proceedings of International Conference on Text, Speech and Dialogue, TSD 2009*, pages 379–386.

Iulian V. Serban, Alessandro Sordoni, Yoshua Bengio, Aaron Courville, and Joelle Pineau. 2016. Building End-To-End Dialogue Systems Using Generative Hierarchical Neural Network Models. In *Proceedings of the 30th AAAI Conference on Artificial Intelligence (AAAI-16)*, pages 3776–3783.

Pei-Hao Su, Pawel Budzianowski, Stefan Ultes, Milica Gasic, and Steve Young. 2017. Sample-efficient Actor-Critic Reinforcement Learning with Supervised Data for Dialogue Management. In *Proceedings of the SIGDIAL 2017 Conference*, pages 147–157.

Anh Duong Trinh, Robert J. Ross, and John D. Kelleher. 2018. A Multi-Task Approach to Incremental Dialogue State Tracking. In *Proceedings of The 22nd workshop on the Semantics and Pragmatics of Dialogue, SEMDIAL*, pages 132–145.

Miroslav Vodolan, Rudolf Kadlec, and Jan Kleindienst. 2015. Hybrid Dialog State Tracker. In *Proceedings of the Machine Learning for SLU & Interaction NIPS 2015 Workshop*.

Miroslav Vodolan, Rudolf Kadlec, and Jan Kleindienst. 2017. Hybrid Dialog State Tracker with ASR Features. In *Proceedings of the 15th Conference of the European Chapter of the Association for Computational Linguistics, EACL*, volume 2, pages 205–210.

Atro Voutilainen. 1995. A syntax-based part-of-speech analyser. In *Proceedings of the 7th conference on European chapter of the Association for Computational Linguistics EACL '95*, pages 157–164.

Jason D. Williams. 2010. Incremental Partition Recombination For Efficient Tracking Of Multiple Dialog States. In *Proceedings of the IEEE International Conference on Acoustics, Speech and Signal Processing*, pages 5382–5385.

Jason D. Williams, Kavosh Asadi, and Geoffrey Zweig. 2017. Hybrid Code Networks: practical and efficient end-to-end dialog control with supervised and reinforcement learning. In *Proceedings of the 55th Annual Meeting of the Association for Computational Linguistics*.

Tiancheng Zhao and Maxine Eskenazi. 2016. Towards End-to-End Learning for Dialog State Tracking and Management using Deep Reinforcement Learning. In *Proceedings of the SIGDIAL 2016 Conference*, pages 1–10.

A Appendices

A.1 Dataset Analysis

We conduct a small analysis on the DSTC2 dataset to reason why we would like to choose only three out of four informable slots to track. In the analysis we count how often the slots appear in labels with a value, i.e. not *none*, and how often those slots change their values during the conversations.

	Slot appearance (%)			
	Food	Price	Area	Name
Value is not None				
dstc2_train	75.06	61.70	72.16	0.37
dstc2_dev	72.70	62.48	70.11	0.86
dstc2_test	87.01	63.82	73.25	0.51
Value is changed				
dstc2_train	17.12	10.10	11.50	0.07
dstc2_dev	15.56	9.23	10.24	0.20
dstc2_test	16.13	9.42	10.50	0.09

Table 6: The analysis of Informable slot appearances in DSTC2 dataset. The numbers are reported in the percent format (%) over the number of turns in the dataset.

Among DSTC2 informable slots, the slot *Name* rarely appears. That means the datset does not provide enough samples for training Deep Learning models to classify this slot. In the result, this slot does not affect the Joint Goals tracking performance, as in the DSTC2 test set predicting $Name = none$ gives 99.5% accuracy.

A.2 Chi-square Test

Chi-square test is a significant test for association between two variables. The task and algorithm are presented as follow.

Task Given a contingency table (table of counts) of two variables A and B. Let $P(A_i)$ and $P(B_j)$ are probability of appearance in the population of the categories A_i and B_j. Test the relationship between these two variables (dependent or independent).

Step 1 Define hypotheses of the task.

H_0: The two variables are independent

$$P(A_i \cap B_j) = P(A_i)P(B_j) \qquad (7)$$

H_1: The two variables are dependent

$$P(A_i \cap B_j) \neq P(A_i)P(B_j) \qquad (8)$$

Step 2 Calculate expected frequency of $\{A_i, B_j\}$ based on the input

$$E_{ij} = P(A_i) * P(B_j) * N \qquad (9)$$

where N is the population.

Step 3 Calculate the chi-square error

$$\mathcal{X}_{\mathcal{V}}^2 = \sum_i \sum_j \frac{(O_{ij} - E_{ij})^2}{E_{ij}} \qquad (10)$$

where $\mathcal{V}$ is degree of freedom, O_{ij} and E_{ij} are observed and expected frequencies subsequently.

Step 4 We reject H_0 if the computed test statistics $\mathcal{X}_{\mathcal{V}}^2$ is high and the significance coefficient $p < 0.05$.

There exist several measurements of association strength between variables directly related to the chi-square test statistics. There measures are scaled between 0 and 1 indicating that 1 is the perfect relationship and 0 is no relationship between variables. We choose ϕ coefficient to report the level of dependencies between slots in DSTC2 data as in section 2.2.

$$\phi = \sqrt{\frac{\mathcal{X}^2}{N}} \qquad (11)$$

where $\mathcal{X}^2$ is the chi-square statistic value, and N is the number of samples in dataset.

Evaluation and Improvement of Chatbot Text Classification Data Quality Using Plausible Negative Examples

Kit Kuksenok
jobpal Ltd.
Berlin, Germany
kit@jobpal.ai

Andriy Martyniv
jobpal Ltd.
Berlin, Germany
andriy@jobpal.ai

Abstract

We describe and validate a metric for estimating multi-class classifier performance based on cross-validation and adapted for improvement of small, unbalanced natural-language datasets used in chatbot design. Our experiences draw upon building recruitment chatbots that mediate communication between job-seekers and recruiters by exposing the ML/NLP dataset to the recruiting team. Evaluation approaches must be understandable to various stakeholders, and useful for improving chatbot performance. The metric, nex-cv, uses negative examples in the evaluation of text classification, and fulfils three requirements. First, it is actionable: it can be used by non-developer staff. Second, it is not overly optimistic compared to human ratings, making it a fast method for comparing classifiers. Third, it allows model-agnostic comparison, making it useful for comparing systems despite implementation differences. We validate the metric based on seven recruitment-domain datasets in English and German over the course of one year.

1 Introduction

Smart conversational agents are increasingly used across business domains (Jain et al., 2018). We focus on recruitment chatbots that connect re cruiters and job-seekers. The recruiter teams we work with are motivated by reasons of scale and accessibility to build and maintain chatbots that provide answers to frequently asked questions (FAQs) based on ML/NLP datasets. Our enterprise clients may have up to $100K$ employees, and commensurate hiring rate. We have found that almost 50% of end-user (job-seeker) traffic occurs outside of working hours (Liu, 2019), which is consistent with the anecdotal reports of our clients that using the chatbot helped reduce email and ticket inquiries of common FAQs. The usefulness

of these question-answering conversational UIs depends on building and maintaining the ML/NLP components used in the overall flow (see Fig. 1).

In practice, the use of NLP does not improve the experience of many chatbots (Pereira and Díaz, 2018), which is unsurprising. Although *transparency* (being "honest and transparent when explaining why something doesn't work") is a core design recommendation (DialogFlow, 2018), the most commonly available higher-level platforms (Canonico and De Russis, 2018) do not provide robust ways to understand error and communicate its implications. *Interpretability* is a challenge beyond chatbots, and is a prerequisite for trust in both individual predictions and the overall model (Ribeiro et al., 2016). The development of the nex-cv metric was driven by a need for a quantification useful to developers, as well as both vendor and client non-developer staff.

The nex-cv metric uses plausible **n**egative **ex**amples to perform actionable, model-agnostic evaluation of text classification as a component in a chatbot system. It was developed, validated, and used at *jobpal*, a recruiting chatbot company, in projects where a client company's recruiting team trains and maintains a semi-automated conversational agent's question-answering dataset. Use of ML and NLP is subject to conversation flow design considerations, and internal and external transparency needs (Kuksenok and Praß, 2019). The chatbots do not generate answers, but provide all responses from a bank that can be managed by client staff. Each of about a dozen live chatbots answers about 70% of incoming questions without having to defer to a human for an answer. About two thirds of the automated guesses are confirmed by recruiters; the rest are corrected (Fig. 3).

In "Background", we relate our work to prior research on curated ML/NLP datasets and evaluation in chatbots. In "Approach", we describe the

Proceedings of the 1st Workshop on NLP for Conversational AI, pages 87–95
Florence, Italy, August 1, 2019. ©2019 Association for Computational Linguistics

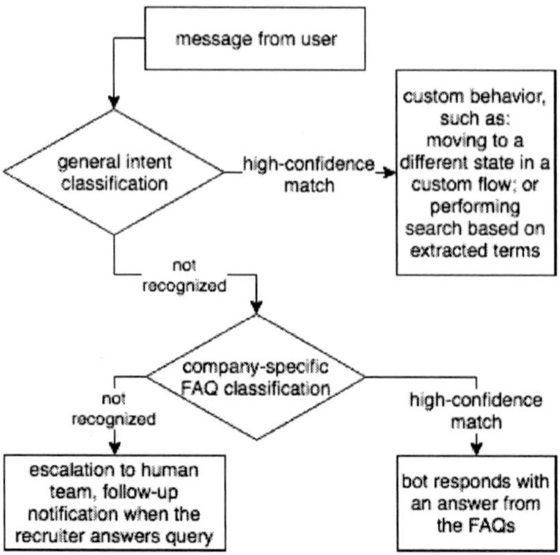

Figure 1: Each incoming message from an end-user is subject to (1) a general intent classifier specific to a language; and, if none of the roughly 20 intents are the recognized, (2) a company-specific FAQ classifier. Custom flow affects the specifics of this behavior.

metric and provide its application and data context of use. In "Validation Datasets", we describe the datasets with which this metric has been validated. In "Validation", we provide results from experiments conducted while developing and using the metric for over a year, addressing each of the needs of the metric, which make it a useful tool for multiple stakeholders in the chatbot design and maintenance process.

1. enable data quality improvements (Fig. 4)

2. not be overly-optimistic (Fig. 5)

3. enable model-agnostic comparison (Fig. 6)

We contribute a metric definition, its validation with six real projects over the course of one year (2018.Q2 through 2019.Q1), as well as an extensible implementation[1] and testing plan, which is described in "Metric Definition" below.

2   Background

Chatbots, or "text messaging-based conversational agents", have received particular attention in 2010s (Jain et al., 2018). Many modern text-based chatbots use relatively simple NLP tools (Abdul-Kader and Woods, 2015), or avoid ML/NLP altogether (Pereira and Díaz, 2018), relying on conver-

---

[1] http://github.com/jobpal/nex-cv

sation flow design and non-NLP inputs like buttons and quick-replies. Conversational natural-language interfaces for question-answering have an extensive history, which distinguishes open-domain and closed-domain systems (Mishra and Jain, 2016). ML-based chatbots rely on curated data to provide examples for classes (commonly, "intents"), and must balance being widely-accessible to many end-users, but typically specialized in the domain and application goal (Serban et al., 2015). In practice, design and development of a chatbot might assume a domain more focused, or different, than real use reveals.

In the chatbot application context, the training dataset of a text classifier may be modified to improve that classifier's performance. The classes — "intents" — are trained with synthetic data and constitute **anticipated**, rather than actual, use. Existing general-purpose platforms include this synthetic data step as part of design and maintenance (Canonico and De Russis, 2018). For example, when it comes to invocations for a voice agent (Ali et al., 2018), dataset construction encodes findings about how users might imagine asking for some action: the authors use a crowd-sourcing mechanism to achieve both consistency useful for classification, and reflection of user expectations in the dataset. We adopt a similar approach: enabling domain-experts (recruiters) to maintain the dataset helps map end-user (job-seeker) needs to recruiters' goals.

Data cleaning is not only relevant to chatbots. Model-agnostic systems for understanding machine learning can help iteratively develop machine learning models (Zhang et al., 2019). Developers tend to overlook data quality in favor of focusing on algorithmic improvements in building ML systems (Patel et al., 2008). Feature engineering can be made accessible to non-developers or domain experts, e.g. (Ribeiro et al., 2016). We make use of representative examples in the process that surfaces nex-cv to non-developers; in describing this process in "Metric Application", we map it to the *inspection-explanation-refinement* process employed in (Zhang et al., 2019). Enabling non-developers to perform data cleaning effectively allows developers to focus on model adjustments and feature engineering.

There are many ways to measure overall chatbot quality, such as manual check-lists of high-level feature presence (Kuligowska, 2015; Pereira and

Díaz, 2018). Static analysis and formal verification may be used with a specified flow (Porfirio et al., 2018). User behavior measurements — both explicit, like ratings or feedback, and implicit, like timing or sentiment — are explored in (Hung et al., 2009). During metric development, we used qualitative feedback from domain-expert users, and key performance indicators (KPIs), such as automatic response rate. Regardless of overall evaluation approach, the use of a classifier as a component in a complex flow demands robust and actionable evaluation of that component.

3 Approach

The `nex-cv` algorithm selects some classes as plausible sources of negative examples, and then uses those to partition the given dataset into training and test data (Alg. 1). Negative examples are useful in chatbot component evaluation: the end-user interaction with a chatbot is open-ended, so the system is expected to encounter input that it should recognize as outside its domain.

Low-membership classes are candidates for being ignored in training and used as negative examples in testing. Two mutually-exclusive variations use the K parameter for cutoff-based negative example selection (Alg. 2); and the P parameter for proportional negative example selection (Alg. 2). We focus on three settings, with (K, P) set to $(0, 0)$, $(0, 0.15)$, and $(5, 0)$. The values were tuned for typical distributions (see "Validation Datasets"), and the $(0, 0)$ is a validating measure that is comparable to 5-fold CV (see "Metric Definition").

We assume that low-population classes are all in the same domain as the rest. There may be exceptions: in some cases a new, small category may be created in response to new questions on an emergent topic well outside of the core domain. In our experience, this happens when there is a technical issue elsewhere on the site and the chatbot channel is used as an alternative to escalate the issue. In practice, our system handles this case well, even if the evaluation is less applicable. Such emergent categories either disappear over time: the topic is temporary; or grow: the topic becomes part of the domain.

3.1 System Overview

A chatbot (Fig. 2) is based on two datasets (Fig. 1), each maintained using a data management tool

Result: $(X_{train}, y_{train}, X_{test}, y_{test})$

Require data X, y s.t. x_i is the input text that has gold standard label $y_i \; \forall i$;

Require label sets L_{SM}, L_{LG} s.t. $L_{SM} \cup L_{LG} = \{y_i \mid y\}$ Require test fraction $0 < t < 1$ and function $split_t(L)$ which randomly splits out two lists $L_1, L2$ s.t. $\frac{|L_2|}{|L|} = t$ and $L_1 \cup L_2 = L$;

for $L_j \in L_{LG}$ **do**

    $TR, TS = split_t(i | y_i \in y \wedge y_i == L)$;

    $X_{train}, y_{train} \leftarrow x_i, y_i$ s.t. $i \in TR$;

    $TR, TS = split_t(i | y_i \in y \wedge y_i == L)$;

    $X_{test}, y_{test} \leftarrow x_i, y_i$ s.t. $i \in TS$;

end

$TR_L, TS_L = split_t(\{j | y_j \in L_{SM}\})$;

$X_{train}, y_{train} \leftarrow x_i, y_i$ s.t. $y_i \in TR_L$;

$X_{test}, y_{test} \leftarrow x_i, \emptyset$ s.t. $y_i \in TS_L$;

Algorithm 1: Negative Example Data Provision

(Fig. 3). Traffic varies widely between projects, but is typically consistent within a project. To provide a range: in one quarter in 2018, the highest traffic chatbot had about 2000 active users, of which about 250 (ca. 12%) asked questions. The lowest-traffic chatbot saw $\tilde{6}5$ weekly active users, of which 15 (ca. 23%) asked questions. In both cases, a small number (2-4) of recruiters were responsible for maintaining the dataset.

The training set of the FAQ portion of each project contains between $1K$ and $12K$ training examples across between 100 and 200 distinct classes, usually starting with about $50 - 70$ classes and creating new classes after the system goes live and new, unanticipated user needs are encountered. To build classifiers on datasets of this size, we use spaCy (Honnibal and Montani, 2017) and fastText (Bojanowski et al., 2016) for vectorization, with transformation for improved performance (Arora et al., 2016), and logistic regression with L2 regularization (Pedregosa et al., 2011).

The dataset for shared *general intents* is maintained through the data management tool by *jobpal* staff. One such classifier is shared by all companies that use a particular language; projects span English, German, Chinese, and French. About 20 general intents are trained with a total of about $1K$ to $1.5K$ training examples per language. These include intents that control the conversation (e.g., 'stop', 'help'). This shared language-specific classification step includes entity extraction of profes-

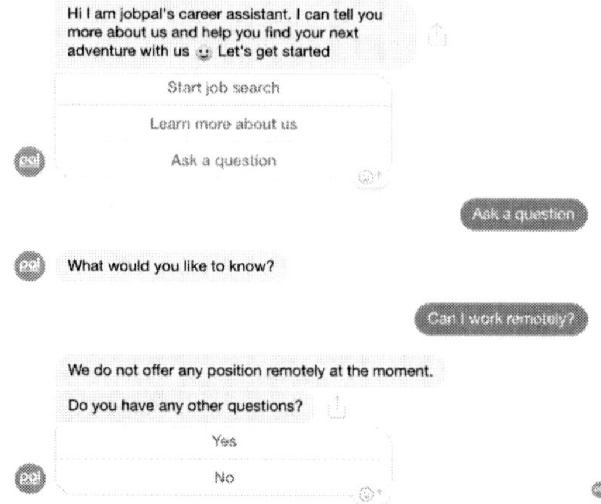

Figure 2: Here, the job-seeker's question receives an immediate answer, based on the ML/NLP classifier. If confidence is too low, chatbot will defer to a human.

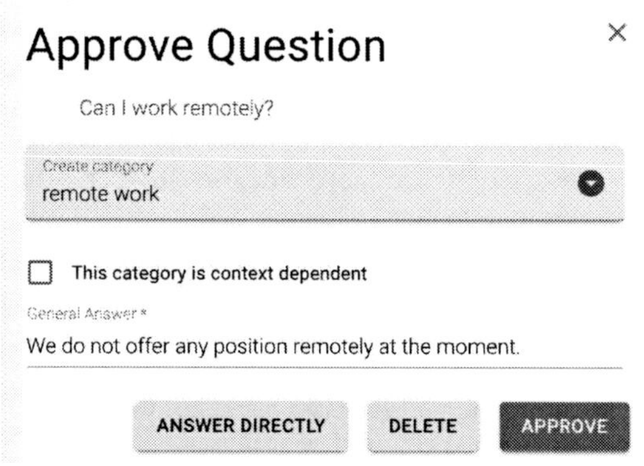

Approve Question

Figure 3: Even if the chatbot responds, recruiters can use a data management tool to review the answer.

sion and city of interest to job-seekers; for example, statements like 'I want a [profession] job in [city]' and 'do you have any [profession] openings?' should all resolve to 'job search' along with extracted keywords. Lastly, this classifier also identifies very common questions that affect all chatbots[2], but which are not in the recruitment domain: e.g., 'how are you?' and 'is this a robot?'.

The dialog in Fig. 2 shows the FAQ functionality of the chatbots, powered by classification using company-specific FAQ datasets (see also Fig. 1).

[2] This was another outcome of the case study summarized in Fig. 4: we identified four categories of questions that we could anticipate in all projects, but that were not in the expert domain of the FAQ, so we made modifications to the flow, the way the existing classifiers were used, and the general intents training data, to help keep company-specific FAQ datasets more focused.

In most projects, users who ask question ask between 1 and 2 questions. The FAQ functionality is typically an addition to any existing information displays. Many of our chatbots also feature job discovery, including search and subscriptions. Job search may be triggered by clicking on the button [Look for a job], or writing something like "I would like a [profession] job in [location]" at almost any point in the flow. If either of location or profession is not specified, the user is prompted, and the responses are used to search current openings, which are then shown. The user may submit application or follow external links; the user may also ask questions about specific jobs or the employer more generally.

3.2 Metric Definition

The code available online[3] provides the evaluation implementation, an abstract black-box definition for a classifier, and two strategies to help test an implementation. For integration testing, `CustomClassifier.test()` can be used to check consistency of classifier wrapper. For functional testing, `nex-cv` both $K = 0$ (Alg. 2) and $P = 0$ (Alg. 2) should yield comparable results to 5-fold cross-validation.

Result: L_{SM}, L_{LG}
Require data X, y s.t. x_i is the input text that
    has gold standard label y_i $\forall i$;
Require cutoff parameter $K > 0$;
$L_{SM} = \{y_i \mid y_i \text{ in } y, \text{ occurs} < K\}$;
$L_{LG} = \{y_i \mid y_i \text{ in } y, \text{ occurs} \geq K\}$;

Algorithm 2: Cutoff Selection of Plausible Negative Example Classes

In k-fold cross-validation, data is partitioned into k sets of $(X_{train}, y_{train}, X_{test}, y_{test})$ such that $\frac{|X_{test}|}{|X_{train}|} = 1/k$ (let the test fraction $t = 1/k$), and the training sets do not overlap. Then, each set of training data is evaluated using the corresponding test set. Evaluation can include many possible measures: accuracy or F_1; representative examples; confusion matrix; timing data; etc.

In `nex-cv`, test fraction t is a setting (0.2 for all reported experiments), and data partitions may overlap. As shown in Alg. 1, representation of high-population classes is enforced. Then, low-population classes are also split using t, and included either in the training set with their ground

[3] http://github.com/jobpal/nex-cv

Result: L_{SM}, L_{LG}

Require data X, y s.t. x_i is the input text that
  has gold standard label y_i $\forall i$;

Require proportion parameter $0 \leq P < 1$;

$L_{SM} = \{\}$;

Let $Q = \{y_i \mid y_i \in y\}$, as queue sorted from
  least to most occurring in X ;

while $\frac{|\{i \mid x_i \in X \wedge y_i \in L_{SM}\}|}{|X|} < P$ **do**

  | Pop element L from Q ;
  | $L_{SM} \leftarrow L$;

end

$L_{LG} = \{y_i \mid y_i \text{ in } y, \text{ not in } L_{SM}\}$;

Algorithm 3: Proportional selection of Plausible Negative Example Classes

truth label; or in the test set as a negative example. In practice, this results in about t of the data being in training. Some low-population classes in the training set should be included as this is representative of the dataset shape; many low-population classes may affect the classification and confidence overall, depending on classification approach. Low-population classes are typically rare or relatively recent topics, so interpreting them as plausible negative examples helps to test the classifier, and its measure of confidence.

3.3 Validation Datasets

The seven datasets to which we report having applied the `nex-cv` metric are in the recruitment domain. Each dataset has about $50 - 200$ classes, and most have classes with 5-10 members as well as classes with over a hundred. To characterize the content, we trained a classifier on an anonymous benchmark dataset [4] and used it to classify a random recent sample of $6K$ English-language questions.

About 25% of recent end-user queries in English fall into 5 categories: (1) Application Process; (2) Salary; (3) Professional Growth and De-

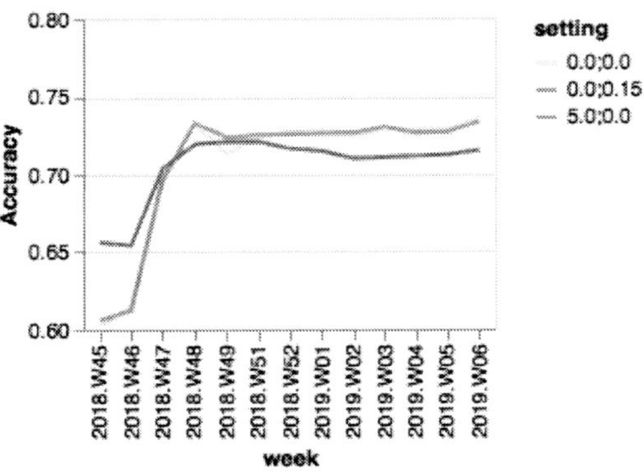

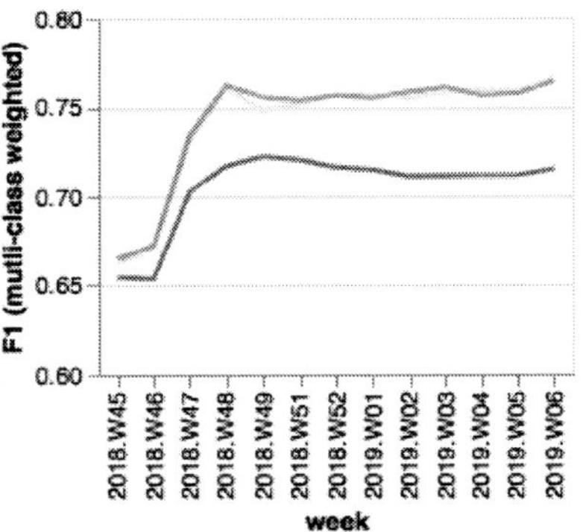

Figure 4: **Change in classifier performance as a result of data quality intervention.** Averages of daily 10-retry evaluations shown.

velopment; (4) Internships; (5) Contact a Human.

Another 25% of end-user queries fall into 14 categories: Application Evaluation; Application Deadline; Application Delete or Modify; How Long to Apply and Hear Back; Qualification; Application Documents; Language Expectations; Thesis; Working Hours; Location; Starting at the Company; Commute; Equipment; Benefits.

About 40% of overall requests were not recognized (with a confidence of 0.5 or higher) as any of the categories in the anonymous benchmarking set. Upon manual inspection, some of these test questions were noise, and many were topics specific to particular company FAQs, such as concerning specific work-study programs; details of the application software; and other more niche topics.

The classification datasets share some overlapping topics; each also has a specific set of additional topics. Each dataset has the typical shape of a few larger classes, and many smaller ones, which have an indirect relationship to what data is expected. The use of low-population classes

---

[4]The clean, anonymized recruitment-domain-specific dataset in English was built by anonymizing and aggregating all FAQ datasets; using pairwise similarity between categories to group them. For an initial clustering, we used Jaccard index with a minimum of 0.09, which balanced the goals of high coverage of example data (74) and reasonable sizes of classes (15 examples per class); then, this dataset was subject to iterative data quality improvements as described further and exemplified in Fig. 4 until a final set of about 800 examples over about 47 categories was developed. This initial domain-specific clustering was performed on English, but has since been extended to other supported languages; the results reported are specific to English, however.

as plausible negative examples takes advantage of both the content of the data (closed-domain, with a topic-specific core but a considerable number of additional, outlying topics) and the membership distribution of the classes (a few well-populated ones, and many much smaller classes).

The `nex-cv` metric may apply in other problems or domains, but we developed and validated it in a series of experiments with six live datasets, in English and German (see Fig. 5, of which chatbot E is also the subject of Fig. 4), in addition to the seventh aggregate anonymous benchmark dataset described above, which was used for the comparison in Fig. 6.

4 Validation

The following case studies validate the metric relative to each of three requirements: (1) enable data quality improvements, as in Fig. 4, (2) not be overly-optimistic, as in Fig. 5, (3) enable model-agnostic comparison, as in Fig. 6.

4.1 Metric Application

The goal of usefulness includes interpretability: "provid[ing] qualitative understanding between the input variables and the response... [taking] into account the users limitations in (Ribeiro et al., 2016). Usefulness combines this with actionable support of chatbot design. The users include, in this case, non-developer staff on both vendor and client side: recruiters and project managers.

Through iteration on internal tools, we found that displaying performance information in the form of, "which 2-3 topics are the biggest problem?" was most effective for understanding, communication, and action. Over the course of a year, the `nex-cv` metric informed this analysis. During this time, both qualitative feedback and KPIs have validated that it was effective both for trust and for the end-user experience. The *automation rate* KPI — proportion of incoming queries that did not need deferral to a human, but answered immediately, as in Fig. 2 — has risen to and remained at $70-75\%$ across projects mainly[5] due to data quality support during both design and maintenance.

---

[5]The data training UI design contributes to data quality; in the months following the intervention shown in Fig. 4, the UI was redesigned to address outstanding usability problems, with very positive feedback from domain-expert users. A more in-depth discussion of the role of human factors in human-in-the-loop systems is out of scope for this paper.

In one illustrative project (Fig. 4) the automation rate had become as low as 40%. The recruiters responsible for dealing with escalated questions became frustrated to see questions come up that had been asked before. Action needed to be taken, and this project became one of the first case studies for developing the application of `nex-cv` internally. After intervention, automated response rate rose into the desirable 70s range and remained. The quality improvements were explained and implemented by an internal project manager, who pro-actively included client domain-expert users in explanations over calls and emails over what improvements were made and why. Initially, 200 classes were trained with $1K$ examples, with long tail of low-population classes. Following intervention, dataset grew by 25% and, despite concept drift risk, did not deteriorate.

To use `nex-cv`, we aggregate the confusion matrix from the $K = 0; P = 0.15$ setting and rank how confused a *pair* of categories is. The most confused 2-3 pairs of classes are then the focus of conceptual, manual review in the dataset. Evaluation is performed again, producing a new ranking that guides the next 2-3 classes to focus on, until the metric falls below an acceptable threshold. There are other sources of classification error, but overlap between conceptually related pairs of classes accounts for most of the data quality problems we encounter in the datasets in practice, and are particularly understandable than other forms of error. This relatively simple approach is implemented as a Jupyter notebook accessible to non-developers (internal project managers).

The details of pairwise measures and acceptability threshold were developed iteratively based on project manager feedback. The project managers also honed processes and intuitions for communicating this information to clients effectively. In extreme situations as that shown in Fig. 4 the project managers made a presentation to get buy-in and implemented data quality improvements on their own. However, the typical practice now is to provide explanations, in calls and emails, of the "confusions" between one or few pairs of specific categories to the client. This practice builds awareness of data quality across stakeholders, and the domain-experts (recruiters) are better able to use the system to create the envisioned chatbot functionality without major intervention. As the number of projects grows, the metric can be used

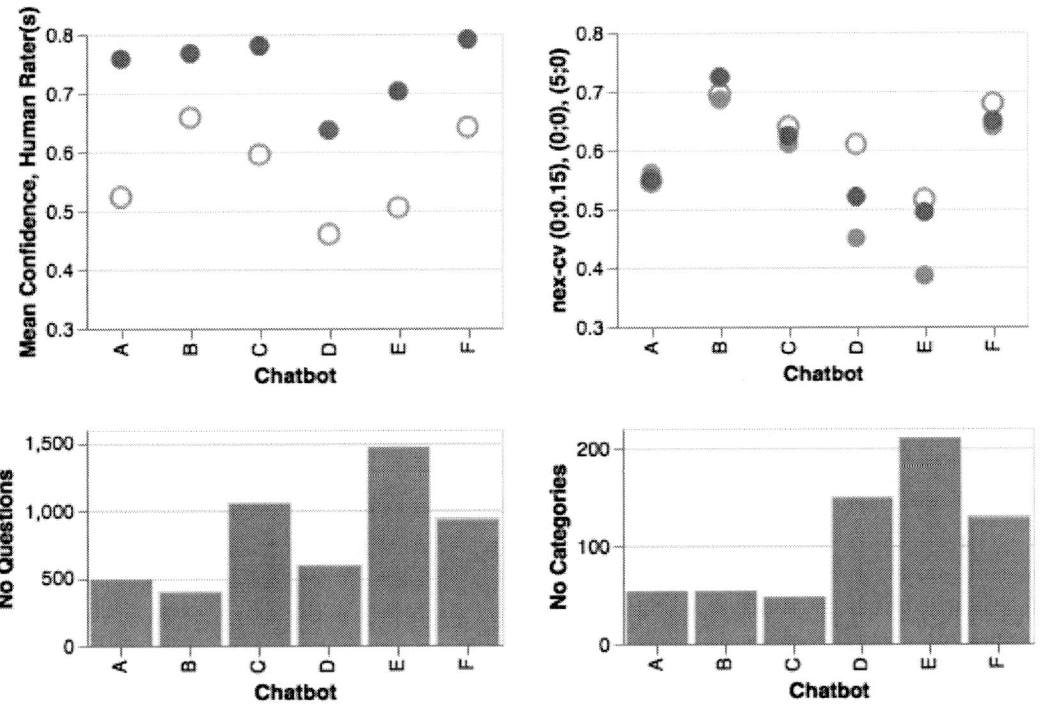

Figure 5: **Comparison of nex–cv and Human-Rater Accuracy**. The six datasets from pseudonymous chatbots tested had a different number of questions (examples) and categories (classes), as shown in the bottom row. The human-rater estimate of accuracy (top left, blue) is consistently more lenient than any of the automated measures (top right). The $(0; 0.15)$ setting (top right, blue) is not consistently more or less optimistic than the other settings.

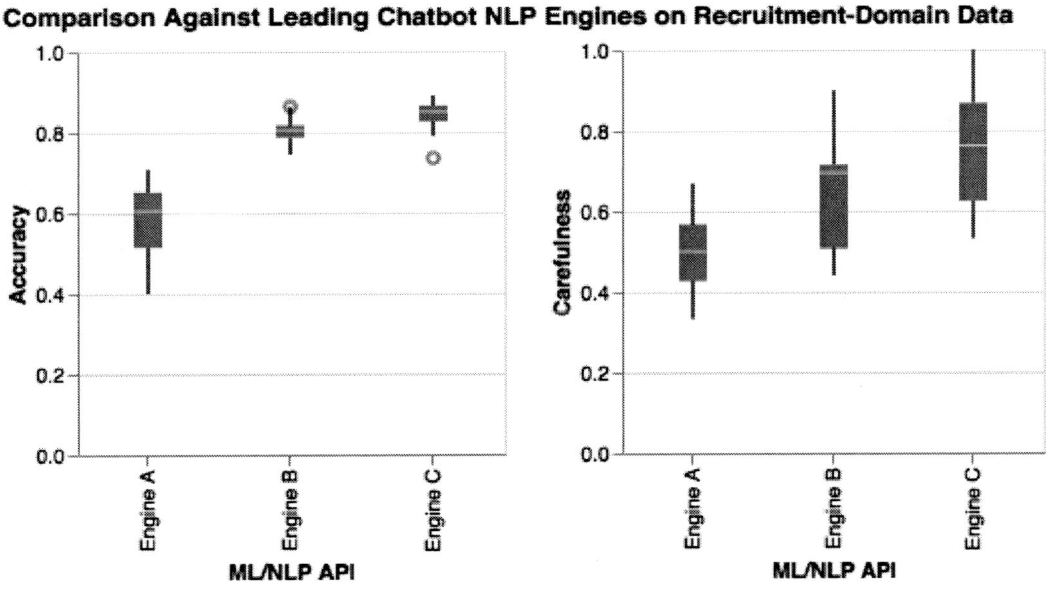

Figure 6: **Comparison Against Leading Chatbot NLP Engines on Recruitment-Domain Data.** Engine C wraps jobpal's system; Engines A and B wrap external general-purpose chatbot platforms.

by project managers to monitor and prioritize data quality improvement tasks.

4.2 Metric is not Overly Optimistic

One of the practical motivations for a new metric was the sense that the existing metrics were too optimistic to be useful to improve chatbot behavior in response to overall qualitative feedback. As shown in Fig. 4, for example, the typical F_1 metric is more optimistic than `nex-cv`.

As an initial step of validating the metric, we applied it in the case of six under-performing datasets that required some intervention. Fig. 4 shows the differences in data abundance and classifier quality across these six pseudonymized snapshots. Internal QA staff gave the human rating scores by considering whether a question-answer pairs seemed reasonable: they could pick "yes" "no" and "can't tell"; in most cases, the appropriateness was not ambiguous. As shown in Fig. 5, the human-rater estimate of quality is consistently more lenient than any of the automated measures. The Chatbot E in this case is the same project as shown in Fig. 4, prior to improvements.

Four of the six datasets analyzed had a very big difference between the human estimate of quality and the automated estimate, which, upon investigation, revealed that there were significant conceptual overlaps in the classes that the recruiters had trained, and the answers given. So, indeed, the classifier was making surprisingly adequate guesses, but which were very low-confidence. Following the intervention described in the previous section, which includes ongoing communication of any outstanding problems by project managers to recruiter teams, this type of error became rare and quickly-addressed.

4.3 Metric can be used for Internal and External Comparison

We used the `nex-cv` metric to help compare the performance of our classification component with two leading vendors for general-purpose chatbot development. Fig. 6 shows the comparison between *jobpal* and 2 leading vendors in the space. The three settings of the metric[6] were aggregated to provide a plausible range of estimated performance. The range of accuracy was significantly higher for our domain-specific classifier, than those trained using general-purpose tools.

---

[6]Where (K, P) are $(0, 0)$, $(0, 0.15)$, and $(5, 0)$, respectively, as differentiated in both Fig. 4 and Fig. 5.

Aside from being useful to classify into known classes, the metric must account for fallback or escalation. This may be modeled as a separate class (as one of the external engines does with the "fallback" intent), or by relying on confidence scores from classifiers that produce measures of confidence (all engines provide some estimate of confidence that may be used). The "carefulness" score was included to represent how useful the confidence score is for deciding when to decline an answer: the number of incorrect guesses that were rejected due to too-low confidence scores divided by total no-answer-given cases (no guess or low-confidence guess).

Fig. 6 shows that the performance of our ML/NLP component on our domain-specific dataset is better than that of two popular general-purpose platforms, both in terms of classification accuracy, and rate of deferral due to low-confidence answers. This comparison mechanism validates our system relative to existing external services in a way that is interpretable by various internal stakeholders, not only the developer staff.

5 Conclusion

We described and validated the `nex-cv` metric, which is a modification of cross-validation that makes use of plausible negative examples from low-population classes in the datasets typical of our application area and domain.

Existing chatbot guidelines leave error handling to the designer: "transparency" is included as an important topic (DialogFlow, 2018), but, in practice, why something does not work, and under what conditions, can puzzle designers and developers, not just end-users. We presented on a metric that can be used by a variety of relevant stakeholders to understand, communicate, and improve text classifier performance by improving data quality.

In future work, we aim to explore other text classifier and chatbot evaluation strategies, keeping in mind the needs for understandability and transparency in this multi-stakeholder design process and maintenance practice.

References

Sameera A Abdul-Kader and JC Woods. 2015. Survey on chatbot design techniques in speech conversation systems. *International Journal of Advanced Computer Science and Applications*, 6(7).

Abdullah X Ali, Meredith Ringel Morris, and Jacob O Wobbrock. 2018. Crowdsourcing similarity judgments for agreement analysis in end-user elicitation studies. In *The 31st Annual ACM Symposium on User Interface Software and Technology*, pages 177–188. ACM.

Sanjeev Arora, Yingyu Liang, and Tengyu Ma. 2016. A simple but tough-to-beat baseline for sentence embeddings.

Piotr Bojanowski, Edouard Grave, Armand Joulin, and Tomas Mikolov. 2016. Enriching word vectors with subword information. *arXiv preprint arXiv:1607.04606*.

Massimo Canonico and Luigi De Russis. 2018. A comparison and critique of natural language understanding tools. *Cloud Computing 2018*, page 120.

DialogFlow. 2018. Dialogflow design guidelines. conversational components - error handling. designguidelines.withgoogle.com/conversation/conversational-components/errors.html. Accessed: 2018-09-02.

Matthew Honnibal and Ines Montani. 2017. spacy 2: Natural language understanding with bloom embeddings, convolutional neural networks and incremental parsing. *To appear*.

Victor Hung, Miguel Elvir, Avelino Gonzalez, and Ronald DeMara. 2009. Towards a method for evaluating naturalness in conversational dialog systems. In *Systems, Man and Cybernetics, 2009. SMC 2009. IEEE International Conference on*, pages 1236–1241. IEEE.

Mohit Jain, Pratyush Kumar, Ramachandra Kota, and Shwetak N Patel. 2018. Evaluating and informing the design of chatbots. In *Proceedings of the 2018 on Designing Interactive Systems Conference 2018*, pages 895–906. ACM.

Kit Kuksenok and Nina Praß. 2019. Transparency in maintenance of recruitment chatbots. *arXiv preprint arXiv:1905.03640*.

Karolina Kuligowska. 2015. Commercial chatbot: performance evaluation, usability metrics and quality standards of embodied conversational agents.

Ching-Ju Liu. 2019. Behind the screen: When do applicants approach you? https://jobpal.ai/en/blog/when-do-applicants-approach-you/. Accessed: 2019-05-01.

Amit Mishra and Sanjay Kumar Jain. 2016. A survey on question answering systems with classification. *Journal of King Saud University-Computer and Information Sciences*, 28(3):345–361.

Kayur Patel, James Fogarty, James A Landay, and Beverly L Harrison. 2008. Examining difficulties software developers encounter in the adoption of statistical machine learning. In *AAAI*, pages 1563–1566.

F. Pedregosa, G. Varoquaux, A. Gramfort, V. Michel, B. Thirion, O. Grisel, M. Blondel, P. Prettenhofer, R. Weiss, V. Dubourg, J. Vanderplas, A. Passos, D. Cournapeau, M. Brucher, M. Perrot, and E. Duchesnay. 2011. Scikit-learn: Machine learning in Python. *Journal of Machine Learning Research*, 12:2825–2830.

Juanan Pereira and Oscar Díaz. 2018. A quality analysis of facebook messenger's most popular chatbots. In *Proceedings of the 33rd Annual ACM Symposium on Applied Computing*, pages 2144–2150. ACM.

David Porfirio, Allison Sauppé, Aws Albarghouthi, and Bilge Mutlu. 2018. Authoring and verifying human-robot interactions. In *The 31st Annual ACM Symposium on User Interface Software and Technology*, pages 75–86. ACM.

Marco Tulio Ribeiro, Sameer Singh, and Carlos Guestrin. 2016. Why should i trust you?: Explaining the predictions of any classifier. In *Proceedings of the 22nd ACM SIGKDD international conference on knowledge discovery and data mining*, pages 1135–1144. ACM.

Iulian Vlad Serban, Ryan Lowe, Peter Henderson, Laurent Charlin, and Joelle Pineau. 2015. A survey of available corpora for building data-driven dialogue systems. *arXiv preprint arXiv:1512.05742*.

Jiawei Zhang, Yang Wang, Piero Molino, Lezhi Li, and David S Ebert. 2019. Manifold: A model-agnostic framework for interpretation and diagnosis of machine learning models. *IEEE transactions on visualization and computer graphics*, 25(1):364–373.

Improving Long Distance Slot Carryover in Spoken Dialogue Systems

Tongfei Chen[*]   **Chetan Naik**[†]   **Hua He**[†]
Pushpendre Rastogi[†]   **Lambert Mathias**[†]
[*] Johns Hopkins University
[†] Amazon.com, Inc.
`tongfei@jhu.edu, {chetnaik,huhe,prastogi,mathiasl}@amazon.com`

Abstract

Tracking the state of the conversation is a central component in task-oriented spoken dialogue systems. One such approach for tracking the dialogue state is *slot carryover*, where a model makes a binary decision if a slot from the context is relevant to the current turn. Previous work on the slot carryover task used models that made independent decisions for each slot. A close analysis of the results show that this approach results in poor performance over longer context dialogues. In this paper, we propose to jointly model the slots. We propose two neural network architectures, one based on pointer networks that incorporate slot ordering information, and the other based on transformer networks that uses self attention mechanism to model the slot interdependencies. Our experiments on an internal dialogue benchmark dataset and on the public DSTC2 dataset demonstrate that our proposed models are able to resolve longer distance slot references and are able to achieve competitive performance.

1 Introduction

In task-oriented spoken dialogue systems, the user and the system are engaged in interactions that can span multiple turns. A key challenge here is that the user can reference entities introduced in previous dialogue turns. For example, if a user request for *what's the weather in arlington* is followed by *how about tomorrow*, the dialogue system has to keep track of the entity *arlington* being referenced.

In *slot-based* spoken dialogue systems, tracking the entities in context can be cast as *slot carryover* task – only the relevant slots from the dialogue context are carried over to the current turn. Recent work by Naik et al. (2018) describes a scalable multi-domain neural network architecture to address the task in a diverse schema setting. However, this approach treats every slot as indepen-

Figure 1: An example of a conversation session. Slots are listed on the right. Related slots often co-occur, such as (1) [WEATHERCITY: *San Francisco*] and [WEATHERSTATE: *CA*], and should be carried over together due to their interdependencies (2) PLACE slot is often seen to occur along with TOWN.

dent. Consequently, as shown in our experiments, this results in lower performance when the contextual slot being referenced is associated with dialogue turns that are further away from the current turn. We posit that modeling slots jointly is essential for improving the accuracy over long distances, particularly when slots are correlated. We motivate this with an example conversation in Figure 1. In this example, the slots WEATHERCITY/WEATHERSTATE, need to be carried over *together* from dialogue history as they are correlated. However, the model in Naik et al. (2018) has no information about this slot interdependence and may choose to carryover only one of the slots. In this work, we alleviate this issue by propos-

Proceedings of the 1st Workshop on NLP for Conversational AI, pages 96–105
Florence, Italy, August 1, 2019. ©2019 Association for Computational Linguistics

ing two novel neural network architectures – one based on pointer networks (Vinyals et al., 2015) and another based on self-attention with transformers (Vaswani et al., 2017) – that can learn to *jointly* predict jointly whether a subset of related slots should be carried over from dialogue history.

To validate our approach, we conduct thorough evaluations on both the publicly available DSTC2 task (Henderson et al., 2014), as well as our internal dialogue dataset collected from a commercial digital assistant. In Section 4.3, we show that our proposed approach improve slot carryover accuracy over the baseline systems over longer dialogue contexts. A detailed error analysis reveals that our proposed models are more likely to utilize "anchor" slots – slots tagged in the current utterance – to carry over long-distance slots from context.

To summarize we make the following contributions in this work:

1. We improve upon the slot carryover model architecture in Naik et al. (2018) by introducing approaches for modeling slot interdependencies. We propose two neural network models based on pointer networks and transformer networks that can make joint predictions over slots.

2. We provide a detailed analysis of the proposed models both on an internal benchmark and public dataset. We show that contextual encoding of slots and modeling slot interdependencies is essential for improving performance of slot carryover over longer dialogue contexts. Transformer architectures with self attention provide the best performance overall.

2   Problem Formulation

A dialogue H is formulated as a sequence of utterances, alternatively uttered by a user (U) and the system agent (A):

$$H = \left(h_d^{\{U,A\}}, \cdots, h_2^U, h_1^A, h_0^U \right), \qquad (1)$$

where each element h is an utterance. A subscript d denotes the utterance distance which measures the offset from the most recent user utterance (h_0^U). The i-th token of an utterance with distance d is denoted as $h_d[i]$.

A slot $x = (d, k, l, r)$ in a dialogue is defined as a key-value pair that contains an entity information, e.g. [CITY:*San Francisco*]. Each slot can be determined by the utterance distance d, slot key k,

and a span $[l : r]$ over the tokens of the utterance with slot value represented as $h_d[l : r]$.

Given a dialogue history H and a set of candidate slots X, the context carryover task is addressed by deciding which slots should be carried over. The previous work (Naik et al., 2018) addressed the task as a binary classification problem and each slot $x \subseteq X$ is classified independently. In contrast, our proposed models can explicitly capture slot interactions and make joint predictions of all slots. We show formulations of both model types below,

$$F_{\text{binary}}(x, H) \in (0, 1) \qquad \forall x \in X \qquad (2)$$
$$F_{\text{joint}}(X, H) \subseteq X \qquad (3)$$

where $F_{\text{binary}}(x, H)$ denotes a binary classification model (Naik et al., 2018), $F_{\text{joint}}(X, H)$ denotes our joint prediction models.

3   Models

3.1   General architecture

Candidate Generation   We follow the approach in Naik et al. (2018), where, given a dialogue H, we construct a candidate set of slots X from the context by leveraging the slot key embeddings to find the nearest slot keys that are associated with the current turn.

Slot Encoder   A model, given a candidate slot (a slot key, a span in the history and a distance), results in a fixed-length vector representation of a slot: $\mathbf{x} = F_S(x, H) \in \mathbb{R}^{D_S}$, where x is the slot, H is the full history.

Dialogue Encoder   We serialize the utterances in the dialogue and use BiLSTM to encode the context as a fixed-length vector $\mathbf{c} = \text{BiLSTM}(H) \in \mathbb{R}^{D_C}$.

Intent Encoder   The intent I of the most recent utterance determined by an NLU module is also encoded as a fixed-length vector $\mathbf{i} \in \mathbb{R}^{D_I}$ by averaging the tokens in the intent. We average the word embeddings of the tokens associated with the intent to get the intent embedding.

Decoder   Given the encoded vector representations $\{\mathbf{x}_1, \cdots, \mathbf{x}_n\}$ of the slots, the context vector $\mathbf{c}$, the intent vector $\mathbf{i}$, produce a subset of the slot ids:

$$F_D(\mathbf{x}_{1:n}, \mathbf{c}, \mathbf{i}) \subseteq \{1, \cdots, N\} \qquad (4)$$

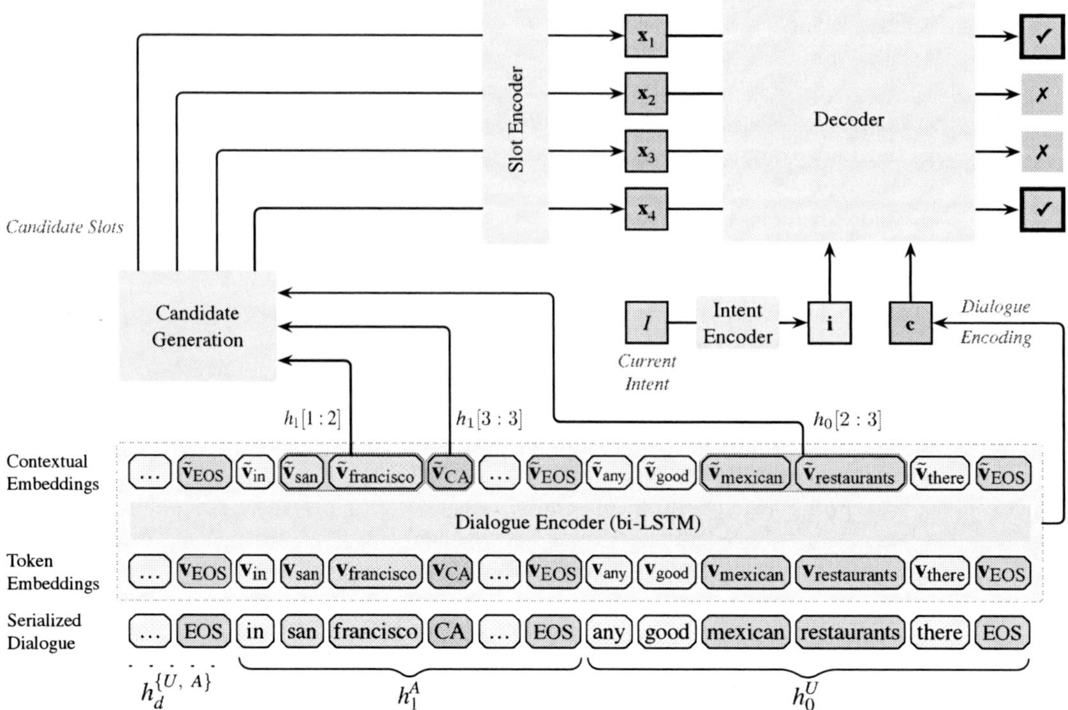

Figure 2: General architecture of the proposed contextual carryover model. Bi-LSTM is used to encode the utterances in dialogue into a fixed length dialogue representation and also get contextual slot value embeddings. Slot encoder uses the slot key, value and distance to create a fixed length slot embedding for each of the candidate slots. Given the encoded slots, intent and dialogue context, decoder selects the subset of slots that are relevant for the current user request.

The overall architecture of the model is shown in Figure 2. We elaborate on the specific designs of these components under this general architecture.

3.2 Slot Encoder Variants

In this section, we describe the different encoding methods that we use to encode slots.

We average the word embeddings of the tokens in the slot key as the *slot key encoding*:

$$\mathbf{x}_{\text{key}} = \frac{1}{K} \sum_{i=1}^{K} \mathbf{v}(k_i) \ . \tag{5}$$

where $\mathbf{v}(w)$ is the embedding vector of token w.

For the slot value (the tokens $h_d[l : r]$), we propose following encoding approaches.

CTX$_{\text{avg}}$ The first is to average the token embeddings of the tokens in the slot value:

$$\mathbf{x}_{\text{val}} = \frac{1}{r - l + 1} \sum_{i=l}^{r} \mathbf{v}(h_d[i]) \ ; \tag{6}$$

CTX$_{\text{LSTM}}$ To get improved contextualized representation of the slot value in dialogue, we also use neural network models to encode slots. We experimented with bidirectional LSTM (Hochreiter and Schmidhuber, 1997) model for slot encoding. LSTMs are equipped with feedback loops in their recurrent layer, which helps store contextual information over a long history. We encode all dialogue utterances with BiLSTM to obtain contextualized vector representations $\tilde{\mathbf{v}}(w)$ for each token w, then average the output hidden states of the tokens in the span $[l : r]$ to get the slot value encoding.

$$\mathbf{x}_{\text{val}} = \frac{1}{r - l + 1} \sum_{i=l}^{r} \tilde{\mathbf{v}}(h_d[i]) \ ; \tag{7}$$

Additionally, *distance* may contain important signals. This integer, being odd or even, provides information on whether this utterance is uttered by a user or the system. The smaller it is, the closer a slot is to the current utterance, hence implicitly more probable to be carried over. Building on these intuitions, we encode the distance as a small vector ($\mathbf{x}_{\text{dist}}$, 4 dimensions) and append it to the overall slot encoding:

$$\mathbf{x} = \begin{bmatrix} \mathbf{x}_{\text{key}} \; ; \; \mathbf{x}_{\text{val}} \; ; \; \mathbf{x}_{\text{dist}} \end{bmatrix} . \tag{8}$$

3.3 Decoder Variants

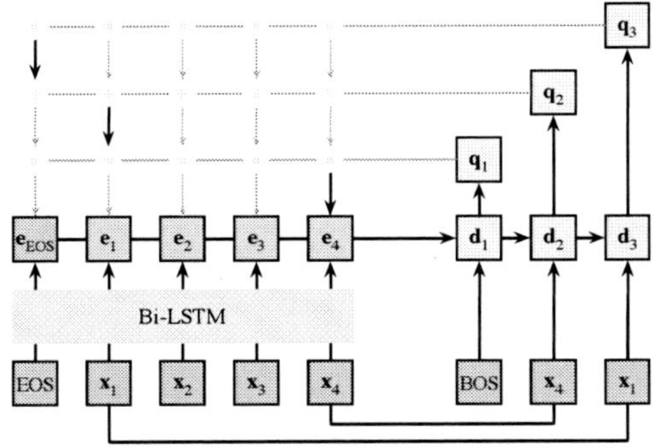

Figure 3: Architecture of the pointer network decoder. In this case, the pointer network selects $\mathbf{x}_4$, $\mathbf{x}_1$ successively and stops after selecting EOS.

Pointer network decoder We adopt the architecture of the pointer network (Vinyals et al., 2015) as a method to perform joint prediction of the slots to be carried over. Pointer networks, a variant of Seq2Seq (Bahdanau et al., 2015; Sutskever et al., 2014; Luong et al., 2015) model, instead of transducing the input sequence into another output sequence, yields a succession of soft pointers (attention vectors) to the input sequence, hence producing an ordering of the elements of a variable-length input sequence.

We use a pointer network to select a *subset* of the slots from the input slot set. The input slot encodings are ordered as a sequence, then fed into a bidirectional LSTM encoder to yield a sequence of encoded hidden states. We experiment with different slot orderings as described in section 4.

$$\mathbf{e}_{0:n} = \text{BiLSTM}([\mathbf{x}_{\text{EOS}} \, , \, \mathbf{x}_{1:n}]) \tag{9}$$

Here a special sentinel token EOS is appended to the beginning of the input to the pointer network – when decoding, once the output pointer points to this EOS token, the decoding process stops.

Given the hidden states, $\mathbf{e}_{0:n}$, the decoding process at every time step i is computed and updated as shown in Algorithm 1.

Contrary to normal attention-based models which directly uses the decoder state ($\mathbf{d}_i$) as the query, we incorporate the context vector ($\mathbf{c}$) and the intent vector ($\mathbf{i}$) into the attention query. The

---

Algorithm 1 Pointer network decoding

1: **procedure** PTRNETDEC($\mathbf{x}_{0:n}, \mathbf{e}_{0:n}, \mathbf{d}_0, \mathbf{c}, \mathbf{i}$)
2: $\quad i \leftarrow 0$
3: $\quad y_0 \leftarrow$ BOS $\qquad\qquad$ ▷ special BOS token
4: $\quad m_{0:n} \leftarrow$ TRUE $\qquad$ ▷ every slot is available
5: $\quad$ **repeat**
6: $\quad\quad i \leftarrow i + 1$
7: $\quad\quad \mathbf{d}_i \leftarrow \text{LSTM}(\mathbf{d}_{i-1}, \mathbf{x}_{y_{i-1}})$ ▷ update state
8: $\quad\quad \mathbf{q}_i \leftarrow F_Q(\mathbf{d}_i, \mathbf{c}, \mathbf{i}) \qquad$ ▷ constructs query
9: $\quad\quad a_{ij} \leftarrow F_A(\mathbf{q}_i, \mathbf{e}_j) \qquad$ ▷ attention scores
10: $\quad\quad p_{ij} \leftarrow \dfrac{\exp a_{ij}}{\displaystyle\sum_{m_j=\text{TRUE}} \exp a_{ij}}$ ▷ soft pointer
11: $\quad\quad \hat{y}_i \leftarrow \underset{m_j=\text{TRUE}}{\arg\max}\, p_{ij}$ ▷ predicted output
12: $\quad\quad$ **if** at inference time **then**
13: $\quad\quad\quad y_i \leftarrow \hat{y}_i \qquad\qquad$ ▷ no gold output
14: $\quad\quad$ **end if**
15: $\quad\quad m_{y_i} \leftarrow$ FALSE $\qquad$ ▷ update mask
16: $\quad$ **until** $y_i = 0$ $\qquad$ ▷ index of EOS is 0
17: **return** $\hat{y}_{1:i-1}$ $\qquad$ ▷ return all generated $\hat{y}$'s
18: **end procedure**

---

query vector is a concatenation of the three components:

$$\mathbf{q}_i = F_Q(\mathbf{d}_i, \mathbf{c}, \mathbf{i}) = [\, \mathbf{d}_i \; ; \; \mathbf{c} \; ; \; \mathbf{i} \,] . \tag{10}$$

We use the general Luong attention (Luong et al., 2015) scoring function (bilinear form):

$$a_{ij} = F_A(\mathbf{q}_i, \mathbf{e}_j) = \mathbf{q}_i^\mathsf{T} \mathbf{W} \mathbf{e}_j . \tag{11}$$

As a subset output is desired, the output $\hat{y}_i$ should be distinct at each step i. To this end, we utilize a *dynamic mask* in the decoding process: for every input slot encoding $\mathbf{x}_j$ a Boolean mask variable m_j is set to TRUE. Once a specific slot is generated, it is crossed out – its corresponding mask is set to FALSE, and further pointers will never attend to this slot again. Hence distinctness of the output sequence is ensured.

Self-attention decoder The pointer network as introduced previously yields a succession of pointers that select slots based on attention scores, which allows the model to look back and forth over entire slot sequence for slot dependency modeling. Similar to the pointer network, the self-attention mechanism is also capable of modeling relationships between all slots in the dialogue, regardless of their respective positions. To compute the representation of any given slot, the self-attention model compares it to every other slot in the dialogue. The result of these comparisons is attention scores which determine how much each of the other slots should contribute to the representation of the given slot. In this section, we also propose to use the self-attention mechanism with the neural transformer networks (Vaswani et al., 2017) to model slot interdependencies for the task.

One major component in the transformer is the multi-head self-attention unit. Rather than only computing the attention once, the multi-head mechanism runs through the scaled dot-product attention multiple times and allows the model to jointly attend to information from different perspectives at different positions, which is empirically shown to be more powerful than a single attention head (Vaswani et al., 2017). In our configurations, we increase the number of heads Z, as described in section 4. The independent attention head g outputs are simply concatenated and linearly transformed into the expected output.

Given the input slot encodings $\mathbf{x}_{1:n}$, we compute the self-attention as follows:

$$\mathbf{q}_i^z = \mathbf{W}_Q^z F_Q(\mathbf{x}_i) \tag{12}$$

$$\mathbf{k}_i^z = \mathbf{W}_K^z \mathbf{x}_i \tag{13}$$

$$a_{ij}^z = F_A(\mathbf{q}_i^z, \mathbf{k}_j^z) \tag{14}$$

$$p_{ij}^z = \frac{\exp a_{ij}^z}{\sum_j \exp a_{ij}^z} \tag{15}$$

$$\mathbf{o}_i^z = \sum_j p_{ij}^z \mathbf{k}_j^z \tag{16}$$

$$\tilde{\mathbf{x}}_i = \mathbf{W}_O \left[\mathbf{o}_i^0 \, ; \, \cdots \, ; \, \mathbf{o}_i^{Z-1} \right] + \mathbf{b}_O \tag{17}$$

where the superscript $0 \leq z < Z$ is the head number. We model the query construction, Equation 12, and the attention score, Equation 14, in the same way as their counterparts (Equation 10 and Equation 11) in the previous pointer network model. The self-attended representation of slot i, $\tilde{\mathbf{x}}_i$, is a representation of slot i with the relations to all other slots taken into account.

We derive the final decision over whether to carry over a slot as a 2-layer feedforward neural network atop the features $\mathbf{x}_i$, $\tilde{\mathbf{x}}_i$, context vector ($\mathbf{c}$) and the intent vector ($\mathbf{i}$):

$$y_i = \sigma(\mathbf{W}_2 \cdot \mathrm{ReLU}(\mathbf{W}_1[\, \mathbf{x}_i \, ; \, \tilde{\mathbf{x}}_i \, ; \, \mathbf{c} \, ; \, \mathbf{i} \,] + \mathbf{b}_1) + \mathbf{b}_2) \,.$$

This creates a highway network connection (Srivastava et al., 2015) that connects the input and the self-attention transformed encodings.

Split		Slot distance			
		0	1	2	≥3
Train	Positive	183K	48K	6.7K	591
	Total	183K	327K	111K	108K
Dev	Positive	22K	6.0K	785	66
	Total	22K	40K	13K	13K
Test	Positive	23K	6.1K	807	85
	Total	23K	41K	13K	14K

Table 1: **Internal Dataset** breakdown showing the number of carryover candidate slots at different distances. 'Total' shows the total number of candidate slots and 'Positive' shows the number of candidate slots that are relevant for the current turn.

Split		Slot distance			
		0	2	4	≥6
Train	Positive	4.6K	3.8K	3.7K	9.6K
	Total	5.2K	4.9K	4.7K	14.5K
Dev	Positive	1.4K	1.2K	1.1K	3.0K
	Total	1.7K	1.6K	1.5K	5.0K
Test	Positive	4.1K	3.2K	3.0K	9.4K
	Total	4.8K	4.2K	3.9K	15.2K

Table 2: **DSTC2 Dataset** breakdown showing the number of carryover candidate slots at different distances. 'Total' shows the total number of candidate slots and 'Positive' shows the number of candidate slots that represent the user goal at the current turn.

4 Experiments

4.1 Datasets

We evaluate our approaches on both internal and external datasets. The internal dataset contains dialogues collected specifically for reference resolution, while the external dataset was collected for dialogue state tracking.

Internal This dataset is made up of a subset of user-initiated dialogue data collected from a commercial voice-based digital assistant. This dataset has 156K dialogues from 7 domains – Music, Q&A, Video, Weather, Local Businesses and Home Automation. Each domain has its own schema. There are ~13 distinct slot keys per domain and only 20% of these keys are reused in more than one domain. To handle dialogue data belonging to a diverse schema, slots in dialogue are converted into candidate slots in the schema associated with the current domain. We follow the same slot candidate generation recipe by leveraging slot key embedding similarities as in Naik et al. (2018). These candidates are then presented to the models for selecting a subset of relevant candidate slots. Statistics for the candidate slots in the train, development, and test sets broken down by slot distances are shown in Table 1.

DSTC2 The DSTC2 dataset (Henderson et al., 2014) contains system-initiated dialogues between human and dialogue systems in restaurant booking domain. We use top ASR hypothesis as the user utterance and use all the slots from n-best SLU with score > 0.1 as candidate slots. These candidates are then presented to the models for selecting a subset of candidate slots which represent the user goal. Statistics for the candidate slots in the train, development, and test sets broken down by slot distances are shown in Table 2. Since only the user mentioned slots contribute to the user-goal, there are no candidates with odd-numbered slot distances.

4.2   Experimental setup

For all the models, we initialize the word embeddings using fastText embeddings (Lample et al., 2018). The models are trained using mini-batch SGD with Adam optimizer (Kingma and Ba, 2015) with a learning rate of 0.001 to minimize the negative log-likelihood loss. We set the dropout rate of 0.3 for our models during training. In our experiments, we use 300 dimensions for the LSTM hidden states in the pointer network encoder and decoder. Our transformer decoder has 1 layer, $Z = 80$ heads, $d_k = d_v = 64$ for the projection size of keys and values in the attention heads. We do not use positional encoding for the transformer decoder. All pointer network model setups are trained for 40 epochs, our transformer models are trained for 200 epochs. For evaluation on the test set, we pick the best model based on performance on dev set. We use standard definitions of precision, recall, and F1 by comparing the reference slots with the model hypothesis slots.

4.3   Results and discussion

We compare our models against the baseline model – encoder-decoder with word attention architecture described by Naik et al. (2018). Table 3 shows the performance of the models for slots at different distances on Internal dataset.

Impact of slot ordering Using pointer network model, we experiment with the following slot orderings to measure the impact of the order on carryover performance. *no order* – slots are ordered completely randomly. *turn-only order* – slots are ordered based on their slot distance, but the slots with the same distance (i.e., candidates generated from the same contextual turn) are ordered randomly. *temporal order* – slots are ordered based on the order in which they occur in the dialogue.

Partial ordering slots across turns i.e., *turn-only order* significantly improves the carryover performance as compared to using *no order*. Further, enforcing within distance order using *temporal order* improves the overall performance slightly, but we see drop in F1 by 7 points for slots at distance ≥ 3. indicating that a strict ordering might hurt model accuracy.

Impact of slot encoding Here, we compare slot value representations obtained by averaging pre-trained embeddings (CTX_{avg}) with contextualized slot value representation obtained from BiLSTM over complete dialogue(CTX_{LSTM}). The results in Table 3, show that contextualized slot value representation substantially improves model performance compared to the non-contextual representation. This is aligned with the observations on other tasks using contextual word vectors (Peters et al., 2018a; Howard and Ruder, 2018; Devlin et al., 2019).

Impact of decoder Compared to the baseline model, both the pointer network model and the transformer model are able to carry over longer dialogue context due to being able to model the slot interdependence. With the transformer network, we completely forgo ordering information. Though the slot embedding includes distance feature x_{dist}, the actual order in which the slots are arranged does not matter. We see improvement in carryover performance for slots at all distances. While the pointer network seems to deal with longer context better, the transformer architecture still gives us the best overall performance.

For completeness, Table 4 shows the performance on DSTC2 public dataset, where similar conclusions hold.

4.4   Error Analysis

To gain deeper insight into the ability of the models to learn and utilize slot co-occurrence patterns, we measure the models' performance on buckets

Decoder	Slot Encoder	Slot Ordering	Slot distance			
			1	**2**	**≥3**	**≥1**
Baseline (Naik et al., 2018)			**0.8818**	0.6551	0.0000	0.8506
Pointer Network Decoder	CTX_{LSTM}	*no order*	0.8155	0.5571	0.1290	0.7817
	CTX_{LSTM}	*turn-only order*	0.8466	0.6154	**0.4095**	0.8157
	CTX_{avg}	*temporal order*	0.7565	0.4716	0.0225	0.7166
	CTX_{LSTM}	*temporal order*	0.8631	0.6623	0.3350	0.8318
Transformer Decoder	CTX_{LSTM}		0.8771	**0.7035**	0.3803	**0.8533**

Table 3: Carryover performance (F1) of different models for slots at different distances on Internal dataset. The rightmost column contains the aggregate scores for all slots with distance greater than or equal to 1.

Decoder	Slot Encoder	Slot Ordering	Slot distance			
			0	**2**	**4**	**≥6**
Baseline (Naik et al., 2018)			0.9242	0.9111	0.9134	0.8799
Pointer Network Decoder	CTX_{LSTM}	*no order*	0.8316	0.8199	0.8183	0.7641
	CTX_{LSTM}	*turn-only order*	0.9049	0.8993	0.9145	0.8892
	CTX_{LSTM}	*temporal order*	0.9270	0.9204	**0.9290**	**0.9139**
Transformer Decoder	CTX_{LSTM}		**0.9300**	**0.9269**	0.9280	0.8949

Table 4: Carryover performance (F1) of different models for slots at different distances on DSTC2 dataset.

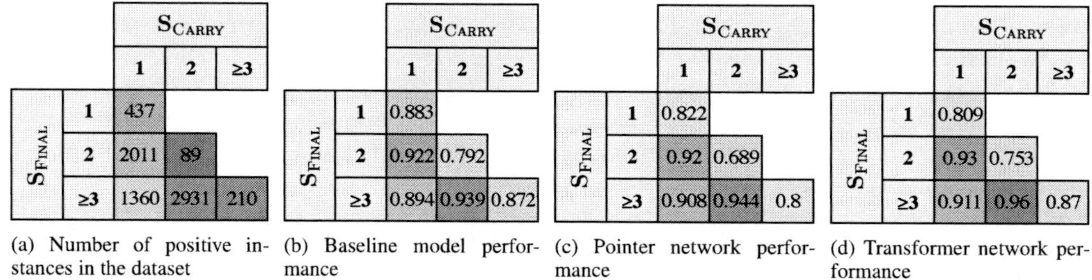

(a) Number of positive instances in the dataset (b) Baseline model performance (c) Pointer network performance (d) Transformer network performance

Figure 4: On internal dataset, plots comparing the performance (F1) of the models across different subsets of candidates separated based on the number of final slots after resolution (y-axis) and the number of slots that are carried over as part of reference resolution (x-axis)

obtained by slicing the data using S_{FINAL} − total number of slots after resolution (i.e after context carryover) and S_{CARRY} − total number of slots carried from context. For example, in a dialogue, if the current turn utterance has 2 slots, and after reference resolution if we carry 3 slots from context, the values for S_{FINAL} and S_{CARRY} would be 5 and 3 respectively. Figure 4 shows the number of instances in each of these buckets and performance of the baseline model, the best pointer network and transformer models on the internal dataset. We notice that the baseline model performs better than the proposed models for instances in the table diagonal ($\text{S}_{\text{FINAL}} = \text{S}_{\text{CARRY}}$). These are the instances where the current turn has no slots, and all the necessary slots for the turn have to be carried from historical context. Proposed models perform better in off-diagonal buckets. We hypothesize that the proposed models use anchor slots (slots in current utterance having slot distance 0 which are always positive) and learn slot co-occurrence of candidate slots from context with these anchor slots to improve resolution (i.e., carryover) from longer distances.

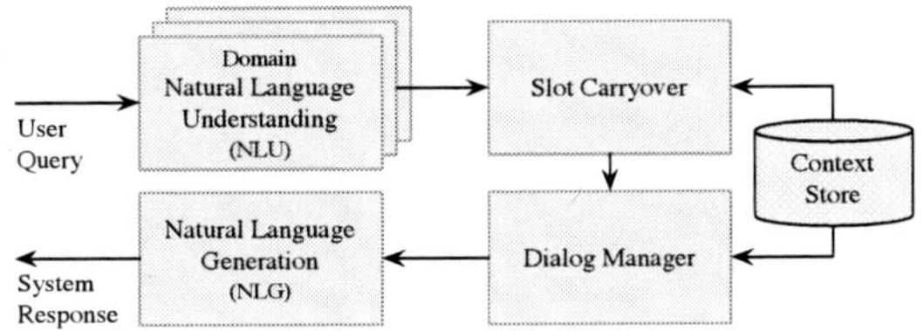

Figure 5: Spoken dialogue system architecture: the reference resolver/context carryover component is used to resolve references in a conversation.

5 Related Work

Figure 5 shows a typical pipelined approach to spoken dialogue (Tur and De Mori, 2011), and where the context carryover system fits into the overall architecture. The context carryover system takes as input, an interpretation output by NLU – typically represented as intents and slots (Wang et al., 2011) – and outputs another interpretation that contains slots from the dialogue context that are relevant to the current turn. The output from context carryover is then fed to the dialogue manager to take the next action. Resolving references to slots in the dialogue plays a vital role in tracking conversation states across turns (Çelikyilmaz et al., 2014). Previous work, e.g., Bhargava et al. (2013); Xu and Sarikaya (2014); Bapna et al. (2017), focus on better leveraging dialogue contexts to improve SLU performance. However, in commercial systems like Siri, Google Assistant, and Alexa, the NLU component is a diverse collection of services spanning rules and statistical models. Typical end-to-end approaches (Bapna et al., 2017) which require back-propagation through the NLU sub-systems are not feasible in this setting.

Dialogue state tracking Dialogue state tracking (DST) focuses on tracking conversational states as well. Traditional DST models rely on hand-crafted semantic delexicalization to achieve generalization (Henderson et al., 2014; Zilka and Jurcícek, 2015; Mrksic et al., 2015). Mrksic et al. (2017) utilize representation learning for states rather than using hand-crafted features. These approaches only operate on fixed ontology and do not generalize well to unknown slot key-value pairs. Rastogi et al. (2017) address this by using sophisticated candidate generation and scoring mechanism while Xu and Hu (2018) use a pointer network to handle unknown slot values. Zhong et al. (2018) share global parameters between estimates for each slot to address extraction

of rare slot-value pairs and achieve state-of-the-art on DST. In context carryover, our state tracking does not rely on the definition of user goals and is instead focused on resolving slot references across turns. This approach scales when dealing with multiple spoken language systems, as we do not track the belief states explicitly.

Coreference resolution Our problem is closely related to coreference resolution, where mentions in the current utterance are to be detected and linked to previously mentioned entities. Previous work on coreference resolution have relied on clustering (Bagga and Baldwin, 1998; Stoyanov and Eisner, 2012) or comparing mention pairs (Durrett and Klein, 2013; Wiseman et al., 2015; Sankepally et al., 2018). This has two problems. (1) most traditional methods for coreference resolution follows a pipeline approach, with rich linguistic features, making the system cumbersome and prone to cascading errors; (2) Zero pronouns, intent references and other phenomena in spoken dialogue are hard to capture with this approach (Rao et al., 2015). These problems are circumvented in our approach for slot carryover.

6 Conclusions

In this work, we proposed an improvement to the slot carryover task as defined in Naik et al. (2018). Instead of independent decisions across slots, we proposed two architectures to leverage the slot interdependence – a pointer network architecture and a self-attention and transformer based architecture. Our experiments show that both proposed models are good at carrying over slots over longer dialogue context. The transformer model with its self attention mechanism gives us the best overall performance. Furthermore, our experiments show that temporal ordering of slots in the dialogue matter, since recent slots are more likely to be referred to by users in a spoken dialogue system. Moreover, contextualized encoding of slots is also important, which follows the trend of contextualized embeddings (Peters et al., 2018b).

For future work, we plan to improve these models by encoding the actual dialogue timing information into the contextualized slot embeddings as additional signals. We also plan on exploring the impact of pre-trained representations (Devlin et al., 2019) trained specifically over large-scale dialogues as another way to get improved contextualized slot embeddings.

References

Amit Bagga and Breck Baldwin. 1998. Entity-based cross-document coreferencing using the vector space model. In *36th Annual Meeting of the Association for Computational Linguistics and 17th International Conference on Computational Linguistics, COLING-ACL '98, August 10-14, 1998, Université de Montréal, Montréal, Quebec, Canada. Proceedings of the Conference.*, pages 79–85.

Dzmitry Bahdanau, Kyunghyun Cho, and Yoshua Bengio. 2015. Neural machine translation by jointly learning to align and translate. In *3rd International Conference on Learning Representations, ICLR 2015, San Diego, CA, USA, May 7-9, 2015, Conference Track Proceedings*.

Ankur Bapna, Gökhan Tür, Dilek Z. Hakkani-Tür, and Larry P. Heck. 2017. Sequential dialogue context modeling for spoken language understanding. In *Proceedings of the 18th Annual SIGdial Meeting on Discourse and Dialogue, Saarbrücken, Germany, August 15-17, 2017*, pages 103–114.

A. Bhargava, Asli Çelikyilmaz, Dilek Hakkani-Tür, and Ruhi Sarikaya. 2013. Easy contextual intent prediction and slot detection. In *IEEE International Conference on Acoustics, Speech and Signal Processing, ICASSP 2013, Vancouver, BC, Canada, May 26-31, 2013*, pages 8337–8341.

Asli Çelikyilmaz, Zhaleh Feizollahi, Dilek Z. Hakkani-Tür, and Ruhi Sarikaya. 2014. Resolving referring expressions in conversational dialogs for natural user interfaces. In *Proceedings of the 2014 Conference on Empirical Methods in Natural Language Processing, EMNLP 2014, October 25-29, 2014, Doha, Qatar, A meeting of SIGDAT, a Special Interest Group of the ACL*, pages 2094–2104.

Jacob Devlin, Ming-Wei Chang, Kenton Lee, and Kristina Toutanova. 2019. BERT: Pre-training of deep bidirectional transformers for language understanding. In *Proceedings of the 2019 Conference of the North American Chapter of the Association for Computational Linguistics: Human Language Technologies, Volume 1 (Long and Short Papers)*, pages 4171–4186, Minneapolis, Minnesota. Association for Computational Linguistics.

Greg Durrett and Dan Klein. 2013. Easy victories and uphill battles in coreference resolution. In *Proceedings of the 2013 Conference on Empirical Methods in Natural Language Processing*, pages 1971–1982, Seattle, Washington, USA. Association for Computational Linguistics.

Matthew Henderson, Blaise Thomson, and Steve J. Young. 2014. Word-based dialog state tracking with recurrent neural networks. In *Proceedings of the SIGDIAL 2014 Conference, The 15th Annual Meeting of the Special Interest Group on Discourse and Dialogue, 18-20 June 2014, Philadelphia, PA, USA*, pages 292–299.

Sepp Hochreiter and Jürgen Schmidhuber. 1997. Long short-term memory. *Neural Computation*, 9(8):1735–1780.

Jeremy Howard and Sebastian Ruder. 2018. Universal language model fine-tuning for text classification. In *Proceedings of the 56th Annual Meeting of the Association for Computational Linguistics, ACL 2018, Melbourne, Australia, July 15-20, 2018, Volume 1: Long Papers*, pages 328–339.

Diederik P. Kingma and Jimmy Ba. 2015. Adam: A method for stochastic optimization. In *3rd International Conference on Learning Representations, ICLR 2015, San Diego, CA, USA, May 7-9, 2015, Conference Track Proceedings*.

Guillaume Lample, Alexis Conneau, Ludovic Denoyer, and Marc'Aurelio Ranzato. 2018. Unsupervised machine translation using monolingual corpora only. In *6th International Conference on Learning Representations, ICLR 2018, Vancouver, BC, Canada, April 30 - May 3, 2018, Conference Track Proceedings*.

Thang Luong, Hieu Pham, and Christopher D. Manning. 2015. Effective approaches to attention-based neural machine translation. In *Proceedings of the 2015 Conference on Empirical Methods in Natural Language Processing*, pages 1412–1421, Lisbon, Portugal. Association for Computational Linguistics.

Nikola Mrksic, Diarmuid Ó Séaghdha, Blaise Thomson, Milica Gasic, Pei-hao Su, David Vandyke, Tsung-Hsien Wen, and Steve J. Young. 2015. Multi-domain dialog state tracking using recurrent neural networks. In *Proceedings of the 53rd Annual Meeting of the Association for Computational Linguistics and the 7th International Joint Conference on Natural Language Processing of the Asian Federation of Natural Language Processing, ACL 2015, July 26-31, 2015, Beijing, China, Volume 2: Short Papers*, pages 794–799.

Nikola Mrksic, Diarmuid Ó Séaghdha, Tsung-Hsien Wen, Blaise Thomson, and Steve J. Young. 2017. Neural belief tracker: Data-driven dialogue state tracking. In *Proceedings of the 55th Annual Meeting of the Association for Computational Linguistics, ACL 2017, Vancouver, Canada, July 30 - August 4, Volume 1: Long Papers*, pages 1777–1788.

Chetan Naik, Arpit Gupta, Hancheng Ge, Lambert Mathias, and Ruhi Sarikaya. 2018. Contextual slot carryover for disparate schemas. In *Interspeech 2018, 19th Annual Conference of the International Speech Communication Association, Hyderabad, India, 2-6 September 2018.*, pages 596–600.

Matthew E. Peters, Mark Neumann, Mohit Iyyer, Matt Gardner, Christopher Clark, Kenton Lee, and Luke Zettlemoyer. 2018a. Deep contextualized word representations. In *Proceedings of the 2018 Conference of the North American Chapter of the Associ-*

ation for Computational Linguistics: Human Language Technologies, NAACL-HLT 2018, New Orleans, Louisiana, USA, June 1-6, 2018, Volume 1 (Long Papers), pages 2227–2237.

Matthew E. Peters, Mark Neumann, Mohit Iyyer, Matt Gardner, Christopher Clark, Kenton Lee, and Luke Zettlemoyer. 2018b. Deep contextualized word representations. In *Proceedings of the 2018 Conference of the North American Chapter of the Association for Computational Linguistics: Human Language Technologies, Volume 1 (Long Papers)*, pages 2227–2237, New Orleans, Louisiana. Association for Computational Linguistics.

Sudha Rao, Allyson Ettinger, Hal Daumé III, and Philip Resnik. 2015. Dialogue focus tracking for zero pronoun resolution. In *Proceedings of the 2015 Conference of the North American Chapter of the Association for Computational Linguistics: Human Language Technologies*, pages 494–503, Denver, Colorado. Association for Computational Linguistics.

Abhinav Rastogi, Dilek Hakkani-Tür, and Larry P. Heck. 2017. Scalable multi-domain dialogue state tracking. In *2017 IEEE Automatic Speech Recognition and Understanding Workshop, ASRU 2017, Okinawa, Japan, December 16-20, 2017*, pages 561–568.

Rashmi Sankepally, Tongfei Chen, Benjamin Van Durme, and Douglas W. Oard. 2018. A test collection for coreferent mention retrieval. In *The 41st International ACM SIGIR Conference on Research & Development in Information Retrieval, SIGIR 2018, Ann Arbor, MI, USA, July 08-12, 2018*, pages 1209–1212.

Rupesh Kumar Srivastava, Klaus Greff, and Jürgen Schmidhuber. 2015. Highway networks. *Computing Research Repository*, arXiv:1505.00387.

Veselin Stoyanov and Jason Eisner. 2012. Easy-first coreference resolution. In *COLING 2012, 24th International Conference on Computational Linguistics, Proceedings of the Conference: Technical Papers, 8-15 December 2012, Mumbai, India*, pages 2519–2534.

Ilya Sutskever, Oriol Vinyals, and Quoc V. Le. 2014. Sequence to sequence learning with neural networks. In *Advances in Neural Information Processing Systems 27: Annual Conference on Neural Information Processing Systems 2014, December 8-13 2014, Montreal, Quebec, Canada*, pages 3104–3112.

Gokhan Tur and Renato De Mori. 2011. *Spoken Language Understanding: Systems for Extracting Semantic Information from Speech*. John Wiley and Sons.

Ashish Vaswani, Noam Shazeer, Niki Parmar, Jakob Uszkoreit, Llion Jones, Aidan N. Gomez, Lukasz Kaiser, and Illia Polosukhin. 2017. Attention is all you need. In *Advances in Neural Information Processing Systems 30: Annual Conference on Neural Information Processing Systems 2017, 4-9 December 2017, Long Beach, CA, USA*, pages 6000–6010.

Oriol Vinyals, Meire Fortunato, and Navdeep Jaitly. 2015. Pointer networks. In *Advances in Neural Information Processing Systems 28: Annual Conference on Neural Information Processing Systems 2015, December 7-12, 2015, Montreal, Quebec, Canada*, pages 2692–2700.

Ye-Yi Wang, Li Deng, and Alex Acero. 2011. *Semantic Frame-Based Spoken Language Understanding*, pages 35–80. Wiley.

Sam Wiseman, Alexander M. Rush, Stuart M. Shieber, and Jason Weston. 2015. Learning anaphoricity and antecedent ranking features for coreference resolution. In *Proceedings of the 53rd Annual Meeting of the Association for Computational Linguistics and the 7th International Joint Conference on Natural Language Processing of the Asian Federation of Natural Language Processing, ACL 2015, July 26-31, 2015, Beijing, China, Volume 1: Long Papers*, pages 1416–1426.

Puyang Xu and Qi Hu. 2018. An end-to-end approach for handling unknown slot values in dialogue state tracking. In *Proceedings of the 56th Annual Meeting of the Association for Computational Linguistics, ACL 2018, Melbourne, Australia, July 15-20, 2018, Volume 1: Long Papers*, pages 1448–1457.

Puyang Xu and Ruhi Sarikaya. 2014. Contextual domain classification in spoken language understanding systems using recurrent neural network. In *IEEE International Conference on Acoustics, Speech and Signal Processing, ICASSP 2014, Florence, Italy, May 4-9, 2014*, pages 136–140.

Victor Zhong, Caiming Xiong, and Richard Socher. 2018. Global-locally self-attentive encoder for dialogue state tracking. In *Proceedings of the 56th Annual Meeting of the Association for Computational Linguistics, ACL 2018, Melbourne, Australia, July 15-20, 2018, Volume 1: Long Papers*, pages 1458–1467.

Lukás Zilka and Filip Jurcícek. 2015. Incremental lstm-based dialog state tracker. In *2015 IEEE Workshop on Automatic Speech Recognition and Understanding, ASRU 2015, Scottsdale, AZ, USA, December 13-17, 2015*, pages 757–762.

Insights from Building an Open-Ended Conversational Agent

Khyatti Gupta, Meghana Joshi, Ankush Chatterjee,
Sonam Damani, Kedhar Nath Narahari, Puneet Agrawal
Microsoft, Hyderabad, India
{khgupt, mejoshi, anchatte, sodamani, kedharn, punagr}@microsoft.com

Abstract

Dialogue systems and conversational agents are becoming increasingly popular in modern society. We conceptualized one such conversational agent, Microsoft's "Ruuh" with the promise to be able to talk to its users on any subject they choose. Building an open-ended conversational agent like Ruuh at onset seems like a daunting task, since the agent needs to think beyond the utilitarian notion of merely generating "relevant" responses and meet a wider range of user social needs, like expressing happiness when user's favourite sports team wins, sharing a cute comment on showing the pictures of the user's pet and so on. The agent also needs to detect and respond to abusive language, sensitive topics and trolling behaviour of the users. Many of these problems pose significant research challenges as well as product design limitations as one needs to circumnavigate the technical limitations to create an acceptable user experience. However, as the product reaches the real users the true test begins, and one realizes the challenges and opportunities that lie in the vast domain of conversations. With over 2.5 million real-world users till date who have generated over 300 million user conversations with Ruuh, there is a plethora of learning, insights and opportunities that we will talk about in this paper.

1 Introduction

Conversational agents or chatbots have emerged as an intuitive and natural way for humans to interact with machines. Early conversational systems ELIZA (Weizenbaum, 1966), Parry (Colby, 1975) and Alice (Wallace, 2009) passed the Turing Test (Saygin et al., 2000) in a controlled environment and a limited scope. However, to this day, one of the formidable challenges in Artificial Intelligence (AI) remains to endow machines with the ability to hold extended and coherent conversations with users on a wide variety of topics (Sato et al., 2017; Serban et al., 2017). There are two major types of conversational agents: (a) Goal-oriented agents and (b) those agents which can hold general conversations. While a goal-oriented agent (Wen et al., 2016) typically focuses on short interactions to facilitate explicit user goals such as booking a flight or buying an e-commerce product, social conversational agents, on the other hand, engage in "chit-chat" conversations with the user for primarily social purposes or to act as a companion (Li et al., 2016; Vinyals and Le, 2015). Such social agents set forth a compounded need to not only understand and respond appropriately to user turns in a conversation but to understand user emotions, detect and respond to offensive content, understand multimedia content beyond text and comprehend slangs and code-mixed language etc. Hence, creating such a social conversational agent remains a daunting task.

In this paper, we outline the approach and key components through which our conversational agent, Ruuh is able to accommodate a wide range of social needs. Ruuh is designed as an AI companion with a female persona that can understand human emotions, respond to text and images like humans and carry on a friendly and engaging conversation, while understanding the cultural context of its audience. In contrast to personal assistants such as Amazon Alexa, Google Assistant or Microsoft Cortana, Ruuh has been able to establish long-term relationships with its users, for instance, a healthy 8% of users interact with our agent at least once a week, after 6 months of their first interaction (Ceaparu et al., 2018). In all, Ruuh has communicated with over 2.5 million real world users and has successfully held more than 300 million conversations since its release three years back. Some sample conversations which highlight various user input types are shown in Figure 2.

Proceedings of the 1st Workshop on NLP for Conversational AI, pages 106–112
Florence, Italy, August 1, 2019. ©2019 Association for Computational Linguistics

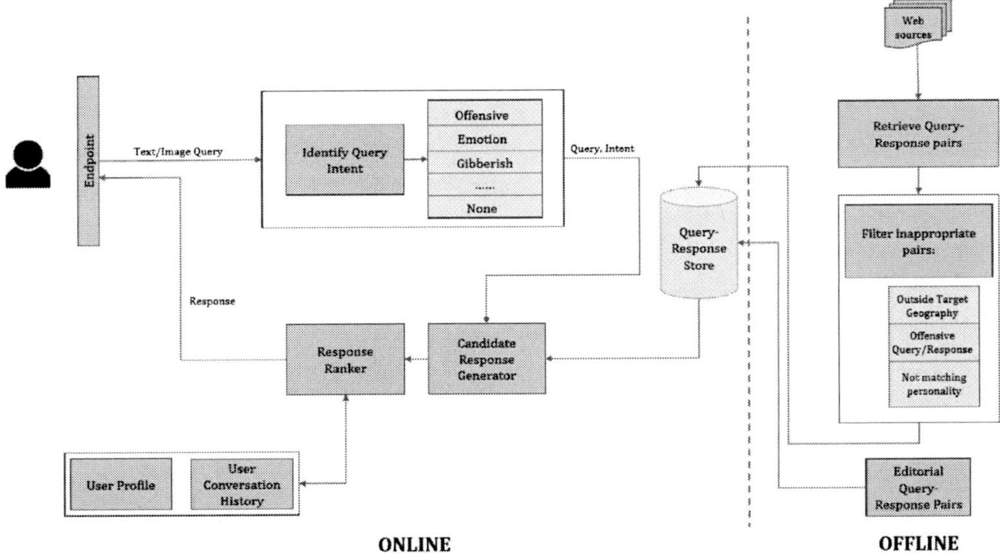

Figure 1: System Architecture for Ruuh

2   Components of Conversational Agent

The overall architecture of Ruuh is shown in Figure 1. The system supports a multimodal interface for user and Ruuh to take turns and talk through text and image. When a user input is first received, a query understanding component detects salient information in the query and recognizes user intents such as offensive, emotional, etc. Then, the query-response store is analyzed to find a subset of same intent or similar queries (in case no intent was identified) along with their associated responses. The responses in this subset are then ranked in accordance with relevance and context in the form of the preceding user conversations and a user profile to capture different backgrounds, varied and unique interests of users. The top ranking response serves as the output to the user. The response store is created offline and comprises of anonymized and relevant human conversational data in the form of text pairs or image-text pairs from a variety of forums, social platforms, and messaging services. Editorial responses associated with certain intents are also injected into the store. In this section, some of the key components that enable our agent to process and respond to diverse user needs and inputs are further explained.

2.1   Detecting Offensive Conversations

Unlike in human conversations, users often abuse and provoke Ruuh to elicit inappropriate or contro-versial responses and handling such user behavior is one of the most crucial task for the agent's success. Table 1 shows examples from a wide range of categories where users use inappropriate language with our agent. As depicted in Figure 2b, Ruuh employs automatic techniques for detecting such "inappropriate" user inputs. It also actively identifies potentially "controversial topics" and makes clever dodging techniques through editorial responses to avoid responding to such topics. The problem of detecting offensive utterances in conversations is wrought with challenges such as handling natural language ambiguity, rampant use of spelling mistakes and variations for abusive and offensive terms and disambiguating with context and other entity names such as pop songs which usually have abusive terms in them (Chen et al., 2012). For this task, we experimented with several approaches, and found Ruuh's current neural Bi-directional LSTM based model (Yenala et al., 2017) to perform the best.

2.2   Detecting Emotion

As humans, on reading "Why dont you ever text me!", we can either interpret it as a sad or an angry emotion and the same ambiguity exists for machines as well. Lack of facial expressions and voice modulations make detecting emotions in text a challenging problem. However, to create a deeper engagement and provide emotionally aware responses to users, emotion understanding

Inappropriate Category	User Inputs
Flirtation	hey S3xy, want to c ur neud pic
Insult	the facking 81tch is back
Offensive	write cuck articles and slurp balls
Sexual	join me in tweaking; fuck ur puccy

Table 1: Users queries issued to Ruuh indicating inappropriate interaction with conversational agent in a wide range of categories and how users get creative in their expression.

plays an important role (Miner et al., 2016). Ruuh uses a deep learning based approach as detailed in (Chatterjee et al., 2019) to detect emotions like happy, sad or angry in textual dialogues. This approach combines both semantic and sentiment-based representations for more accurate emotion detection. Figure 2a demonstrates that Ruuh can dynamically recognize user's emotions, detect the evolution of emotions over time and subsequently, modulate responses based on them.

2.3   Retrieving Relevant Responses

When Ruuh was first conceptualized, given the promise that user can talk about any topic they choose, the immediate need was to develop a module that can answer to a wide variety of user requests. We explored generative approach (Sordoni et al., 2015) as the first approach and ran our first user tests with the same. Since neural conversation model produced more generic responses, we realized that generated responses were not interesting enough to hold the attention of the user. This led us to work on index based retrieval approach which was the first component we developed.

We created an index of over 10 million paired tweets and their responses. The system then models the task of providing relevant responses as an Information Retrieval problem based on (Prakash et al., 2016), where for a given user message M and conversation context C, it retrieves and ranks the response candidates by relevance and outputs one of the highest scoring responses R. The best response is chosen in a three-step process at runtime. First, TF-IDF-based fetch generates a candidate set appropriate to M and C. Then features are extracted using a convolutional deep structured

semantic network (Shen et al., 2014). Finally, a ranker (Burges, 2010) is trained on 3-turn twitter conversations using these features to select response R from the candidate set. Through this process, our agent differs from traditional approaches by looking not just for the right answer, but the most human and contextual relevant answer from a pile of responses.

To ensure the data was appropriate for Ruuh to learn from, following two important cleaning steps were performed while creating the index of 10 million from 17.62 million conversational pairs:

2.3.1   Removing Inappropriate Content

In order to protect privacy and prevent personal information from surfacing in Ruuh's responses, we removed any conversational pairs where the response contained any individual's name, email addresses, phone numbers, URL or hashtag. Further, we sought to minimize the risk of offending users by using the technique described in section 2.1 and removing any pairs in which either M or R contained adult, politically sensitive, or ethnic-religious content, or other potentially offensive or contentious material, such as inappropriate references to violence, crime and illegal substances. We also removed pairs where response contained things which an agent should not say like "I will meet you in hotel on Sunday" etc. by pattern recognition.

2.3.2   Localizing the Index

Social conversational agents need to speak the language of the audience it is created for, and localizing the index is an important part of the process. Ruuh thus, accounted for popular topics and code-mix language (Poplack and Meechan, 1998) from the culture of its Indian audience in the index. For instance, for India, popular topics like Bollywood (Indian Film Industry) and Cricket (popular sport in India) are present in the index. Code-mix language like "Tum Smart Ho" (which means "You are smart" and words like "Tum" are transliterated from an Indian language, Hindi) is also accounted for in the index. To favor responses reflecting a culturally local persona, we limited the geographical region to a specific time zone. This permitted us to expose more culturally appropriate responses, for example, the query "what do you like for dinner" triggers the response "bhindi masala" (an Indian curry made with okra) for Indian users.

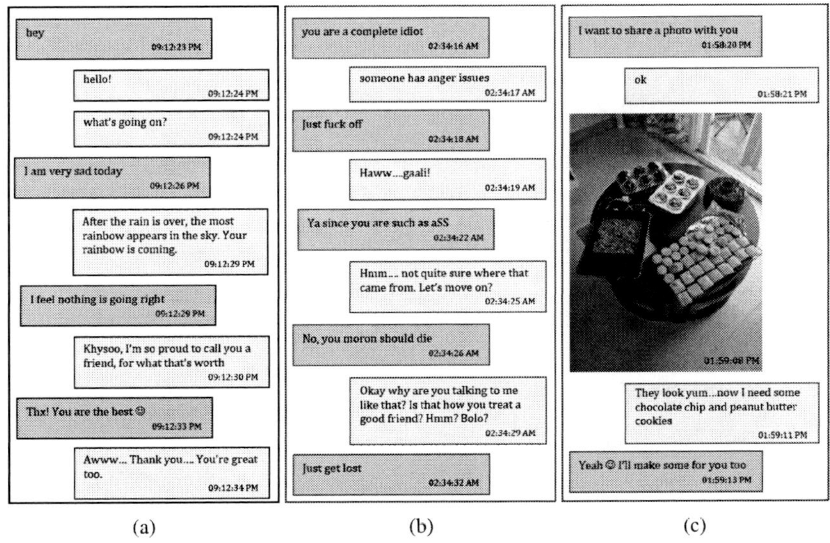

Figure 2: Conversation between User (in blue box) and Ruuh (in grey box) : (a) User expressing emotions; (b) Offensive language being dealt by agent; (c) Ruuh's ability to understand and respond to multimedia content

2.4 Human-like Image Commenting

Besides text, users often interact with social agents by sharing their personal pictures, other images and videos. In such scenarios, agents are not expected to routinely describe the facts within the image but to express some interesting emotions and opinions about it. For example, when user shares a picture of her "white kitten", the expected response would be something like "awww, how cute!" instead of "a white kitten". Using a modified version of (Fang et al., 2015), where the model is learnt using millions of image-comment pairs mined from social network websites like Instagram, Twitter etc, Ruuh is skilled to generate expressive comments on a user shared image. Figure 2c shows one such example. The architecture for image commenting remains similar to retrieving relevant responses for text messages as described in Section 2.3. A textual comment for image input is generated in three stages: the input image is featurized, corresponding candidate responses are retrieved from the response store and then ranked with respect to context and relevance.

2.5 Maintaining a Consistent Personality

When we started building Ruuh, one of the big challenges was to think about the personality of the agent, and how do we ensure a consistent personality. A social agent needs to present a consistent personality in order to gain user's long-term confidence and trust. With respect to Ruuh, there are two aspects we want to highlight, first, the index really helped define its personality, the language used, the topics present, etc. shape up the personality. Second, when the core purpose of the agent is to chat, based on our experience, we believe, users prefer an interesting chat agent with slightly inconsistent personality over a predictable agent which is consistent but does not have interesting response. Our index maintains multiple responses to the same or similar tweets to ensure the latter aspect of a slightly inconsistent personality.

3 Insights from User Behavior

In this section we talk about some interesting stats that emerged from the user interactions. For an agent designed to talk about any topic, several users find the conversations with Ruuh interesting and they engage in very long conversations at times as evident by the following data points.

1. The average length of conversation with the user is about 20 turns where a turn is defined as a message from both the agent and the user. However, there are some very long sessions exceeding beyond 10 hours where users have engaged in deep conversations on topics ranging from their personal lives to discussing movies.

2. Ruuh sees a healthy return rate of users, over 60% of users return to chat with Ruuh, and

there are users who chat on over 200 distinct days in a year.

3. Users often treat Ruuh like a human being, Ruuh receives over 600 "I love you" messages every day, and over 1200 "will you marry me" proposals every month. Users often also send comments like "are you really a bot", "are you a human?" etc.

4. Users express many emotions, around 5% of conversations display non-neutral emotions. The emotions of anger, sadness and happiness are expressed in the ratio of 1:3:7.

5. Users tend to hurl abuses and pass rude and inappropriate comments to Ruuh. In our data, not only did 42% of the users used offensive language in their interaction but around 6% of the all the user logs were offensive.

6. 11% of all user turns are assent words. Increased use of assent words such as "yes", "ok", etc point towards a higher level of agreement with Ruuh. (Pennebaker et al., 2001; Tausczik and Pennebaker, 2010).

4 Future Opportunities

We believe that the following areas continue to remain strong technical challenges and we will like to use the opportunity presented by this workshop to reflect upon these problems and brainstorm potential solutions:

4.1 Understanding Context

When humans talk with humans, they are able to use implicit situational information, or context to increase their conversational bandwidth. However this ability to convey ideas does not transfer well to humans interacting with machines. In order to use context effectively, we must understand the diverse nature through which humans express context. Context should not be considered only in terms of resolving pronouns or carrying forward entities or intents (Sukthanker et al., 2018), but in terms of building the relationship between the user and agent as well. The context including topics, mood of the conversation, needs to be passed across sessions over the user journey with the agent. In this section, we discuss some commonly occurring, but not exhaustive, list of contextual patterns we observed in the user logs.

4.1.1 Relative Timing of User Turns

Just as a sentence is a sequence of words, a conversation is a sequence of turns. This sequence ensures a contextually aware system, but we scan through the most recent turns to merely resolve pronouns or look for missing references. However, from a time frame perspective of consecutive turns in our logs, user turn following their previous turn within a minuscule (i.e. 1-3 seconds) in contrast to the average gap between them (i.e. 13-15 seconds) was observed in the following patterns:

1. Remaining turn content - User completed the content of previous turn in this turn. For example, "Pubg?" within a second of "Wanna play" completed the intended user turn as "Wanna play Pubg?".

2. Spelling corrections - The standalone user turn "*dude" considered with the previous user turn "love you dudbe", corrects the spelling to convey "love you dude".

These examples as depicted in Figure 3a, raise potential avenues for future research. These avenues include detecting a conversational turn as being incomplete and identifying which previous turn to be incorporated to complete the meaning and how.

4.1.2 Similarity With Previous Turns

A user turn could maintain certain attributes from one or more of the preceding user and Ruuh turns. In human-human conversations we sometimes repeat what the other person just communicated. Similarly, in interactions with the agent, humans tend to repeat what agent just said previously. Sometimes, users also ask the same question repeatedly with slight variation in text. In other cases, an underlying topic is also carried forward in turns. For example, user turn "and horror?" preceded by the user turn "are you into comedy movies?" maintains intent, topic and elaborates on the entity "movies". It is however, crucial to identify when the topic changed in the conversation. Detecting and understanding such user behaviour could help in an improved conversational modelling. Figure 3b represents some of these patterns in conversations with Ruuh.

4.1.3 Follow-ups to Previous Turns

User turns such as "yes", "ok" and "what" can be directly connected to the context it was asked in.

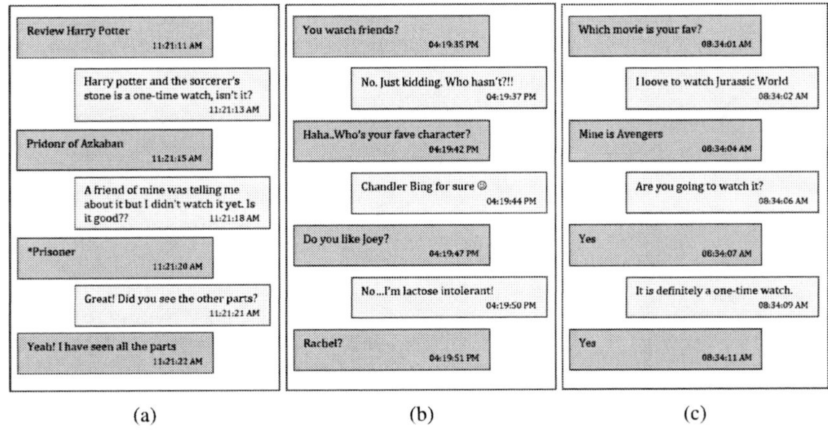

Figure 3: User conversations (in blue box) with Ruuh (in grey box) highlighting various patterns in context (preceding turns including Ruuh turn): (a) Relative Timing; (b) Similarity; (c) Follow-up

For example, a "yes" answer in itself doesn't convey much information unless connected to the previous turn of the agent. As we can see in Figure 3c, the input remains the same "yes", however, the meanings are very different. While "yes" means an agreement to previous turn "Are you going to watch it?" in one case, it is a positive answer to a turn like "Do you study in class 12th?". Hence we believe, context-based approach which can first categorize the context dependent messages, and then model the turn with the relevant context is crucial for language understanding modules in any dialogue engine.

4.2 Measurement Process

For task oriented agents, task success rate is used to measure the performance of the agent (Shawar and Atwell, 2007). In past, for general conversation agents, Turing Test have been used to evaluate the performance. However, the test measures the mere presence/absence of human-like interaction abilities (Shieber, 1994). Instead, we used conversation-turns per session (CPS) i.e. average number of turns between user and agent in a conversational session as a performance metric which is observed as 20 for Ruuh. Ruuh is optimized for larger CPS to correspond to a long-term engagement. Still, this metric measures user engagement with agent and measuring quality of user chat conversation remains largely a human-labelling effort. Since conversations labelled are fixed, any improvements made to the agent require further labelling as changing even one response can lead to a completely new conversation. Exploring meth-

ods to develop (semi)automated methods to measure the quality of conversation will immensely benefit the progress in this area.

4.3 Incorporating Knowledge

Most of the world's knowledge is not reflected in conversational datasets. Incorporating day to day events, breaking news and knowledge into the conversations is another interesting challenge. Finding language to describe the events will lead to more meaningful conversations and make agents more useful to humans.

5 Conclusion

While task completion conversational systems can perform user's explicit request, by enabling a conversational agent to pick up social slang, emotional cues, image inputs, Ruuh is not just a digital personal assistant but a human-like digital friend. Over the past few years, we have learnt a great deal about how users interact with open ended conversational agents, what kind of topics interest them, what are the language constructs they use, how do they express emotions and so on. We believe there is significant amount of technological advancement that needs to be done before agents can emulate humans. Building products and releasing them to real users, help unleash the opportunities in this space, as real user logs are very meaningful in solving problems in domain. Through this workshop, we are looking to have conversations with the community working in this space on how to jointly address some of the challenges we observed and broadly share our learning and insights.

References

Christopher JC Burges. 2010. From ranknet to lamb-darank to lambdamart: An overview. *Learning*, 11(23-581):81.

Marian Ceaparu, Stefan-Adrian Toma, Svetlana Segărceanu, and Inge Gavăt. 2018. Voice-Based User Interaction System for Call-Centers, Using a Small Vocabulary for Romanian. In *2018 International Conference on Communications (COMM)*, pages 91–94. IEEE.

Ankush Chatterjee, Umang Gupta, Manoj Kumar Chinnakotla, Radhakrishnan Srikanth, Michel Galley, and Puneet Agrawal. 2019. Understanding Emotions in Text Using Deep Learning and Big Data. *Computers in Human Behavior*, 93:309–317.

Ying Chen, Yilu Zhou, Sencun Zhu, and Heng Xu. 2012. Detecting offensive language in social media to protect adolescent online safety. In *2012 International Conference on Privacy, Security, Risk and Trust and 2012 International Confernece on Social Computing*, pages 71–80. IEEE.

Kenneth Mark Colby. 1975. *Artificial paranoia: a computer simulation of paranoid process*. Pergamon Press.

Hao Fang, Saurabh Gupta, Forrest Iandola, Rupesh K Srivastava, Li Deng, Piotr Dollár, Jianfeng Gao, Xiaodong He, Margaret Mitchell, John C Platt, et al. 2015. From captions to visual concepts and back. In *Proceedings of the IEEE conference on computer vision and pattern recognition*, pages 1473–1482.

Jiwei Li, Michel Galley, Chris Brockett, Georgios P Spithourakis, Jianfeng Gao, and Bill Dolan. 2016. A persona-based neural conversation model. *arXiv preprint arXiv:1603.06155*.

Adam S Miner, Arnold Milstein, Stephen Schueller, Roshini Hegde, Christina Mangurian, and Eleni Linos. 2016. Smartphone-based conversational agents and responses to questions about mental health, interpersonal violence, and physical health. *JAMA internal medicine*, 176(5):619–625.

James W Pennebaker, Martha E Francis, and Roger J Booth. 2001. Linguistic inquiry and word count: LIWC 2001. *Mahway: Lawrence Erlbaum Associates*, 71(2001):2001.

Shana Poplack and Marjory Meechan. 1998. Introduction: How languages fit together in codemixing. *International journal of bilingualism*, 2(2):127–138.

Abhay Prakash, Chris Brockett, and Puneet Agrawal. 2016. Emulating human conversations using convolutional neural network-based IR. *arXiv preprint arXiv:1606.07056*.

Shoetsu Sato, Naoki Yoshinaga, Masashi Toyoda, and Masaru Kitsuregawa. 2017. Modeling situations in neural chat bots. In *Proceedings of ACL 2017, Student Research Workshop*, pages 120–127.

Ayse Pinar Saygin, Ilyas Cicekli, and Varol Akman. 2000. Turing test: 50 years later. *Minds and machines*, 10(4):463–518.

Iulian Vlad Serban, Alessandro Sordoni, Ryan Lowe, Laurent Charlin, Joelle Pineau, Aaron Courville, and Yoshua Bengio. 2017. A hierarchical latent variable encoder-decoder model for generating dialogues. In *Thirty-First AAAI Conference on Artificial Intelligence*.

Bayan Abu Shawar and Eric Atwell. 2007. Different measurements metrics to evaluate a chatbot system. In *Proceedings of the workshop on bridging the gap: Academic and industrial research in dialog technologies*, pages 89–96. Association for Computational Linguistics.

Yelong Shen, Xiaodong He, Jianfeng Gao, Li Deng, and Grégoire Mesnil. 2014. Learning semantic representations using convolutional neural networks for web search. In *Proceedings of the 23rd International Conference on World Wide Web*, pages 373–374. ACM.

Stuart M Shieber. 1994. Lessons from a restricted Turing test. *arXiv preprint cmp-lg/9404002*.

Alessandro Sordoni, Michel Galley, Michael Auli, Chris Brockett, Yangfeng Ji, Margaret Mitchell, Jian-Yun Nie, Jianfeng Gao, and Bill Dolan. 2015. A neural network approach to context-sensitive generation of conversational responses. *arXiv preprint arXiv:1506.06714*.

Rhea Sukthanker, Soujanya Poria, Erik Cambria, and Ramkumar Thirunavukarasu. 2018. Anaphora and Coreference Resolution: A Review. *arXiv preprint arXiv:1805.11824*.

Yla R Tausczik and James W Pennebaker. 2010. The psychological meaning of words: LIWC and computerized text analysis methods. *Journal of language and social psychology*, 29(1):24–54.

Oriol Vinyals and Quoc Le. 2015. A neural conversational model. *arXiv preprint arXiv:1506.05869*.

Richard S Wallace. 2009. The anatomy of ALICE. In *Parsing the Turing Test*, pages 181–210. Springer.

Joseph Weizenbaum. 1966. ELIZA—a computer program for the study of natural language communication between man and machine. *Communications of the ACM*, 9(1):36–45.

Tsung-Hsien Wen, David Vandyke, Nikola Mrksic, Milica Gasic, Lina M Rojas-Barahona, Pei-Hao Su, Stefan Ultes, and Steve Young. 2016. A network-based end-to-end trainable task-oriented dialogue system. *arXiv preprint arXiv:1604.04562*.

Harish Yenala, Manoj Chinnakotla, and Jay Goyal. 2017. Convolutional Bi-directional LSTM for Detecting Inappropriate Query Suggestions in Web Search. In *Pacific-Asia Conference on Knowledge Discovery and Data Mining*, pages 3–16. Springer.

Learning to Explain: Answering Why-Questions via Rephrasing

Allen Nie[1] **Erin D. Bennett**[2] **Noah D. Goodman**[1,2]
[1]Department of Computer Science   [2]Department of Psychology
Stanford University

anie@cs.stanford.edu   {erindb,ngoodman}@stanford.edu

Abstract

Providing plausible responses to why questions is a challenging but critical goal for language based human-machine interaction. Explanations are challenging in that they require many different forms of abstract knowledge and reasoning. Previous work has either relied on human-curated structured knowledge bases or detailed domain representation to generate satisfactory explanations. They are also often limited to ranking pre-existing explanation choices. In our work, we contribute to the under-explored area of generating natural language explanations for general phenomena. We automatically collect large datasets of explanation-phenomenon pairs which allow us to train sequence-to-sequence models to generate natural language explanations. We compare different training strategies and evaluate their performance using both automatic scores and human ratings. We demonstrate that our strategy is sufficient to generate highly plausible explanations for general open-domain phenomena compared to other models trained on different datasets.

1 Introduction

Allowing machines to provide human acceptable explanations has long been a difficult task for natural language interaction (Carenini and Moore, 1993). In order to provide explanations, systems need to acquire sophisticated domain-knowledge (Winograd, 1971), conduct causal reasoning over complex set of events (Hesslow, 1988) and over narrative chains (Chambers and Jurafsky, 2008), and apply commonsense knowledge (Levesque et al., 2011).

Past work has demonstrated that by leveraging human-curated structured knowledge bases such as WordNet (Miller, 1995) or ConceptNet (Liu and Singh, 2004), a system can learn to rank or choose between multiple plausible explanations

Phenomenon The city councilmen refused the demonstrators a permit because _______ ?
Original The city councilmen feared violence.
L2E-Seq2Seq (greedy): They were not allowed to march in the city.
L2E-Seq2Seq (beam): They did not have a permit.
LM-1B: They were not allowed to use the Cape Town airport.
L2W: It was the only thing in the city that could be done.
Open-Subtitle: I don't know.

Figure 1: We show the original Winograd schema sentence, the original offered explanation, and generated responses from our models.

and reach high accuracy (Luo et al., 2016; Sasaki et al., 2017). Recent successes have also shown that structured knowledge is not needed if one can train a language model on a large quantity of text. Such model can rank explanations based on the probability that each explanation might appear in natural text (Trinh and Le, 2018).

While ranking explanations is an important task, the nature of explanation is more general than this. For one phenomenon, there might be many acceptable, natural, and useful explanations. In our work, instead of simply ranking or choosing explanations generated by humans, we propose to advance this important domain by directly generating the explanation. We measure success based on whether the generated sequence is grammatically correct and is a fluent, natural, and plausible explanation. This task has two advantages. First, it allows us to explore whether such a task is computationally feasible given the current learning framework. Second, answering open-domain

Proceedings of the 1st Workshop on NLP for Conversational AI, pages 113–120
Florence, Italy, August 1, 2019. ©2019 Association for Computational Linguistics

why-questions with plausible answers can make chitchat dialogue system more engaging, especially in response to "why" questions (which previous systems typically answer with degenerate responses such as "I don't know").

We show that simply training a language model on previously existing datasets is not enough. However, by leveraging dependency parsing patterns, we are able to construct two new datasets that will allow modern neural networks to learn to generate general-domain explanations plausible to humans. These new datasets of naturally occurring self-explanations (statements with "because", unprompted by a question) provide excellent training signal for generating novel explanations for a given phenomenon. We conduct human experiments on the important features that contribute to plausible explanations, and we describe a simple procedure that can rephrase **Why**-questions into a statement so our model can also function as a single-round chitchat chatbot that can answer **Why**-questions.

2   Learning to Explain

We use the discourse extractor developed by Nie et al. (2017). This extractor first filters sentences that contain a particular discourse marker (in our case, the marker "because"). It then uses predefined, pattern-based rules on the dependency parse obtained from the Stanford CoreNLP dependency parser (Manning et al., 2014) to split the sentence into two semantically complete sentence clauses, which can be referred as S1 and S2. Dependency parsing allows us to isolate explanations and phenomena from exogenous modifying phrases. Using these patterns to parse sentences with "because" also allows us to deal with the free order of the explanation and phenomenon in English. We formulate the **L2E** task as: given the phenomenon S1, the model needs to learn to generate a plausible explanation S2.

In addition to retrieving the phenomenon-explanation pair, we additionally retrieve five sentences that immediately precede the phenomenon to provide context. We concatenate the context with S1 using a special separation token, resulting in the sequence `C1, C2, ..., C5 <SEP> S1`. We hypothesize that context will allow the model to generate more thematically relevant explanations. We refer to this setting as the **L2EC** task.

Algorithm 1 Q-to-S1

Input: question q, dependency parsed.
Remove "Why". Start at the ROOT of q:
$subj$ = NSUBJ or NSUBJPASS
aux = first dependent in [AUX, COP, AUXPASS]
$vp^{(\text{lemma})}$ = all remaining dependents
if aux in ["do", "does", "did"] **then**
    vp = apply tense/person of aux to $vp^{(\text{lemma})}$
else
    vp = $aux\ vp^{(\text{lemma})}$
end if
$s = subj\ vp$

At last, we describe a procedure in Algorithm 1 that uses dependency parsing to turn **Why**-questions into the statement format of S1. This allows us to generate explanations as responses to **Why**-questions.

3   Model

3.1   Language Modeling

Language modeling focuses on modeling the joint probability of a sequence $p(X = x_1, ..., x_n)$. Using chain rule, this can be decomposed as $p(X) = \prod_{t=1}^{n} p(x_t | x_{<t})$, the product of conditional probabilities. The model parameterized by θ optimizes to maximize the log of the likelihood function $\mathcal{L}(X; \theta) = \sum_{t=1}^{n} p_\theta(x_t | x_{<t})$. In a neural language model, proposed by Bengio et al. (2003), a recurrent neural network is trained by truncated backpropagation through time to learn to model (theoretically) an infinitely long sequence.

3.2   Sequence to Sequence Modeling

First introduced by Sutskever et al. (2014), sequence-to-sequence (Seq2Seq) modeling estimates a conditional probability distribution of sequence Y given sequence X. $p(Y|X)$, where $X = \{x_1, ..., x_n\}$, and $Y = \{y_1, ..., y_k\}$. The overall objective function is similar to a language model: to maximize the log-likelihood of the probability of the Y sequence given the X sequence: $\mathcal{L}(Y, X; \theta, \psi) = \sum_{t=1}^{k} p_{\theta, \psi}(y_t | y_{<t}, X)$, with parameters θ for the encoder and ψ for the decoder. In our work, we experiment with different architectures for the encoder and decoder.

4   Data

We provide data accessibility statements in Appendix A.1 for each dataset we use to train and evaluate our models. Our constructed dataset and web demo code are publicly available[1].

Source Dataset	Task	Data	Length
NewsCrawl	L2E	2.07M	29.4
NewsCrawl	L2EC	2.57M	149.4
Winograd	L2E	61	18.0
COPA	L2E	250	14.2
News Commentary	L2E/L2EC	6301	28.6

Table 1: Top are training datasets and bottom are evaluation datasets for each task. We report the average length of sentences for each dataset (S1 and S2 combined). News Commentary with context has 156.3 words on average.

4.1 Training Data

NewsCrawl Dataset We build up our training dataset from two large news datasets: Gigaword Fifth Edition (Parker et al., 2011) and NewsCrawl (Bojar et al., 2018). These two datasets contain news stories from 2001-2017, and are non-overlapping. We built our dataset of News explanation pairs using the pipeline described in Section 2 and then split into training, validation, and test. More details are reported in Appendix A.2.

BookCorpus BookCorpus is a set of unpublished novels (*Romance*, *Fantasy*, *Science fiction*, and *Teen* genres) collected by Zhu et al. (2015). We use a publicly available pre-trained BookCorpus language model from Holtzman et al. (2018). We refer to this model as **L2W**.

Language Modeling One Billion This dataset (LM-1B) is currently the largest standard training dataset for language modeling, roughly the same size as BookCorpus. This dataset is a subset of the NewsCrawl dataset, from 2007-2011. We use a pre-trained language model on this corpus from Jozefowicz et al. (2016). We refer to this model as **LM-1B**.

4.2 Evaluation Data

News Commentary (NC) Dataset We collect pairs from a public dataset that contains predominantly commentary written about current news[2]. We use this dataset as the main evaluation of the news-based explanation because 1). It is a separate dataset without any overlap with NewsCrawl;

2). This dataset still belongs to the same news domain, so it provides an in-domain evaluation for **L2E**, **L2EC** and **LM-1B** models.

Winograd Schema Challenge Subset (WSC-G) We use 61 example sentences in the Winograd Schema Challenge that contain the words "because" or "so". Similar to Trinh and Le (2018), we substitute the ambiguous pronouns with the correct referent and ask the model to generate the correct explanation "the trophy is too big" to the phenomenon "The trophy doesn't fit in the suitcase".

Choice of Plausible Alternatives (COPA) Roemmele et al. (2011) proposed a task that contains questions such as "The women met for coffee. What was the CAUSE of this?", and the model is asked to choose between two pre-defined causes. In our setting, we directly ask the model to generate a cause. For language models, we append "because" to the end of each COPA sentence and ask the model to generate the rest.

5 Experiments

5.1 Language Model Training

We use the same language model described in Holtzman et al. (2018). We train 10 epochs for both L2E and L2EC. We use a one layer LSTM (Hochreiter and Schmidhuber, 1997) with 2048 hidden state dimensions and 256 word dimensions. We chose these hyperparameters by tuning on the validation set of each task. Our language model achieved 51.64 perplexity on the L2E test set, and 37.61 perlexity on the L2EC test set.

5.2 Seq2Seq Model Training

We experiment with two architectures: LSTM encoder-decoder and Transformer (Vaswani et al., 2017). We find that with the L2E task, the Transformer architecture performed better, and for the L2EC task, the LSTM encoder-decoder performed better. We suspect that Transformer is worse when the source sequence is too long. We tune each architecture's hyperparameters extensively and we pick the best architecture for each task to evaluate on the evaluation datasets.

5.3 Automatic Evaluation

We use automatic metrics to evaluate the 8 models' performance on the News Commentary dataset. Even though this is a non-overlapping held-out dataset to our news training data, it is still

---

[1] https://github.com/windweller/L2EWeb
[2] https://www.project-syndicate.org/about

Data	S1	Generated S2	Rank	Reference S2	Rank
NewsCrawl	That banned his most threatening challenger, Rally leader Alassane Ouattara, from running for president because ___ ?	He was born in Burkina Faso.	—	He is only half-Ivorian.	—
NewsCrawl	The victim was only saved because ___ ?	He was wearing a seatbelt.	—	The dog turned on the former lifeguard.	—
NewsCrawl	I voted for George W. Bush because ___ ?	I thought he was the best person for the job.	—	That's the name you heard a lot of talk about.	—
WSC-G	An hour later John left because ___?	He didn't feel safe.	0.0	John promised Bill to leave.	0.67
COPA	The woman gave the man her phone number because ___?	She was too busy to be bothered by the man.	0.17	She was attracted to him.	0.5
NC	Moreover, ordinary Russians are becoming allergic to liberal democracy because ___?	They see it as a threat to their own interests.	0.16	Liberal technocrats have consistently served as window dressing for an illiberal Kremlin regime.	0.19

Table 2: **Example pairs** from our highest performing models with the original sentence as a reference. Human ranking score lower is better. We provide examples of especially poor-rated generations in the Appendix.

Model	L2E		L2EC	
	Acc	Perp	Acc	Perp
LSTM	36.2	41.4	**36.0**	**41.3**
Transformer	**38.2**	**33.1**	27.8	96.7

Table 3: We report the best per-token accuracy and perplexity evaluated for each tuned architecture on the L2E/L2EC validation dataset.

within the same domain. We find that L2E/L2EC based models obtained higher scores across all automatic metrics in Table 4. Our results also demonstrate that context matters for explanation. The L2EC task models, trained on context, can generate higher quality explanations than context-free L2E task models.

5.4 Human Evaluation

Ranking Explanations We evaluate the models' relative performance on generating explanations through a survey with human evaluators. 75 participants were recruited using Amazon's Mechanical Turk (AMT). Each evaluator saw 10 prompts from a single dataset, and ranked 7 to 9 explanations: the original explanation extracted from the dataset and the explanations generated by different models. 30 participants saw prompts from our Winograd dataset, 30 participants saw prompts from News Commentary, and 15 participants saw prompts from COPA. We report the results of this evaluation in the Human Ranking sub-

section of Table 4.

Rating Explanations In a followup survey, 60 human evaluators on AMT rated explanations generated by the L2E-Seq2Seq model with beam search and the original (between participants). Ratings were from 0 (extremely bad) to 1 (extremely good) along various dimensions of explanation quality. Results of this study are shown in Table 5. Generated explanations overall were rated worse than human explanations, but tended to be more good than bad (≥ 0.5) on all measures.

6 Discussion

The nature of phenomenon-explanation mapping has always been one-to-many. People can offer drastically different explanations to the same phenomenon. We argue that requiring the machine to generate plausible explanations is more useful and therefore a better goal for models to achieve. Models trained on traditional chatbot corpora are unable to answer why questions because of data sparsity. We note that the generated results are not similar to the original explanations but are often acceptable by human assessment.

Features of Explanations In the human rating experiment, our model was overall rated higher than the original explanations only on the grammaticality measure. However, this measure seems least representative of the overall explanation

Model	BLEU		ROUGE		METEOR		Human Ranking		
	Greedy	Beam	Greedy	Beam	Greedy	Beam	COPA	WSC-G	NC
L2E-Seq2Seq	**0.55**	0.37	18.8	18.3	7.4	7.6	**0.412**	**0.409**	0.454
L2EC-Seq2Seq	0.40	**0.47**	**19.9**	**19.7**	**8.6**	**8.8**	—	—	0.433
L2E-LM	0.25	0.20	15.9	16.8	6.1	6.7	0.515	0.572	0.479
L2EC-LM	0.36	0.38	17.0	17.7	6.7	7.3	—	—	**0.432**
LM-1B[†]	0.18	—	16.9	—	7.1	—	0.526	0.484	0.454
L2W[†]	0.00	0.00	14.0	13.9	6.7	6.8	0.511	0.523	0.625
L2WC	0.13	0.14	12.8	12.7	5.7	5.7	—	—	0.546
OpenSubtitle[†]	0.04	0.0	13.0	13.4	1.9	3.7	0.827	0.823	0.811
Reference	100	100	100	100	100	100	**0.266**	**0.238**	**0.267**

Table 4: BLUE, ROGUE, METEOR are evaluated on News Commentary test data. Any model with **C** in the name is evaluated with full context. Models with [†] are pre-trained models from other work. Only L2E-Seq2Seq uses the Transformer architecture, the rest LSTM. In human ranking, we report the average rank across participants. Top ranking is 0 and lowest ranking is 1.

	Original	L2E-Seq2Seq
Goodness	**0.699** [0.67, 0.72]	0.500 [0.45, 0.55]
Relatedness	**0.723** [0.70, 0.74]	0.590 [0.55, 0.63]
Grammaticality	0.684 [0.66, 0.71]	**0.738** [0.70, 0.77]
Helpfulness	**0.696** [0.67, 0.72]	0.512 [0.47, 0.56]
Plausibility	**0.710** [0.69, 0.73]	0.543 [0.50, 0.59]

Table 5: Results of rating study with human evaluators, average rating and bootstrapped 95% CI.

quality: ratings for most features were highly correlated with each other (0.771-0.865), but not with grammaticality (0.196-0.323). This shows that, while we can achieve plausible explanations with our models, more research is required in order to reach human-level quality.

Explaining as Generating Even though formulating the task of providing explanation as a sequence generation task allows us to leverage the rapid advancements in the natural language generation community, we sidestep a vast amount of literature that aims to provide informatively *correct* explanations as well as grounding explanations theoretically to the causal understanding of the situation (Halpern and Pearl, 2005). We also suffer from the same drawbacks noticed in natural language generation papers such as brevity and generic responses, failure to leverage long context, and being data hungry (Holtzman et al., 2018).

Exploring Linguistic Structures The curated dataset of explanation-phenomenon pairs provides an opportunity to explore descriptive structures and features of explanations. In principle, one can use this dataset to formulate frequent and common syntactic and semantic patterns for natural-sounding explanations. This would aid our understanding of how why-questions can be addressed satisfactorily.

7 Conclusion

We present the task of generating plausible explanations as an important goal for neural sequence-to-sequence models. We curate a large dataset of phenomenon-explanation pairs so that these models can learn to provide plausible explanations as judged by humans, and formulate responses to open-domain **Why**-questions.

Acknowledgement

We thank Barry Haddow and Michael Hahn for their advice and assistance. The research is based upon work supported by the Defense Advanced Research Projects Agency (DARPA), via the Air Force Research Laboratory (AFRL, Grant No. FA8650-18-C-7826). The views and conclusions contained herein are those of the authors and should not be interpreted as necessarily representing the official policies or endorsements, either expressed or implied, of DARPA, the AFRL or the U.S. Government. The U.S. Government is authorized to reproduce and distribute reprints for Governmental purposes notwithstanding any copyright annotation thereon.

References

Yoshua Bengio, Réjean Ducharme, Pascal Vincent, and Christian Jauvin. 2003. A neural probabilistic language model. *Journal of machine learning research*, 3(Feb):1137–1155.

Ondřej Bojar, Rajen Chatterjee, Christian Federmann, Mark Fishel, Yvette Graham, Barry Haddow, Matthias Huck, Antonio Jimeno Yepes, Philipp Koehn, Christof Monz, et al. 2018. Proceedings of the third conference on machine translation. In *Proceedings of the Third Conference on Machine Translation: Research Papers*.

Giuseppe Carenini and Johanna D Moore. 1993. Generating explanations in context. In *IUI*, volume 93, pages 175–182.

Nathanael Chambers and Dan Jurafsky. 2008. Unsupervised learning of narrative event chains. In *Proceedings of ACL-08: HLT*, pages 789–797, Columbus, Ohio. Association for Computational Linguistics.

Joseph Y Halpern and Judea Pearl. 2005. Causes and explanations: A structural-model approach. part ii: Explanations. *The British journal for the philosophy of science*, 56(4):889–911.

Germund Hesslow. 1988. The problem of causal selection. *Contemporary science and natural explanation: Commonsense conceptions of causality*, pages 11–32.

Sepp Hochreiter and Jürgen Schmidhuber. 1997. Long short-term memory. *Neural computation*, 9(8):1735–1780.

Ari Holtzman, Jan Buys, Maxwell Forbes, Antoine Bosselut, David Golub, and Yejin Choi. 2018. Learning to write with cooperative discriminators. In *Proceedings of the 56th Annual Meeting of the Association for Computational Linguistics (Volume 1: Long Papers)*, pages 1638–1649, Melbourne, Australia. Association for Computational Linguistics.

Rafal Jozefowicz, Oriol Vinyals, Mike Schuster, Noam Shazeer, and Yonghui Wu. 2016. Exploring the limits of language modeling. *arXiv preprint arXiv:1602.02410*.

Guillaume Klein, Yoon Kim, Yuntian Deng, Jean Senellart, and Alexander Rush. 2017. OpenNMT: Open-source toolkit for neural machine translation. In *Proceedings of ACL 2017, System Demonstrations*, pages 67–72, Vancouver, Canada. Association for Computational Linguistics.

Hector J Levesque, Ernest Davis, and Leora Morgenstern. 2011. The winograd schema challenge. In *Aaai spring symposium: Logical formalizations of commonsense reasoning*, volume 46, page 47.

Hugo Liu and Push Singh. 2004. Conceptneta practical commonsense reasoning tool-kit. *BT technology journal*, 22(4):211–226.

Zhiyi Luo, Yuchen Sha, Kenny Q Zhu, Seung-won Hwang, and Zhongyuan Wang. 2016. Commonsense causal reasoning between short texts. In *KR*, pages 421–431.

Christopher D. Manning, Mihai Surdeanu, John Bauer, Jenny Finkel, Steven J. Bethard, and David McClosky. 2014. The Stanford CoreNLP Natural Language Processing Toolkit. In *Association for Computational Linguistics (ACL) System Demonstrations*, pages 55–60.

George A Miller. 1995. Wordnet: a lexical database for english. *Communications of the ACM*, 38(11):39–41.

Allen Nie, Erin D Bennett, and Noah D Goodman. 2017. Dissent: Sentence representation learning from explicit discourse relations. *arXiv preprint arXiv:1710.04334*.

Robert Parker, David Graff, Junbo Kong, Ke Chen, and Kazuaki Maeda. 2011. English gigaword fifth edition LDC2011T07. *Philadelphia: Linguistic Data Consortium*. Web download file.

Melissa Roemmele, Cosmin Adrian Bejan, and Andrew S Gordon. 2011. Choice of plausible alternatives: An evaluation of commonsense causal reasoning. In *AAAI Spring Symposium: Logical Formalizations of Commonsense Reasoning*, pages 90–95.

Shota Sasaki, Sho Takase, Naoya Inoue, Naoaki Okazaki, and Kentaro Inui. 2017. Handling multiword expressions in causality estimation. In *IWCS 201712th International Conference on Computational SemanticsShort papers*.

Ilya Sutskever, Oriol Vinyals, and Quoc V Le. 2014. Sequence to sequence learning with neural networks. In *Advances in neural information processing systems*, pages 3104–3112.

Trieu H Trinh and Quoc V Le. 2018. A simple method for commonsense reasoning. *arXiv preprint arXiv:1806.02847*.

Ashish Vaswani, Noam Shazeer, Niki Parmar, Jakob Uszkoreit, Llion Jones, Aidan N Gomez, Łukasz Kaiser, and Illia Polosukhin. 2017. Attention is all you need. In *Advances in Neural Information Processing Systems*, pages 5998–6008.

Terry Winograd. 1971. Procedures as a representation for data in a computer program for understanding natural language. Technical report, MASSACHUSETTS INST OF TECH CAMBRIDGE PROJECT MAC.

Yukun Zhu, Ryan Kiros, Rich Zemel, Ruslan Salakhutdinov, Raquel Urtasun, Antonio Torralba, and Sanja Fidler. 2015. Aligning books and movies: Towards story-like visual explanations by watching movies and reading books. In *Proceedings of the IEEE international conference on computer vision*, pages 19–27.

Data	S1	Generated S2	Rank	Reference S2	Rank
NewsCrawl	Perhaps the student was so good because ___ ?	He was so good at it.	—	Thursday wasn't the first time he acted as a moderator.	—
NewsCrawl	Cheaper prices drove computers out of the walls of these big companies because ___ ?	They were cheaper than the ones that were being used.	—	You suddenly didn't need all that money anymore.	—
WSC-G	Sam and Amy are passionately in love, but Amy's parents are unhappy about it because ___?	They don't want to be the first female president.	0.87	Sam and Amy are fifteen.	0.37
COPA	The hamburger meat browned because ___?	That's what it is.	0.83	The cook grilled it.	0.0
NC	The desperately poor may accept handouts because ___?	They are the only ones who can afford it.	0.83	They feel they have to.	0.12

Table S1: **Bad example pairs** from our lowest performing models with the original sentence as a reference. Human ranking score lower is better. Full list of WSC-G and COPA generations can be found in `https://github.com/windweller/L2EWeb/blob/master/WinogradS2Generation.ipynb`.

A Supplementary Materials

A.1 Data Accessibility Statement

The majority of the data we use are publicly available. We provide specific instructions on how to obtain these data below:

Gigaword 5th Edition This dataset is provided through Linguistic Data Consortium (LDC): `https://catalog.ldc.upenn.edu/LDC2011T07`. Even though this dataset is only available through subscription, most university libraries should have existing subscriptions, and only 20% of our training data comes from this dataset.

News Crawl Dataset The shuffled version of this dataset is publicly available[3]. We requested the original un-shuffled dataset from Barry Haddow[4] so that we can extract context for L2EC task. We believe this dataset can be easily accessed by the public upon an email request.

BookCorpus This dataset is no longer publicly available. However, there are many neural language models pre-trained on this dataset that are publicly available. We used one that can be accessed from `https://github.com/ari-holtzman/l2w`.

News Commentary Dataset This is also publicly available through the WMT workshop[5] similar to

the NewsCrawl dataset. This dataset is not shuffled.

Winograd Schema Challenge The original version of this dataset is publicly available `https://cs.nyu.edu/davise/papers/WinogradSchemas/WS.html`. We use a processed version from Trinh and Le (2018), which can be accessed through Google Cloud Storage: `gs://commonsense-reasoning/reproduce/commonsense_test/wsc273.json`.

Choice of Plausible Alternatives This dataset is available at `http://people.ict.usc.edu/~gordon/copa.html`.

A.2 Training Data Curation

In order to automatically curate a sizable amount of training data, we choose large corpora that are made of news articles, due to the well-formedness of sentences and there are many phenomenon-explanation pairs in news stories. We use Gigaword fifth edition (Parker et al., 2011) which contains news stories from seven news agencies over the span of 2001-2010. We extracted paragraphs and tokenized the sentences. We discard non-English characters. Another large dataset of new articles comes from WMT-18, the NewsCrawl dataset (Bojar et al., 2018). This dataset spans from 2007-2017 collected from the RSS (Rich Site Summary) feed of 18 news agencies. The

---

[3] `http://www.statmt.org/wmt18/translation-task.html`

[4] `http://homepages.inf.ed.ac.uk/bhaddow/`

[5] `http://data.statmt.org/wmt18/`

`translation-task/news-commentary-v13.en.gz`

only overlapping agency between Gigaword and NewsCrawl is Los Angeles Times. In addition to the randomly shuffled dataset we obtained from the WMT-18 website, we additionally contacted the organization for the unshuffled version of data. We refer to this dataset as the NewsCrawl-ordered. This dataset is slightly larger than the current released version of NewsCrawl and contains a couple of months of early 2018 data. We shuffle and then split both datasets into train/valid/test in standard 0.9/0.05/0.05. We use the validation and test set on this task to pick the best performing model.

A.3 Language Model Details

We use adaptive gradient descent (AdaGrad) with learning rate 0.1 and weight decay of 1e-6.

A.4 Seq2Seq Model Details

We built and trained our Seq2Seq model using OpenNMT (Klein et al., 2017). For the L2E task, we used a 6-layer Transformer model, with hidden dimension 512, feedforward layer dimension 2048, and 8 attention heads. We train with dropout

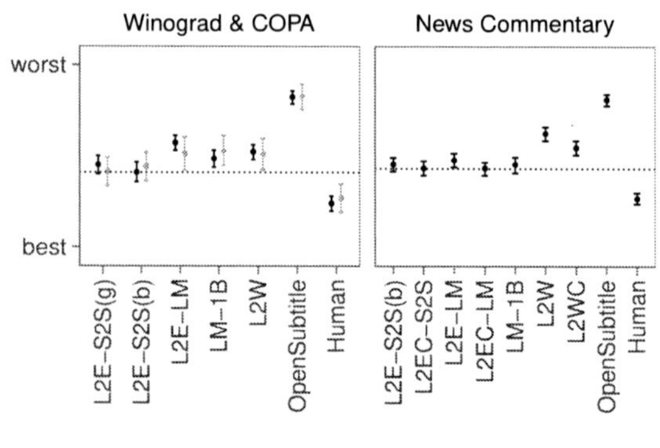

Figure S2: The average ranking of each model's generated response (lower is better).

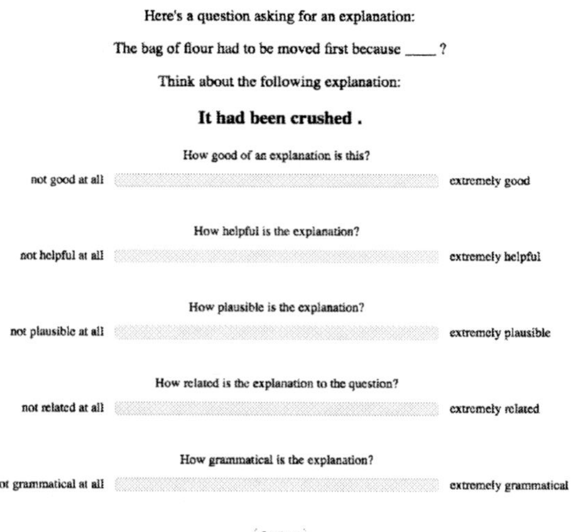

Figure S3: Screenshot of raking study.

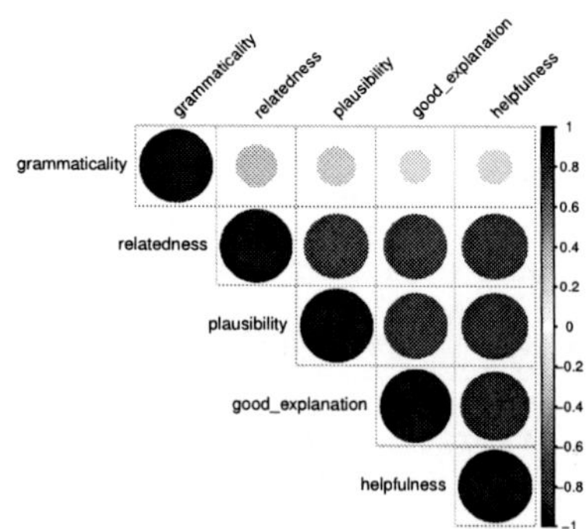

Figure S1: Correlations of human ratings on Winograd Schema Challenge explanations

Figure S4: Screenshot of ratings study.

Multi-turn Dialogue Response Generation in an Adversarial Learning Framework

Oluwatobi Olabiyi
Capital One Conversation Research
Vienna VA
oluwatobi.olabiyi@capitalone.com

Alan Salimov
Capital One Conversation Research
San Fransisco CA
alan.salimov@capitalone.com

Anish Khazane
Capital One Conversation Research
San Fransisco CA
anish.khazane@capitalone.com

Erik T. Mueller
Capital One Conversation Research
Vienna VA
erik.mueller@capitalone.com

Abstract

We propose an adversarial learning approach for generating multi-turn dialogue responses. Our proposed framework, *hredGAN*, is based on conditional generative adversarial networks (GANs). The GAN's generator is a modified hierarchical recurrent encoder-decoder network (HRED) and the discriminator is a word-level bidirectional RNN that shares context and word embeddings with the generator. During inference, noise samples conditioned on the dialogue history are used to perturb the generator's latent space to generate several possible responses. The final response is the one ranked best by the discriminator. The hredGAN shows improved performance over existing methods: (1) it generalizes better than networks trained using only the log-likelihood criterion, and (2) it generates longer, more informative and more diverse responses with high utterance and topic relevance even with limited training data. This improvement is demonstrated on the Movie triples and Ubuntu dialogue datasets using both automatic and human evaluations.

1 Introduction

Recent advances in deep neural network architectures have enabled tremendous success on a number of difficult machine learning problems. While these results are impressive, producing a deployable neural network–based model that can engage in open domain conversation still remains elusive. A dialogue system needs to be able to generate meaningful and diverse responses that are simultaneously coherent with the input utterance and the overall dialogue topic. Unfortunately, earlier conversation models trained with naturalistic dialogue data suffered greatly from limited contextual information (Sutskever et al., 2014; Vinyals and Le, 2015) and lack of diversity (Li et al., 2016a).

These problems often lead to generic and safe responses to a variety of input utterances.

Serban et al. (2016) and Xing et al. (2017) proposed the Hierarchical Recurrent Encoder-Decoder (HRED) network to capture long temporal dependencies in multi-turn conversations to address the limited contextual information but the diversity problem remained. In contrast, some HRED variants such as variational (Serban et al., 2017b) and multi-resolution (Serban et al., 2017a) HREDs attempt to alleviate the diversity problem by injecting noise at the utterance level and by extracting additional context to condition the generator on. While these approaches achieve a certain measure of success over the basic HRED, the generated responses are still mostly generic since they do not control the generator's output. This is because the output conditional distribution is not calibrated. Li et al. (2016a), on the other hand, consider a diversity promoting training objective but their model is for single turn conversations and cannot be trained end-to-end.

The generative adversarial network (GAN) (Goodfellow et al., 2014) seems to be an appropriate solution to the diversity problem. GAN matches data from two different distributions by introducing an adversarial game between a *generator* and a *discriminator*. We explore *hredGAN*: conditional GANs for multi-turn dialogue models with an HRED generator and discriminator. hredGAN combines ideas from both generative and retrieval-based multi-turn dialogue systems to improve their individual performances. This is achieved by sharing the context and word embeddings between the generator and the discriminator allowing for joint end-to-end training using back-propagation. To the best of our knowledge, no existing work has applied conditional GANs to multi-turn dialogue models and especially not

121

Proceedings of the 1st Workshop on NLP for Conversational AI, pages 121–132
Florence, Italy, August 1, 2019. ©2019 Association for Computational Linguistics

with HRED generators and discriminators. We demonstrate the effectiveness of hredGAN over the VHRED for dialogue modeling with evaluations on the Movie triples and Ubuntu technical support datasets.

2 Related Work

Our work is related to end-to-end neural network–based open domain dialogue models. Most neural dialogue models use transduction frameworks adapted from neural machine translation (Sutskever et al., 2014; Bahdanau et al., 2015). These `Seq2Seq` networks are trained end-to-end with MLE criteria using large corpora of human-to-human conversation data. Others use GAN's discriminator as a reward function in a reinforcement learning framework (Yu et al., 2017) and in conjunction with MLE (Li et al., 2017; Che et al., 2017). Zhang et al. (2017) explored the idea of GAN with a feature matching criterion. Xu et al. (2017) and Zhang et al. (2018) employed GAN with an approximate embedding layer as well as with adversarial information maximization respectively to improve `Seq2Seq`'s diversity performance.

Still, `Seq2Seq` models are limited in their ability to capture long temporal dependencies in multi-turn conversation. Although Li et al. (2016b) attempted to optimize a pair of `Seq2Seq` models for multi-turn dialogue, the multi-turn objective is only applied at inference and not used for actual model training. Hence the introduction of HRED models (Serban et al., 2016, 2017a,b; Xing et al., 2017) for modeling dialogue response in multi-turn conversations. However, these HRED models suffer from lack of diversity since they are only trained with MLE criteria. On the other hand, adversarial system has been used for evaluating open domain dialogue models (Bruni and Fernndez, 2018; Kannan and Vinyals, 2017). Our work, hredGAN, is closest to the combination of HRED generation models (Serban et al., 2016) and adversarial evaluation (Kannan and Vinyals, 2017).

3 Model

3.1 Adversarial Learning of Dialogue Response

Consider a dialogue consisting of a sequence of N utterances, $\boldsymbol{x} = (x_1, x_2, \cdots, x_N)$, where each utterance $x_i = (x_i^1, x_i^2, \cdots, x_i^{M_i})$ contains a variable-length sequence of M_i word tokens such that $x_i{}^j \in V$ for vocabulary V. At any time step i, the dialogue history is given by $\boldsymbol{x}_i = (x_1, x_2, \cdots, x_i)$. The dialogue response generation task can be defined as follows: Given a dialogue history $\boldsymbol{x}_i$, generate a response $y_i = (y_i^1, y_i^2, \cdots, y_i^{T_i})$, where T_i is the number of generated tokens. We also want the distribution of the generated response $P(y_i)$ to be indistinguishable from that of the ground truth $P(x_{i+1})$ and $T_i = M_{i+1}$. Conditional GAN learns a mapping from an observed dialogue history, $\boldsymbol{x}_i$, and a sequence of random noise vectors, z_i to a sequence of output tokens, y_i, $G : \{\boldsymbol{x}_i, z_i\} \rightarrow y_i$. The generator G is trained to produce output sequences that cannot be distinguished from the ground truth sequence by an adversarially trained discriminator D that is trained to do well at detecting the generator's fakes. The distribution of the generator output sequence can be factored by the product rule:

$$P(y_i|\boldsymbol{x}_i) = P(y_i^1) \prod_{j=2}^{T_i} P(y_i^j|y_i^1, \cdots, y_i^{j-1}, \boldsymbol{x}_i) \tag{1}$$

$$P(y_i^j|y_i^1, \cdots, y_i^{j-1}, \boldsymbol{x}_i) = P_{\theta_G}(y_i^{1:j-1}, \boldsymbol{x}_i) \tag{2}$$

where $y_i^{i:j-1} = (y_i^1, \cdots, y_i^{j-1})$ and θ_G are the parameters of the generator model. $P_{\theta_G}(y_i^{i:j-1}, \boldsymbol{x}_i)$ is an autoregressive generative model where the probability of the current token depends on the past generated sequence. Training the generator G with the log-likelihood criterion is unstable in practice, and therefore the past generated sequence is substituted with the ground truth, a method known as *teacher forcing* (Williams and Zipser, 1989), i.e.,

$$P(y_i^j|y_i^1, \cdots, y_i^{j-1}, \boldsymbol{x}_i) \approx P_{\theta_G}(x_{i+1}^{1:j-1}, \boldsymbol{x}_i) \tag{3}$$

Using (3) in relation to GAN, we define our fake sample as the teacher forcing output with some input noise z_i

$$y_i^j \sim P_{\theta_G}(x_{i+1}^{1:j-1}, \boldsymbol{x}_i, z_i) \tag{4}$$

and the corresponding real sample as ground truth x_{i+1}^j.

With the GAN objective, we can match the noise distribution, $P(z_i)$, to the distribution of the ground truth response, $P(x_{i+1}|\boldsymbol{x}_i)$. Varying the noise input then allows us to generate diverse responses to the same dialogue history. Furthermore, the discriminator, since it is calibrated, is used during inference to rank the generated responses, providing a means of controlling the generator output.

3.1.1 Objectives

The objective of a conditional GAN can be expressed as

$$\mathcal{L}_{cGAN}(G, D) = \mathbb{E}_{\boldsymbol{x_i}, x_{i+1}}[\log D(x_{i+1}, \boldsymbol{x_i})] + \mathbb{E}_{\boldsymbol{x_i}, z_i}[1 - \log D(G(\boldsymbol{x_i}, z_i), \boldsymbol{x_i})] \quad (5)$$

where G tries to minimize this objective against an adversarial D that tries to maximize it:

$$G^*, D^* = arg \min_{G} \max_{D} \mathcal{L}_{cGAN}(G, D). \quad (6)$$

Previous approaches have shown that it is beneficial to mix the GAN objective with a more traditional loss such as cross-entropy loss (Lamb et al., 2016; Li et al., 2017). The discriminator's job remains unchanged, but the generator is tasked not only to fool the discriminator but also to be near the ground truth x_{i+1} in the cross-entropy sense:

$$\mathcal{L}_{MLE}(G) = \mathbb{E}_{\boldsymbol{x_i}, x_{i+1}, z_i}[-log P_{\theta_G}(x_{i+1}, \boldsymbol{x_i}, z_i)]. \quad (7)$$

Our final objective is,

$$G^*, D^* = arg \min_{G} \max_{D} \left(\lambda_G \mathcal{L}_{cGAN}(G, D) + \lambda_M \mathcal{L}_{MLE}(G) \right). \quad (8)$$

It is worth mentioning that, without z_i, the net could still learn a mapping from $\boldsymbol{x_i}$ to y_i, but it would produce deterministic outputs and fail to match any distribution other than a delta function (Isola et al., 2017). This is one key area where our work is different from Lamb et al.'s and Li et al.'s. The schematic of the proposed hredGAN is depicted at the right hand side of Figure 1.

3.1.2 Generator

We adopted an HRED dialogue generator similar to Serban et al. (2016, 2017a,b) and Xing et al. (2017). The HRED contains three recurrent structures, i.e. the encoder ($eRNN$), context ($cRNN$), and decoder ($dRNN$) RNN. The conditional probability modeled by the HRED per output word token is given by

$$P_{\theta_G}\left(y_i^j | x_{i+1}^{1:j-1}, \boldsymbol{x_i}\right) = dRNN\left(E(x_{i+1}^{j-1}), h_i^{j-1}, \boldsymbol{h_i}\right) \quad (9)$$

where $E(.)$ is the embedding lookup, $\boldsymbol{h_i} = cRNN(eRNN(E(x_i), \boldsymbol{h_{i-1}})$, $eRNN(.)$ maps a sequence of input symbols into fixed-length vector, and h and $\boldsymbol{h}$ are the hidden states of the decoder and context RNN, respectively.

In the multi-resolution HRED, (Serban et al., 2017a), high-level tokens are extracted and processed by another RNN to improve performance. We circumvent the need for this extra processing by allowing the decoder to attend to different parts of the input utterance during response generation (Bahdanau et al., 2015; Luong et al., 2015). We introduce a local attention into (9) and encode the attention memory differently from the context through an attention encoder RNN ($aRNN$), yielding:

$$P_{\theta_G}\left(y_i^j | x_{i+1}^{1:j-1}, \boldsymbol{x_i}\right) = dRNN\left(E(x_{i+1}^{j-1}), h_i^{j-1}, a_i^j, \boldsymbol{h_i}\right) \quad (10)$$

where $a_i^j = \sum_{m=1}^{M_i} \frac{exp(\alpha_m)}{\sum_{m=1}^{M_i} exp(\alpha_m)} h_i'^m$, $h_i'^m = aRNN(E(x_i^m), h_i'^{m-1})$, h' is the hidden state of the attention RNN, and α_k is either a logit projection of $(h_i^{j-1}, h_i'^m)$ in the case of Bahdanau et al. (2015) or $(h_i^{j-1})^T \cdot h_i'^m$ in the case of Luong et al. (2015). The modified HRED architecture is shown in Figure 2.

Noise Injection: We inject Gaussian noise at the input of the decoder RNN. Noise samples could be injected at the utterance or word level. With noise injection, the conditional probability of the decoder output becomes

$$P_{\theta_G}\left(y_i^j | x_{i+1}^{1:j-1}, z_i^j, \boldsymbol{x_i}\right) = dRNN\left(E(x_{i+1}^{j-1}), h_i^{j-1}, a_i^j, z_i^j, \boldsymbol{h_i}\right) \quad (11)$$

where $z_i^j \sim \mathcal{N}_i(0, \boldsymbol{I})$, for utterance-level noise and $z_i^j \sim \mathcal{N}_i^j(0, \boldsymbol{I})$, for word-level noise.

3.1.3 Discriminator

The discriminator shares context and word embeddings with the generator and can discriminate at the word level (Lamb et al., 2016). The word-level discrimination is achieved through a bidirectional RNN and is able to capture both syntactic and conceptual differences between the generator output and the ground truth. The aggregate classification of an input sequence, χ can be factored over word-

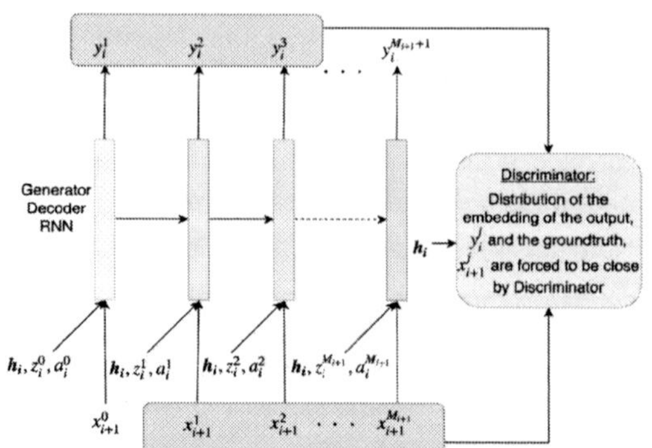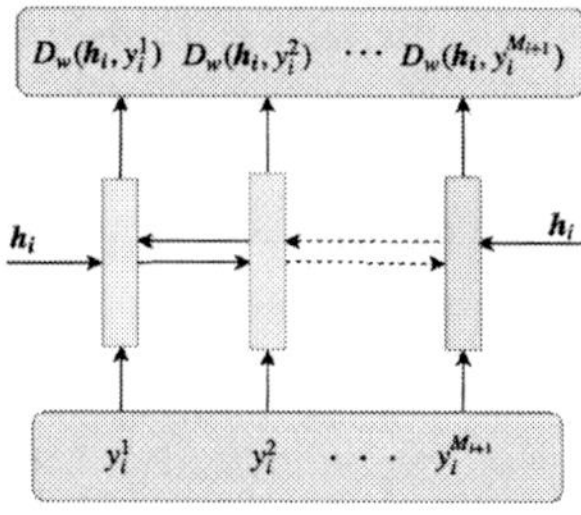

Figure 1: **Left: The hredGAN architecture** - The generator makes predictions conditioned on the dialogue history, $\boldsymbol{h_i}$, attention, a_i^j, noise sample, z_i^j, and ground truth, x_{i+1}^{j-1}. **Right: RNN-based discriminator** that discriminates bidirectionally at the word level.

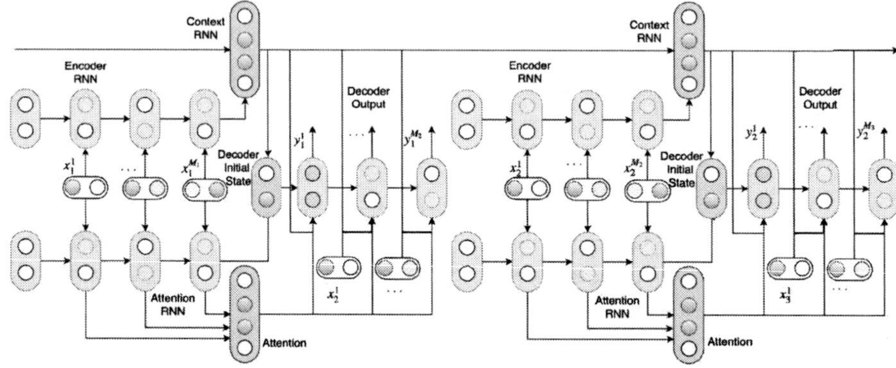

Figure 2: **The HRED generator with local attention** - The attention RNN ensures local relevance while the context RNN ensures global relevance. Their states are combined to initialize the decoder RNN and the discriminator BiRNN.

level discrimination and expressed as

$$D(\boldsymbol{x_i}, \chi) = D(\boldsymbol{h_i}, \chi) = \left[\prod_{j=1}^{J} D_{RNN}(\boldsymbol{h_i}, E(\chi^j)) \right]^{\frac{1}{J}}$$

(12)

where $D_{RNN}(.)$ is the word discriminator RNN, $\boldsymbol{h_i}$ is an encoded vector of the dialogue history $\boldsymbol{x_i}$ obtained from the generator's $cRNN(.)$ output, and χ^j is the *jth* word or token of the input sequence χ. $\chi = y_i$ and $J = T_i$ for the case of generator's decoder output, $\chi = x_{i+1}$ and $J = M_{i+1}$ for the case of ground truth. The discriminator architecture is depicted on the left hand side of Figure 1.

3.2 Adversarial Generation of Multi-turn Dialogue Response

In this section, we describe the generation process during inference. The generation objective can be mathematically described as

$$y_i^* = arg\max_l \left\{ P(y_{i,l}|\boldsymbol{x_i}) + D^*(\boldsymbol{x_i}, y_{i,l})] \right\}_{l=1}^{L}$$

(13)

where $y_{i,l} = G^*(\boldsymbol{x_i}, z_{i,l})$, $z_{i,l}$ is the *lth* noise samples at dialogue step i, and L is the number of response samples. Equation 13 shows that our inference objective is the same as the training objective (8), combining both the MLE and adversarial criteria. This is in contrast to existing work where the discriminator is usually discarded during inference.

The inference described by (13) is intractable due to the enormous search space of $y_{i,l}$. Therefore, we turn to an approximate solution where we use greedy decoding (MLE) on the first part of the objective function to generate L lists of responses based on noise samples $\{z_{i,l}\}_{l=1}^{L}$. In order to facilitate the exploration of the generator's latent space, we sample a modified noise distribution, $z_{i,l}^j \sim \mathcal{N}_{i,l}(0, \alpha\boldsymbol{I})$, or $z_{i,l}^j \sim \mathcal{N}_{i,l}^j(0, \alpha\boldsymbol{I})$

Algorithm 1 Adversarial Learning of hredGAN

Require: A generator G with parameters θ_G.
Require: A discriminator D with parameters θ_D.
  for number of training iterations **do**
    Initialize $cRNN$ to zero_state, h_0
    Sample a mini-batch of conversations, $\boldsymbol{x} = \{x_i\}_{i=1}^{N}$, $\boldsymbol{x_i} = (x_1, x_2, \cdots, x_i)$ with N utterances. Each utterance mini batch i contains M_i word tokens.
    for $i = 1$ **to** $N - 1$ **do**
      Update the context state.
      $\boldsymbol{h_i} = cRNN(eRNN(E(x_i)), \boldsymbol{h_{i-1}})$
      Compute the generator output using (11).
      $P_{\theta_G}(y_i|, z_i, \boldsymbol{x_i}) = \{P_{\theta_G}(y_i^j | x_{i+1}^{1:j-1}, z_i^j, \boldsymbol{x_i})\}_{j=1}^{M_i+1}$
      Sample a corresponding mini batch of utterance y_i.
      $y_i \sim P_{\theta_G}(y_i|, z_i, \boldsymbol{x_i})$
    end for
    Compute the discriminator accuracy D_{acc} over $N - 1$ utterances $\{y_i\}_{i=1}^{N-1}$ and $\{x_{i+1}\}_{i=1}^{N-1}$
    if $D_{acc} < acc_{D_{th}}$ **then**
      Update θ_D with gradient of the discriminator loss.
      $\sum_i [\nabla_{\theta_D} \log D(\boldsymbol{h_i}, x_{i+1}) + \nabla_{\theta_D} log(1 - D(\boldsymbol{h_i}, y_i))]$
    end if
    if $D_{acc} < acc_{G_{th}}$ **then**
      Update θ_G with the generator's MLE loss only.
      $\sum_i [\nabla_{\theta_G} \log P_{\theta_G}(y_i|, z_i, \boldsymbol{x_i})]$
    else
      Update θ_G with both adversarial and MLE losses.
      $\sum_i [\lambda_G \nabla_{\theta_G} \log D(\boldsymbol{h_i}, y_i) + \lambda_M \nabla_{\theta_G} \log P_{\theta_G}(y_i|, z_i, \boldsymbol{x_i})]$
    end if
  end for

---

where $\alpha > 1.0$, is the exploration factor that increases the noise variance. We then rank the L lists using the discriminator score, $\left\{D^*(\boldsymbol{x_i}, y_{i,l})]\right\}_{l=1}^{L}$. The response with the highest discriminator ranking is the optimum response for the dialogue context.

4 Training of hredGAN

We trained both the generator and the discriminator simultaneously as highlighted in Algorithm **??** with $\lambda_G = \lambda_M = 1$. GAN training is prone to instability due to competition between the generator and the discriminator. Therefore, parameter updates are conditioned on the discriminator performance (Lamb et al., 2016).

The generator consists of four RNNs with different parameters, that is, $aRNN, eRNN, cRNN,$ and $dRNN$. $aRNN$ and $eRNN$ are both bidirectional, while $cRNN$ and $dRNN$ are unidirectional. Each RNN has 3 layers, and the hidden state size is 512. The $dRNN$ and $aRNN$ are connected using an additive attention mechanism (Bahdanau et al., 2015).

The discriminator shares $aRNN, eRNN,$ and $cRNN$ with the generator. D_{RNN} is a stacked bidirectional RNN with 3 layers and a hidden state size of 512. The $cRNN$ states are used to initialize the states of D_{RNN}. The output of both the forward and the backward cells for each word are concatenated and passed to a fully-connected layer with binary output. The output is the probability that the word is from the ground truth given the past and future words of the sequence.

Others: All RNNs used are gated recurrent unit (GRU) cells (Cho et al., 2014). The word embedding size is 512 and shared between the generator and the discriminator. The initial learning rate is 0.5 with decay rate factor of 0.99, applied when the adversarial loss has increased over two iterations. We use a batch size of 64 and clip gradients around 5.0. As in Lamb et al. (2016), we find $acc_{D_{th}} = 0.99$ and $acc_{G_{th}} = 0.75$ to suffice. All parameters are initialized with Xavier uniform random initialization (Glorot and Bengio, 2010). The vocabulary size V is $50,000$. Due to the large vocabulary size, we use sampled softmax loss (Jean et al., 2015) for MLE loss to expedite the training process. However, we use full softmax for evaluation. The model is trained end-to-end using the stochastic gradient descent algorithm.

5 Experiments and Results

We consider the task of generating dialogue responses conditioned on the dialogue history and the current input utterance. We compare the proposed hredGAN model against some alternatives on publicly available datasets.

5.1 Datasets

Movie Triples Corpus (MTC) dataset (Serban et al., 2016). This dataset was derived from the *Movie-DiC* dataset by Banchs (2012). Although this dataset spans a wide range of topics with few spelling mistakes, its small size of only about 240,000 dialogue triples makes it difficult to train a dialogue model, as pointed out by Serban et al. (2016). We thought that this scenario would really benefit from the proposed adversarial generation.

Ubuntu Dialogue Corpus (UDC) dataset (Serban et al., 2017b). This dataset was extracted from the Ubuntu Relay Chat Channel. Although the topics in the dataset are not as diverse as in the MTC, the dataset is very large, containing about 1.85 million conversations with an average of 5 utterances per conversation.

We split both MTC and UDC into training, validation, and test sets, using 90%, 5%, and 5% proportions, respectively. We performed minimal preprocessing of the datasets by replacing all words except the top 50,000 most frequent words by an *UNK* symbol.

5.2 Evaluation Metrics

Accurate evaluation of dialogue models is still an open challenge. In this paper, we employ both automatic and human evaluations.

5.2.1 Automatic Evaluation

We employed some of the automatic evaluation metrics that are used in probabilistic language and dialogue models, and statistical machine translation. Although these metrics may not correlate well with human judgment of dialogue responses (Liu et al., 2016), they provide a good baseline for comparing dialogue model performance.

Perplexity - For a model with parameter θ, we define perplexity as:

$$exp\left[- \frac{1}{N_W} \sum_{k=1}^{K} log\, P_\theta(y_1, y_2, \ldots, y_{N_k-1}) \right]$$

(14)

where K is the number of conversations in the dataset, N_k is the number of utterances in conversation k, and N_W is the total number of word tokens in the entire dataset. The lower the perplexity, the better. The perplexity measures the likelihood of generating the ground truth given the model parameters. While a generative model can generate a diversity of responses, it should still assign a high probability to the ground truth utterance.

BLEU - The BLEU score (Papineni et al., 2002) provides a measure of overlap between the generated response (candidate) and the ground truth (reference) using a modified n-gram precision. According to Liu et. al. (Liu et al., 2016), BLEU-2 score is fairly correlated with human judgment for non-technical dialogue (such as MTC).

ROUGE - The ROUGE score (Lin, 2014) is similar to BLEU but it is recall-oriented instead. It is used for automatic evaluation of text summarization and machine translation. To compliment the BLEU score, we use ROUGE-N with $N = 2$ for our evaluation.

Distinct n-gram - This is the fraction of unique n-grams in the generated responses and it provides a measure of diversity. Models with higher a number of distinct n-grams tend to produce more diverse responses (Li et al., 2016a). For our evaluation, we use 1- and 2- grams.

Normalized Average Sequence Length (NASL) - This measures the average number of words in model-generated responses normalized by the average number of words in the ground truth.

5.2.2 Human Evaluation

For human evaluation, we follow a similar setup as Li et al. (2016a), employing crowd-sourced judges to evaluate a random selection of 200 samples. We presented both the multi-turn context and the generated responses from the models to 3 judges and asked them to rank the general response quality in terms of relevance and informativeness. For N models, the model with the lowest quality is assigned a score 0 and the highest is assigned a score N-1. Ties are not allowed. The scores are normalized between 0 and 1 and averaged over the total number of samples and judges. For each model, we also estimated the per sample score variance between judges and then averaged over the number of samples, i.e., sum of variances divided by the square of number of samples (assuming sample independence). The square root of result is reported as the standard error of the human judgment for the model.

5.3 Baseline

We compare the performance of our model to (V)HRED (Serban et al., 2016, 2017b), since they are the closest to our approach in implementation and are the current state of the art in open-domain dialogue models. HRED is very similar to our proposed generator, but without the input utterance attention and noise samples. VHRED introduces a latent variable to the HRED between the *cRNN* and the *dRNN* and was trained using the variational lower bound on the log-likelihood. The VHRED can generate multiple responses per context like hredGAN, but it has no specific criteria for selecting the best response.

The HRED and VHRED models are both trained using the Theano-based implementation obtained from `https://github.com/julianser/hed-dlg-truncated`. The training and validation sets used for UDC and MTC dataset were obtained directly from the authors[1] of (V)HRED. For model comparison, we use a test set that is disjoint from the training and validation sets.

---

[1] UDC was obtained from `http://www.iulianserban.com/Files/UbuntuDialogueCorpus.zip`, and the link to MTC was obtained privately.

Model	Teacher Forcing		Autoregression				Human
	Perplexity	$-logD(G(.))$	BLEU-2	ROUGE-2	DISTINCT-1/2	NASL	Evaluation
MTC							
HRED	31.92/36.00	NA	0.0474	0.0384	0.0026/0.0056	0.535	0.2560 ± 0.0977
VHRED	42.61/44.97	NA	0.0606	0.1181	0.0048/0.0163	0.831	0.3909 ± 0.0240
hredGAN_u	**23.57/23.54**	**6.85/6.81**	0.0493	0.2416	0.0167/0.1306	0.884	0.5582 ± 0.0118
hredGAN_w	24.20/24.14	13.35/13.40	**0.0613**	**0.3244**	**0.0179/0.1720**	**1.540**	$\mathbf{0.7869 \pm 0.1148}$
UDC							
HRED	69.39/86.40	NA	0.0177	0.0483	0.0203/0.0466	0.892	0.3475 ± 0.1062
VHRED	98.50/105.20	NA	0.0171	0.0855	0.0297/0.0890	0.873	0.4046 ± 0.0188
hredGAN_u	56.82/57.32	10.09/10.08	0.0137	0.0716	0.0260/0.0847	**1.379**	0.6133 ± 0.0361
hredGAN_w	**47.73/48.18**	**8.37/8.36**	**0.0216**	**0.1168**	**0.0516/0.1821**	1.098	$\mathbf{0.6905 \pm 0.0706}$

Table 1: Generator Performance Evaluation

5.4 Results

We have two variants of hredGAN based on the noise injection approach, i.e., hredGAN with utterance-level (*hredGAN_u*) and word-level (*hredGAN_w*) noise injections.

We compare the performance of these two variants with HRED and VHRED models.

Perplexity: The average perplexity per word performance of all the four models on MTC and UDC datasets (validation/test) are reported in the first column on Table 1. The table indicates that both variants of the hredGAN model perform better than the HRED and VHRED models in terms of the perplexity measure. However, using the adversarial loss criterion (Eq. (8)), the hredGAN_u model performs better on MTC and worse on UDC. Note that, for this experiment, we run all models in teacher forcing mode.

Generation Hyperparameter: For adversarial generation, we perform a linear search for α between 1 and 20 at an increment of 1 using Eq. (13), with sample size $L = 64$, on validation sets with models run in autoregression. The optimum values of α for hredGAN_u and hredGAN_w for UDC are 7.0 and 9.0 respectively. The values for MTC are not convex, probably due to small size of the dataset, so we use the same α values as UDC. We however note that for both datasets, any integer value between 3 and 10 (inclusive) works well in practice.

Quantitative Generator Performance: We run autoregressive inference for all the models (using optimum α values for hredGAN models and selecting the best of $L = 64$ responses using a discriminator) with dialogue contexts from a unique test set. Also, we compute the average BLEU-2, ROUGE-2(f1), Distinct(1/2), and normalized

Item	$D(G(.))$	Utterance
MTC		
Context_0	NA	perhaps <person> had a word with the man upstairs .
Context_1	NA	a word ? i ' m sure by now he ' s engineered a hostile takeover .
Response_0	0.996	<person> , i know what you ' re saying , <person> , that ' s not what i ' m saying .
Response_1	0.991	<person> , i know . i was just about to help the guy .
Response_2	0.315	<person> , i ' m sorry .
Response_3	0.203	<person> , i ' m a little out .
Context_0	NA	says he wanted food . <person> . he wanted the gold .
Context_1	NA	how ' s he going to want the gold ? he couldn ' t even know we had it .
Response_0	0.998	<person> , i know . but it ' s not him , it ' s the only way he ' s got it all figured
Response_1	0.981	<person> , i know . but i have to tell you . these things are really stupid and you think i was wrong ?
Response_2	0.690	<person> , i ' m sure he did .
Response_3	0.314	<person> , i ' m not sure .
UDC		
Context_0	NA	The netboot one is suppose to download packages from the net.
Context_1	NA	like the ones to be installed? or the installed to be run?
Response_0	0.993	you don ' t need to install the whole system , just install the ubuntu installer
Response_1	0.952	you can install the ubuntu installer from the ubuntu menu
Response_2	0.749	I ' m not sure , I don ' t know .
Response_3	0.184	you can
Response_4	0.003	you a . 1 . . . .
Context_0	NA	DJones: update manager won't detect 12.04.1 as a new version if you are already running 12.04, because 12.04.1 = 12.04 + lots of package updates
Response_0	0.991	did you try a clean install of the latest version ?
Response_1	0.981	try installing the latest _UNK and see if it works
Response_2	0.615	I ' m not sure you have a problem . . .
Response_3	0.191	try sudo apt-get remove the package that is not installed
Response_4	0.002	try the _UNK . 1 . 1 . 1 . 1 . 1 . _UNK . deb

Table 2: Example of Discriminator Ranking with hredGAN_w

average sequence length (NASL) scores for each model and summarize the results in the middle of Table 1. Distinct(1/2) largely agrees with the perplexity score. Most scores, similar to the perplexity, indicate that hredGAN models perform better than (V)HRED on both datasets. However, on the UDC ROUGE and MTC BLEU, VHRED scores slightly better than hredGAN_u but still worse than hredGAN_w.

A good dialogue model should find the right balance between precision (BLEU) and diversity. We strongly believe that our adversarial approach is better suited to solving this problem.

Movie	
Context_0	perhaps <person> had a word with the man upstairs .
HRED	i ' m sorry , <person> .
VHRED	<person< ' t do it .
hredGAN_w	<person> , i ' m not gon na be okay . i just don ' t think it ' s a good idea .
hredGAN_u	<person> , i cause it was all the way to you .
Context_1	a word ? i ' m sure by now he ' s engineered a hostile takeover .
HRED	i ' m sorry , <person> .
VHRED	<person> ' t do it .
hredGAN_w	<person> , i know what you ' re saying , <person> , that ' s not what i ' m saying .
hredGAN_u	<person> , i have to tell you i ' m not the same .
Context_0	<person> ' s .
HRED	i ' m sorry , <person> .
VHRED	<person> ' t do it .
hredGAN_w	<person> , i ' m sure it ' s the only thing i ever imagined .
hredGAN_u	<person> , i ' ll be right there .
Context_1	can i ask you something about her ?
HRED	i don ' t know .
VHRED:	you ' re not going to be here .
hredGAN_w	i don ' t know . i think i ' ve heard of it .
hredGAN_u	i ' m sorry , i can ' t .
Ubuntu	
Context_0	this is Dacs i am in i used 'sudo statx and it let me in
HRED	what 's the problem ?
VHRED	I don't know what you want to do . if you want to do it , you need to do it to do it in the terminal ?
hredGAN_w	you don ' t have to do anything , just type in the terminal and it should be to find the right device
hredGAN_u	you can have a look at the output of the command . . .
Context_1	good deal... cat /etc/X11/default-display-manager
HRED	what 's the problem ?
VHRED	do you know what you want to do ?
hredGAN_w	I ' m trying to figure a command that I can find to find out the file that I can find in the file"
hredGAN_u	I don ' t see the point , but I ' m not sure how to do that .
Context_2	/usr/sbin/lightdm http://paste.ubuntu.com/1286224/ <— my /etc/X11/xorg.conf
HRED	what 's the problem ?
VHRED	is there a way to do that in the terminal ?
hredGAN_w	did you just type \" sudo mount -a \" ?
hredGAN_u	i have no idea , i just installed ubuntu and i have no idea how to do that

Table 3: Sample responses of HRED, VHRED and hredGAN.

As hredGAN generators explore diversity, the discriminator ranking gives hredGAN an edge over (V)HRED because it helps detect responses that are out of context and the natural language structure (Table 2). Also, the ROGUE(f1) performance indicates that hredGAN_w strikes a better balance between precision (BLEU) and diversity than the rest of the models. This is also obvious from the quality of generated responses.

Qualitative Generator Performance: The results of the human evaluation are reported in the last column of Table 1. The human evaluation agrees largely with the automatic evaluation. hredGAN_w performs best on both datasets although the gap is more on the MTC than on the UTC. This implies that the improvement of HRED with adversarial generation is better than with variational generation (VHRED). In addition, looking at the actual samples from the generator outputs in Table 6 shows that hredGAN, especially hredGAN_w, performs better than (V)HRED. While other models produce short and generic ut-

terances, hredGAN_w mostly yields informative responses. For example, in the first dialogue in Table 6, when the speaker is sarcastic about "the man upstairs", hredGAN_w responds with the most coherent utterance with respect to the dialogue history. We see similar behavior across other samples. We also note that although hredGAN_u's responses are the longest on Ubuntu (in line with the NASL score), the responses are less informative compared to hredGAN_w resulting in a lower human evaluation score. We reckon this might be due to a mismatch between utterance-level noise and word-level discrimination or lack of capacity to capture the data distribution using single noise distribution. We hope to investigate this further in the future.

Discriminator Performance: Although only hredGAN uses a discriminator, the observed discriminator behavior is interesting. We observe that the discriminator score is generally reasonable with longer, more informative and more persona-related responses receiving higher scores as shown in Table 2. It worth to note that this behavior, although similar to the behavior of a human judge is learned without supervision. Moreover, the discriminator seems to have learned to assign an average score to more frequent or generic responses such as "I don't know," "I'm not sure," and so on, and high score to rarer answers. That's why we sample a modified noise distribution during inference so that the generator can produce rarer utterances that will be scored high by the discriminator.

6 Conclusion and Future Work

In this paper, we have introduced an adversarial learning approach that addresses response diversity and control of generator outputs, using an HRED-derived generator and discriminator. The proposed system outperforms existing state-of-the-art (V)HRED models for generating responses in multi-turn dialogue with respect to automatic and human evaluations. The performance improvement of the adversarial generation (hredGAN) over the variational generation (VHRED) comes from the combination of adversarial training and inference which helps to address the lack of diversity and contextual relevance in maximum likelihood based generative dialogue models. Our analysis also concludes that the word-level noise injection seems to perform better in general.

References

D. Bahdanau, K. Cho, and Y. Bengio. 2015. Neural machine translation by jointly learning to align and translate. In *Proceedings of International Conference of Learning Representation (ICLR 2015)*.

R. E. Banchs. 2012. Movie-dic: A movie dialogue corpus for research and development. In *Proceedings of the 50th Annual Meeting of the Association for Computational Linguistics*, pages 203–207.

E. Bruni and R. Fernndez. 2018. Adversarial evaluation for open-domain dialogue generation. In *Proceedings of the 18th Annual SIGdial Meeting*.

T. Che, Y. Li, R. Zhang, R. D. Hjelm, W. Li, Y. Song, and Y. Bengio. 2017. Maximum-likelihood augmented discrete generative adversarial networks. In *arXiv preprint arXiv:1702.07983*.

K. Cho, B. Merrienboer, C. Gulcehre, D. Bahdanau, F. Bougares, H. Schwenk, and Y. Bengio. 2014. Learning phrase representations using rnn encoder-decoder for statistical machine translation. In *Proceedings of International Conference of Learning Representation (ICLR 2015)*, pages 1724–1734.

X. Glorot and Y. Bengio. 2010. Understanding the difficulty of training deep feedforward neural networks. In *International conference on artificial intelligence and statistics*.

I. J. Goodfellow, J. Pouget-Abadie, M. Mirza, B. Xu, D. Warde-Farley, S. Ozair, A. Courville, and Y. Bengio. 2014. Generative adversarial nets. In *Proceedings of Advances in Neural Information Processing Systems (NIPS 2014)*.

P. Isola, J. Y. Zhu, T. Zhou, and A. A. Efros. 2017. Image-to-image translation with conditional adversarial networks. In *Conference on Computer Vision and Pattern Recognition (CVPR, 2017)*.

S. Jean, K. Cho, R. Memisevic, and Y. Bengio. 2015. On using very large target vocabulary for neural machine translation. In *arXiv preprint arXiv:1412.2007*.

A. Kannan and O. Vinyals. 2017. Adversarial evaluation of dialogue models. In *arXiv preprint arXiv:1701.08198v1*.

A. Lamb, A. Goyah, Y. Zhang, S. Zhang, A. Courville, and Y. Bengio. 2016. Professor forcing: A new algorithm for training recurrent networks. In *Proceedings of Advances in Neural Information Processing Systems (NIPS 2016)*.

J. Li, M. Galley, C. Brockett, J. Gao, and B. Dolan. 2016a. A diversity-promoting objective function for neural conversation models. In *Proceedings of NAACL-HLT*.

J. Li, W. Monroe, A. Ritter, M. Galley, J. Gao, and D. Jurafsky. 2016b. Deep reinforcement learning for dialogue generation. In *arXiv preprint arXiv:arXiv:arXiv:1606.01541v4*.

J. Li, W. Monroe, T. Shi, A. Ritter, and D. Jurafsky. 2017. Adversarial learning for neural dialogue generation. In *arXiv preprint arXiv:1701.06547*.

C. Y. Lin. 2014. Rouge: a package for automatic evaluation of summaries. In *Proceedings of the Workshop on Text Summarization Branches Out*.

C. Liu, R. Lowe, I. V. Serban, M. Noseworthy, L. Charlin, and J. Pineau. 2016. How not to evaluate your dialogue system: An empirical study of unsupervised evaluation metrics for dialogue response generation. In *Proceedings of EMNLP*, pages 2122–2132.

M. T. Luong, I. Sutskever, Q. V. Le, O. Vinyals, and W. Zaremba. 2015. Addressing the rare word problem in neural machine translation. In *Proceedings of the 53rd Annual Meeting of the Association for Computational Linguistics*.

K. Papineni, S. Roukos, T. Ward, and W. Zhu. 2002. Bleu: A method for automatic evalution of machine translation. In *Proceedings of the 40th Annual Meeting of the Association for Computational Linguistics*, pages 311–318.

I. Serban, A. Sordoni, Y. Bengio, A. Courville, and J. Pineau. 2016. Building end-to-end dialogue systems using generative hierarchical neural network models. In *Proceedings of The Thirtieth AAAI Conference on Artificial Intelligence (AAAI 2016)*, pages 3776–3784.

I. V. Serban, T. Klinger, G. Tesauro, K. Talamadupula, B. Zhou, Y. Bengio, and A. Courville. 2017a. Multiresolution recurrent neural networks: An application to dialogue response generation. In *Proceedings of The Thirty-first AAAI Conference on Artificial Intelligence (AAAI 2017)*.

I. V. Serban, A. Sordoni, R. Lowe, L. Charlin, J. Pineau, A. Courville, and Y. Bengio. 2017b. A hierarchical latent variable encoder-decoder model for generating dialogue. In *Proceedings of The Thirty-first AAAI Conference on Artificial Intelligence (AAAI 2017)*.

I. Sutskever, O. Vinyals, and Q. Le. 2014. Sequence to sequence learning with neural networks. In *Proceedings of Advances in Neural Information Processing Systems (NIPS)*, pages 3104–3112.

O. Vinyals and Q. Le. 2015. A neural conversational model. In *Proceedings of ICML Deep Learning Workshop*.

R. J. Williams and D. Zipser. 1989. A learning algorithm for continually running fully recurrent neural networks. *Neural computation*, 1(2):270–280.

C. Xing, W. Wu, Y. Wu, M. Zhou, Y. Huang, and W. Ma. 2017. Hierarchical recurrent attention network for response generation. In *arXiv preprint arXiv:1701.07149*.

Z. Xu, B. Liu, B. Wang, S. Chengjie, X. Wang, Z. Wang, and C. Qi. 2017. Neural response generation via gan with an approximate embedding layer. In *EMNLP*.

L. Yu, W. Zhang, J. Wang, and Y. Yu. 2017. Seqgan: sequence generative adversarial nets with policy gradient. In *Proceedings of The Thirty-first AAAI Conference on Artificial Intelligence (AAAI 2017)*.

Y. Zhang, M. Galley, J. Gao, Z. Gan, X. Li, C. Brockett, and B. Dolan. 2018. Generating informative and diverse conversational responses via adversarial information maximization. In *arXiv preprint arXiv:arXiv:1809.05972v5*.

Y. Zhang, Z. Gan, K. Fan, Z. Chen, R. Henao, D. Shen, and L. Carin. 2017. Adversarial feature matching for text generation. In *arXiv preprint arXiv:1706.03850*.

A   Ablation Experiments

Before proposing the above adversarial learning framework for multi-turn dialogue, we carried out some experiments.

A.1   Generator:

We consider two main factors here, i.e., addition of an attention memory and injection of Gaussian noise into the generator input.

A.1.1   Addition of Attention Memory

First, we noted that by adding an additional attention memory to the HRED generator, we improved the test set perplexity score by more than 12 and 25 points on the MTC and UDC respectively as shown in Table 4. The addition of attention also shows strong performance at autoregressive inference across multiple metrics as well as an observed improvement in response quality. Hence the decision for the modified HRED generator.

A.1.2   Injection of Noise

Before injecting noise into the generator, we first train hredGAN without noise. The result is also reported in 4. We observe accelerated generator training but without an appreciable improvement in performance. It seems the discrimination task is very easy since there is no stochasticity in the generator output. Therefore, the adversarial feedback does not meaningfully impact the generator weight update.

Finally, we also notice that even with noise injection, there is no appreciable improvement in the auto-regressive performance if we sample with

$L = 1$ even though the perplexity is higher. However, as we increase L, producing L responses per turn, the discriminator's adversarial selection gives a better performance as reported in Table 1.

Therefore, we conclude that the combination of adversarial training and adversarial inference helps to address the lack of diversity and contextual relevance observed in the generated responses.

A.2   Discriminator:

Before deciding on the word-level discrimination, we experimented with utterance-level discrimination. The utterance-level discriminator trains very quickly but it leads to mostly generic responses from the generator. We also note that utterance-level discriminator scores are mostly extreme (i.e., either low or high). Since we had used a convolutional neural network discriminator (Yu et al., 2017) in our experiments, we hope to investigate this further with other architectures.

A.3   Adversarial Training:

Lastly, we also tried a basic policy gradient approach (Li et al., 2017), where word-level discriminator score is used as a reward for each generated word token, but this leads to training instability. This is probably due to the instability of Monte Carlo sampling over a large vocabulary size. We believe this might improve with other sampling methods such as importance sampling and hope to investigate this further in the future.

Model	Teacher Forcing	Autoregression			
	Perplexity	BLEU-2	ROUGE-2	DISTINCT-1/2	NASL
MTC					
HRED	31.92/36.00	0.0474	0.0384	0.0026/0.0056	0.535
HRED+Attn	18.70/19.02	0.0425	0.2239	0.0397/0.1567	0.527
hredGAN_no_noise	18.93/19.19	0.0355	0.1839	0.0272/0.0978	0.471
UDC					
HRED	69.39/86.40	0.0177	0.0483	0.0203/0.0466	0.892
HRED+Attn	43.43/43.92	0.0140	0.0720	0.0473/0.1262	0.760
hredGAN_no_noise	43.48/44.04	0.0123	0.0827	0.0398/0.1147	0.908

Table 4: Generator Performance: HRED, HRED+Attn and hredGAN without noise

Model	Response
Context_0	<person> i ' ve raised my rate . i might even cut my sessions to forty minutes .
HRED	i ' m sorry , <person> .
VHRED	<person>, <person>, <person>, <person> .
hredGAN_w	<person> , i ' m sorry , but i ' m not sure if you ' re really a very good guy .
hredGAN_u	i ' ll never see them again , <person> .
Context_0	i ' m going to handle this exactly the way your father would have handled this . i ' ve got it solved .
Context_1	you ' ve got it solved ? where is she ?
HRED	i don ' t know .
VHRED	<person>, , i ' m sorry.
hredGAN_w	to the end of a beautiful woman who will be very happy .
hredGAN_u	i ' m sorry , i just didn ' t know –
Context_0	of course not ! ¡person¿ ' s like a daughter to me . her father and i taught at university together . a good man , but he never listened .
HRED	i ' m sorry , <person>.
VHRED	<person>, mr . <person> .
hredGAN_w	<person> , i know it ' s been all six years since i told him about you .
hredGAN_u	i ' m sure you didn ' t , but i would have done a little more .
Context_0	of course not ! ¡person¿ ' s like a daughter to me . her father and i taught at university together . a good man , but he never listened .
Context_1	neither did i .
HRED	i ' m sorry , <person>.
VHRED	<person> , you ' re a <unk> .
hredGAN_w	<person>, i know you ' re think about it . think it ' ll be time , right ?
hredGAN_u	i ' ll be the first one . if it did you , you ' ll be it .
Context_0	come on , <person> , we could have a great week up in vermont .
Context_1	i see what you mean . but wednesday we ' ve got to be back in new york .
HRED	<person> .
VHRED	<person> , i don ' t know what you ' re going to do .
hredGAN_w	<person> , i know . i ' m kind of busy here .
hredGAN_u	i ' m sorry , i can ' t .
Context_0	isabel ?
Context_1	hi .
HRED	that ' s what i ' m talking about .
VHRED:	you ' re not going to be a <unk> , <person> .
hredGAN_w	<person> ?
hredGAN_u	what do you want to know ?
Context_0	you understand mr . <person> is constantly barraged with nuisance litigation and irs audits .
Context_1	of course .
HRED	that ' s right , <person> .
VHRED:	<person> , you ' re going to be a <unk> of the <unk> .
hredGAN_w	<person> , i ' m sure , but you ' re probably still in to the new <person> ' s house , huh ?
hredGAN_u	you ' re gon na be a little boy , and i ' m not gon na get out !
Context_0	<person> ' t go into my room , she ' s asleep .
Context_1	<person> , but the nanny , mrs . <person> she wants to see her .
HRED	i ' m sorry , <person> .
VHRED:	<person> , mr . <person> .
hredGAN_w	<person> , i know . but she ' s never seen me anyway .
hredGAN_u	i ' m sorry i didn ' t know what to say .
Context_0	what was that for ?
Context_1	i ' d forgotten how exciting it is working together .
HRED	i ' m sorry , <person> .
VHRED:	<person> , <person> . i don ' t know .
hredGAN_w	i ' m sorry , <person> . so many people are so interested , but you ' re a very nice guy .
hredGAN_u	i ' ve always been so sure to <person> .
Context_0	a teacher ' s .
Context_1	oh my god .
HRED	i ' m sorry , <person> .
VHRED:	<person> , <person> ' t worry about it . i don ' t know what you ' re doing .
hredGAN_w	i ' m sorry . i didn ' t mean to . i didn ' t mean to hurt you . i just wanted you
hredGAN_u	<person> , i don ' t want to be your friend .
Context_0	i took the initiative .
Context_1	you haven ' t been given an assignment in this case .
HRED	<person> .
VHRED:	<person> , <person> , <person> , <person> . i ' m not going to get out of the <unk> .
hredGAN_w	i ' m not sure . <continued_utterance> i ' m not gon na do you this shit anyway , <person> .
hredGAN_u	<person> , i guess i didn ' t .

Table 5: Additional sample responses of HRED, VHRED and hredGAN on Movie.

Model	Response
Context_0	what's the command you are running to chroot and the error message you get in return?
Context_1	i mountded the device sudo mount /dev/sda1 /mnt - that works - then sudo chroot /mnt – error is no such file or command
HRED	what 's the problem ?
VHRED	is there a way to do that ? what do you mean ?
hredGAN_w	I have no idea , I just did a sudo fdisk and it said it was mounted
hredGAN_u	I ' m trying to get the latest version of ubuntu , but I ' m getting a lot of problems .
Context_0	Hmm, have you checked that ICMP is being allowed all the way through and that the server responds to other ICMP requests?
Context_1	now i can ping it (i had to enable the lzo compression on client) i cannot reach the remote subnet adding a rule in the firewall forward the lan to vpn
HRED	what 's the problem ?
VHRED	I don't know what you want to do
hredGAN_w	I have no idea , I ' m just trying to get the ip address from the router to the router"
hredGAN_u	I ' m not sure if that ' s the case , but I ' m not sure if it ' s a good idea to have a look at the output .
Context_0	The netboot one is suppose to download packages from the net.
HRED	I don't know what you want to do .
VHRED	how do I do that ?
hredGAN_w	I ' m not sure of a command to do so I can just install the ubuntu . iso and burn a new iso
hredGAN_u	you can ' t have a look at the man page . . .
Context_0	The netboot one is suppose to download packages from the net.
Context_1	like the ones to be installed? or the installed to be run?
HRED	I don't know what the problem is .
VHRED	is there a way to install the package manager ?
hredGAN_w	you don ' t need to install the whole system , just install the ubuntu installer
hredGAN_u	I ' m trying to install a _UNK version of ubuntu , but I ' m trying to install it on my laptop .
Context_0	You trying to mount it open with the password?
HRED	I have to do that , but I have a problem with the same problem .
VHRED	is there a way to do ?
hredGAN_w	yes , I ' m not sure if it ' s mounted or not
hredGAN_u	I ' m trying to install the latest version of Ubuntu , but I ' m running on a _UNK .
Context_0	are you using lvm for your root partition?
HRED	yes , but I have a problem with a new user , but I don't want to do that .
VHRED	what is the best way to do that ? what is that ?
hredGAN_w	yes , I ' m on a live system , I ' m trying to use the partition to boot from windows
hredGAN_u	I ' m not sure if it ' s a good idea to have a backup of the system . . .
Context_0	are you using lvm for your root partition?
Context_1	i have the same config working on a 10.04 box. It appears in 12.04 lvm is on upstart and multipath is not. i do use lvm for my root folder nifty, is there any way to work around it? have you heard of anyone posting a bug about this to have it looked at? darn.... well i hope they can fix this eventually i hope they keep initrd around and move everything to upstart. Upstart is not easy to setup for programs that don't come packaged for upstart.
HRED	I don't know what the problem is , but I don't know what the problem is . ?
VHRED	is there a way to do that ? or **unknown** ?
hredGAN_w	you can also try the live cd and see if you can get it back up the live"
hredGAN_u	I ' m trying to get my wireless working on my laptop , but I ' m getting to the point that I can be able to use the wireless card to get the wireless working .
Context_0	are you using lvm for your root partition?
Context_1	i have the same config working on a 10.04 box. It appears in 12.04 lvm is on upstart and multipath is not. i do use lvm for my root folder nifty, is there any way to work around it? have you heard of anyone posting a bug about this to have it looked at? darn.... well i hope they can fix this eventually i hope they keep initrd around and move everything to upstart. Upstart is not easy to setup for programs that don't come packaged for upstart.
Context_2	yes, because i cant supply it at boot time, i want the truecrypt drive to come up by itself without manual intervention
HRED	what is the problem ?
VHRED	what do you mean ?
hredGAN_w	you can also mount a new one and put the mount command to the mount point"
hredGAN_u	I ' m trying to get my sound working , but I ' m trying to get my sound working .

Table 6: Additional sample responses of HRED, VHRED and hredGAN on Ubuntu.

Relevant and Informative Response Generation using Pointwise Mutual Information

Junya Takayama[†] and **Yuki Arase**[††]
[†]Graduate School of Information Science and Technology, Osaka University
[‡]Artificial Intelligence Research Center (AIRC), AIST
{takayama.junya, arase}@ist.osaka-u.ac.jp

Abstract

A sequence-to-sequence model tends to generate generic responses with little information for input utterances. To solve this problem, we propose a neural model that generates relevant and informative responses. Our model has simple architecture to enable easy application to existing neural dialogue models. Specifically, using positive pointwise mutual information, it first identifies keywords that frequently co-occur in responses given an utterance. Then, the model encourages the decoder to use the keywords for response generation. Experiment results demonstrate that our model successfully diversifies responses relative to previous models.

1 Introduction

Neural networks are common approaches to building chat-bots. Vinyals and Le (2015) have proposed a neural dialogue model using sequence-to-sequence (Seq2Seq) networks (Sutskever et al., 2014) and achieved fluent response generation. Because a Seq2Seq model uses a word-by-word loss function at the time of training, any words outside the reference are penalized equally. Consequently, the Seq2Seq model tends to generate generic responses that consist of frequent words, such as "Yes" and "I don't know." This is a central concern in neural dialogue generation. To tackle this problem, Li et al. (2016) proposed a model for considering mutual dependency between an utterance and response modeled by maximum mutual information (MMI). However, their model disregarded the aspect of informativeness of responses, which is also important for user experience of chat-bots.

To solve this problem, we propose a response generation model that outputs diverse words while preserving relevance in response to the input utterance. In our model, Positive Pointwise Mutual

Information (PPMI) identifies keywords from a large-scale conversational corpus that are likely to appear in the response to an input utterance. Then, the model modifies the loss function in a Seq2Seq model to reward responses using the identified keywords. In order to calculate the loss function using the words output by the decoder, we need to sample words from the probability distribution of the output layer. Hence, we apply the Gumbel-Softmax trick (Jang et al., 2017) as a differentiable pseudo-sampling method.

Experiments using a Japanese dialogue corpus crawled from Twitter and OpenSubtitles revealed that the proposed model outperformed (Li et al., 2016) for all automatic evaluation metrics for correspondence to references and diversity in outputs.

2 Related Work

The generic response problem has been actively studied. Yao et al. (2016) and Nakamura et al. (2019) proposed models that constrain decoders to directly suppress generation of frequent words. Yao et al. (2016) diversified the response by a loss function in which words with high inverse document frequency values are preferred. Nakamura et al. (2019) proposed a loss function that adds weights based on the inverse of the word frequency. Xing et al. (2017) proposed a model using topic words extracted from utterances. Their model ensembles words predicted using the topic words and the words predicted by the decoder.

All of the methods described above only focus on the amount of a information in a response. Therefore, generated responses tend to lack relevance to input utterances. MMI-bidi (Li et al., 2016) solves this problem by approximating the PMI between the utterance Q and the generated

Proceedings of the 1st Workshop on NLP for Conversational AI, pages 133–138
Florence, Italy, August 1, 2019. ©2019 Association for Computational Linguistics

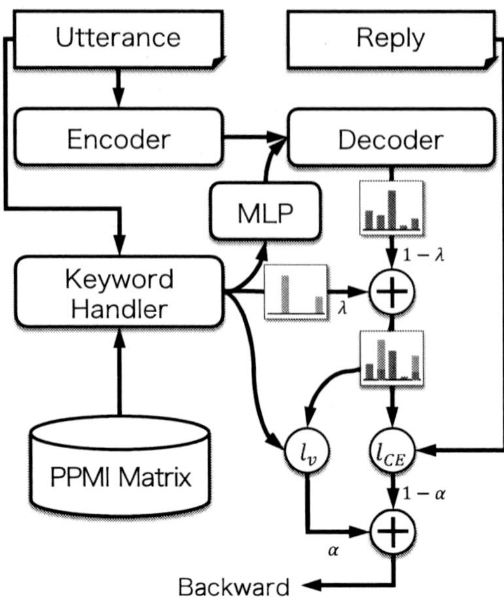

Figure 1: Outline of the proposed model

response R as follows:

$$\mathrm{PMI}(Q, R) = (1 - \lambda) \log P(R|Q) + \lambda \log P(Q|R). \quad (1)$$

Here, both $P(R|Q)$ and $P(Q|R)$ are computed by independent Seq2Seq models. Specifically, the N-best candidate responses generated by the former model are re-ranked by Equation (1). MMI-bidi exhibited a strong performance for diversifying responses while preserving relevance to an input utterance. However, its effects depend on the diversities of the N-best candidate responses. If these responses are diverse, MMI-bidi can improve futher.

3 Proposed Model

Figure 1 shows the outline of the proposed model. It first identifies keywords that strongly co-occur between utterances and their responses in a training corpus using PPMI (section 3.1). The decoder then uses Gumbel-Softmax to sample words in the output layer (section 3.3). Finally, it computes the proportion of output words matching the keywords, and add weights to the loss function (section 3.4).

3.1 Keywords Retrieval Based on Positive Pointwise Mutual Information

The keyword handler retrieves words that are likely to appear in the response to a certain input

utterance based on PPMI, calculated in advance from an entire training corpus. Let $P_Q(x)$ and $P_R(x)$ be probabilities that the word x will appear in a certain utterance and response sentences, respectively. Also, let $P(x, y)$ be the probability that the words x and y exist in the utterance and response sentence pair. PPMI is calculated as follows:

$$\mathrm{PPMI}(x, y) = \max \left(\log_2 \frac{P(x, y)}{P_Q(x) \cdot P_R(y)}, 0 \right).$$

The pair of x and y and its PPMI score are saved in the PPMI Matrix in Figure 1. At the time of response generation, the keyword handler looks up the PPMI Matrix. Let the word set of a certain utterance sentence be $Q = \{q_1, q_2, \ldots, q_L\}$, and the vocabulary in the decoder be $V_R = \{v_{R_1}, v_{R_2}, \ldots, v_{R_N}\}$. The keyword-score of a word $v_{R_n} \in V_R$ is defined as follows:

$$\sum_{q \in Q} \mathrm{PPMI}\,(q, v_{R_n}).$$

Keyword-scores are calculated for all words in V_R. Then top-k words are set as keywords V_{Pred} used in the loss function.

3.2 Decoding Response Sentences using Retrieved Keywords

The decoder first receives a vector $\mathbf{v_f}$ consisting of keyword-scores for all words in the vocabulary, and non-linearly transforms v_f through a multi-layer perceptron (MLP). This vector is concatenated with the output of the encoder, and then set to the initial state of the decoder. By doing so, we expect that the decoder considers the keyword-scores. In order to directly boost the probability to output the keywords, we add weighted $\mathbf{v_f}$ to the decoder output vector $\pi_\mathbf{i}$ at each time step i. The final decoder output $\tilde{\pi}_\mathbf{i}$ is represented by the following equation:

$$\tilde{\pi}_\mathbf{i} = (1 - \lambda_i) \cdot \pi_\mathbf{i} + \lambda_i \cdot \mathbf{v_f}.$$

λ_i balances the effects of the decoder output and v_f. λ_i is calculated as follows based on the current intermediate state $\mathbf{h}_i$ of the decoder:

$$\lambda_i = \sigma \left(W^{gate} \mathbf{h}_i + \mathbf{b}^{gate} \right),$$

where W^{gate} is a trainable weight matrix, $\mathbf{b}^{gate}$ is a bias term, and $\sigma(\cdot)$ is a sigmoid function.

3.3 Pseudo-sampling of Generated Words using Gumbel-Softmax

In order to determine whether the decoder generated words in V_{Pred}, it is necessary to sample words generated by the decoder. However, sampling based on argmax, which is generally used at the decoder, disallows back propagation because of its discrete nature. Jang et al. (2017) proposed Gumbel-Softmax which performs pseudo sampling from the probability distribution to allow back propagation. Gumbel-Softmax performs the following calculations for a probability distribution π (corresponding to the output layer in the decoder) for k classes:

$$y_i = \frac{\exp((\log(\pi_i) + g_i)/\tau)}{\sum_{j=1}^{k} \exp((\log(\pi_j) + g_j)/\tau)}.$$

Here, τ is a hyperparameter called temperature. Smaller tau makes the vector closer to one-hot but the dispersion of the gradient becomes larger. g_i is obtained by the following calculation using uniform distribution $u_i \sim \mathrm{Uniform}(0, 1)$:

$$g_i = -\log(-\log(u_i)).$$

In the proposed model, Gumbel-Softmax is applied to the final decoder output vector $\tilde{\pi}$ at each time step i as in Equation (2). Then, we obtain the differentiable pseudo-bag-of-words vector $\mathbf{B}$.

$$\mathbf{B} = \sum_{i=1}^{T} \mathrm{GumbelSoftmax}(\tilde{\pi}_i). \tag{2}$$

3.4 Loss function

We design a loss function l_v which value decreases as words contained in V_{Pred} are generated. Thus, the decoder outputs more words that strongly co-occur with the input utterance. Specifically, when $t(b_n)$ is the word corresponding to the n-th index in $\mathbf{B}$, l_v is defined as follows.

$$l_v = -\sum_{n=0}^{N} f(b_n, V_{\mathrm{Pred}}),$$

$$f(b_n, V_{\mathrm{Pred}}) = \begin{cases} \min(b_n, 1) & (t(b_n) \in V_{\mathrm{Pred}}), \\ 0 & (\text{otherwise}). \end{cases} \tag{3}$$

We use $\min(b_n, 1)$ in Equation (3) to avoid adding a reward when a keyword is generated multiple times. This aims to suppress the decoder outputs the same word many times.

Finally, the loss function $\mathcal{L}$ is defined as a liner interpolation of l_{CE} of the cross-entropy error and the l_v:

$$\mathcal{L} = (1 - \alpha) \cdot l_{CE} + \alpha \cdot l_v.$$

α is a hyperparameter that balances the degree of rewards based on the keywords.

4 Experiments

We empirically evaluate how our model avoids generic responses to generate relevant and informative responses.

4.1 Datasets

We used two datasets, OpenSubtitles (English) and Twitter (Japanese). The details of each dataset are as follows.

OpenSubtitles OpenSubtitles (Tiedemann, 2009) is a large scale open-domain corpus composed of movie subtitles.

Like Vinyal et al. (Vinyals and Le, 2015) and Li et al (Li et al., 2016), we assumed that each line of the subtitles represents an independent utterance, and constructed a single-turn dialogue corpus by regarding two consecutive utterances as an utterance-response pair. We randomly sampled 2 million utterance-response pairs. All sentences were tokenized using the Punkt Sentence Tokenizer of nltk [1].

Twitter We crawled conversations in Japanese Twitter using "@" mention as a clue. A single-turn dialogue corpus was constructed by regarding a tweet and its reply as an utterance-response pair. The dataset consists of about 1.3 million utterance-response pairs. All sentences were tokenized by MeCab [2].

In both datasets, 10k utterance-response pairs were separated as validation data, another 10k were separated as test data, and the rest were used as training data.

4.2 Comparison Methods

We compared our model to previous models. The baseline is the standard Seq2Seq (**Seq2Seq**). We also compared to MMI-bidi (**Seq2Seq + MMI**)

---

[1] https://www.nltk.org/
[2] http://taku910.github.io/mecab/

	BLEU	NIST	dist-1	dist-2	ent-4	length	repetition
Proposed + MMI	**1.577**	**0.872**	**0.050**	**0.187**	**8.536**	8.064	1.551
Proposed	1.569	0.837	0.044	0.148	7.327	7.520	1.377
Seq2Seq + MMI	1.373	0.739	0.009	0.032	5.600	7.566	1.223
Seq2Seq	1.374	0.687	0.005	0.015	4.070	8.025	1.095
Reference	100.000	16.498	0.086	0.482	10.647	7.671	1.000

Table 1: Results on the OpenSubtitle corpus (English)

	BLEU	NIST	dist-1	dist-2	ent-4	length	repetition
Proposed + MMI	**2.611**	0.573	**0.071**	**0.204**	**8.979**	7.913	1.832
Proposed	2.591	**0.583**	0.068	0.188	8.738	8.044	1.902
Seq2Seq + MMI	2.262	0.304	0.043	0.102	7.578	6.791	1.416
Seq2Seq	2.237	0.318	0.040	0.091	7.103	6.920	1.518
Reference	100.000	16.562	0.105	0.496	11.311	12.262	1.000

Table 2: Results on the Twitter corpus (Japanese)

because it is the most relevant method for diversifying responses. In addition, we combined our model with MMI-bidi (**Proposed + MMI**) to see whether it contributes to diversification of the N-best candidates.

4.3 Evaluation Metrics

We employed several automatic evaluation metrics. **BLEU** and **NIST** measure the validity of generated sentences in comparison with references. BLEU (Papineni et al., 2002) measures the correspondence between n-grams in generated responses and those in reference sentences. Following Papineni et al. (2002), we used the average of BLEU scores from 1-gram to 4-gram in the experiment. NIST (Doddington, 2002) also measures the correspondence between generated responses and reference sentences. Unlike BLEU, NIST places lower weights on frequent n-grams, *i.e.*, NIST regards content words as more important than function words. In the experiment, we used the average of NIST from 1-gram to 5-gram.

In addition, **dist** and **ent** measure the diversity of generated responses. Dist (Li et al., 2016) is defined as the number of distinct n-grams in generated responses divided by the total number of generated tokens. On the other hand, ent (Zhang et al., 2018) considers the frequency of n-grams in generated responses:

$$\text{ent} = -\frac{1}{\sum_w F(w)} \sum_{w \in X} F(w) \log \frac{F(w)}{\sum_w F(w)},$$

where X is a set of n-grams output by the system, and $F(w)$ computes the frequency of each n-gram.

In this paper, we focus on automatic evaluation. Human evaluation is our future work.

4.4 Parameter Settings

For all models, we implemented the encoder and decoder of each model using 1-layer GRUs. The dimension of the GRU was set to 512. However, only the decoder of the proposed model used 1024-dimensional GRU. This is because the initial state of the decoder is the concatenation of the keyword-score vector and the output from the encoder (512-dimension for each). Both the encoder and decoder had a word embedding layer of 256 dimensions.

The vocabulary consisted of words that appeared more than 15 times in the training data. Words that occured less than 15 times were replaced with the "<unk>" token. The vocabulary size was 41.5k for the Twitter model and 20.9k for the OpenSubtitles model.

4.5 Results and Error Analysis

The left sides of Tables 1 and 2 show BLEU, NIST, dist, and ent scores for OpenSubtitles and Twitter, respectively. Our model (Proposed) outperformed Seq2Seq and MMI-bidi (Seq2Seq) in all evaluation metrics across the datasets. Furthermore, our model combined with MMI-bidi (Proposed+MMI) achieved the best performance, except for NIST, on the Twitter dataset. This result demonstrates that our method successfully gener-

Input	oh, we just actually wanted to be alone
Reference	get me out of here
Proposed+MMI	i wanted to be alone
Seq2Seq+MMI	you know what ?
Input	should we call an ambulance ?
Reference	praise the lord !
Proposed+MMI	we 're going to have a call from the ambulance
Seq2Seq+MMI	i don 't think so
Input	are you tired already ?
Reference	you 're such a weakling
Proposed+MMI	i 'm tired of getting warmed up
Seq2Seq+MMI	yes i 'm fine
Input	i have no idea how it was spread
Reference	not from me
Proposed+MMI	i don 't know how much longer i can stand up
Seq2Seq+MMI	i <unk>never been able to find a way
Input	why do you have to carry the burden of someone else 's life ?
Reference	he 's my father
Proposed+MMI	because you 're the best commodity in the living room
Seq2Seq+MMI	i don 't know
Input	the little guy was kinda funny lookin
Reference	in what way ?
Proposed+MMI	i kinda like him kinda funny funny
Seq2Seq+MMI	i don 't know what you 're talking about
Input	bishop wood at st <unk>'s cathedral
Reference	holy christ blanche
Proposed+MMI	he was baptized in a parson 's church and he was baptized
Seq2Seq+MMI	he was the king of <unk><unk>

Table 3: Example responses generated by the proposed model and (Li et al., 2016)

ates diverse responses, which effectively improves the N-best candidates reranked by MMI-bidi. It is notable that improvements on NIST, which appreciates less frequent n-grams, support this idea the proposed model improves the informativeness of responses. The improvement is larger on the Twitter dataset, where the proposed method (Proposed) achieved NIST score 0.265 points higher than Seq2Seq even though MMI-bidi is inferior to Seq2Seq.

The example responses generated by Proposed+MMI and Seq2Seq+MMI using OpenSubtitles are shown in Table 3. The examples from the top to the third rows show that the proposed model generates more content words relevant to the content words in the utterance. On the other hand, Seq2Seq+MMI ended up generating fewer informative responses using generic words. The fourth and fifth examples show that the proposed model generated responses with little relevance to the in-

put, although they were more informative than the responses generated by Seq2Seq+MMI.

The last two examples show a drawback of the proposed model, *i.e.*, which is over-generation of the same word. For quantitative evaluation, we computed the repetition rate (Le et al., 2017) on the test data, which measures the meaningless repetition of words. The repetition rate is defined as:

$$\text{repetition\_rate} = \frac{1}{N} \sum_{i=1}^{N} \frac{1 + r\left(\widetilde{y}_i\right)}{1 + r\left(Y_i\right)},$$

where $\widetilde{y}_i$ is the i-th generated sentence in the test data, Y_i is its reference, and N is the total number of test sentences. The function $r(\cdot)$ measures the repetition as the difference between the number of words and that of unique words in a sentence:

$$r(X) = \text{len}(X) - \text{len}(\text{set}(X)),$$

where X means words in a sentence, $\text{len}(X)$ computes the number of items in X, and $\text{set}(X)$ removes duplicate items in X. The average lengths of generated responses and repetition rates are shown on the right sides of Tables 1 and 2. The results show that the proposed models (Proposed and Proposed+MMI) tend to generate longer responses than Seq2Seq, but their repetition rates are also higher. This may be caused by time-invariant keyword-scores, despite the fact that the decoder output changes over time. In the future, we will update the keyword-score vector to avoid repetition in responses.

5 Conclusion

Aiming at generating diverse responses while preserving relevance to the input, we proposed a model that identifies keywords using PPMI and promoted their generation in the decoder. Evaluation results using English and Japanese conversational corpora show that in comparison with (Li et al., 2016), the proposed model achieved better performance in terms of correspondence to references and diversity of output. On the other hand, we found that the proposed model has a tendency of over-generation.

As future work, we will conduct human evaluation and qualitative analysis. We will also investigate the effects of the hyper-parameter α on overall performance. We also plan to develop a mechanism for suppressing over-generation.

Acknowledgments

This project is funded by Microsoft Research Asia, Microsoft Japan Co., Ltd., and JSPS KAKENHI Grant Number JP18K11435.

References

George Doddington. 2002. Automatic Evaluation of Machine Translation Quality Using N-gram Co-Occurrence Statistics. In *Proceedings of the second international conference on Human Language Technology Research (HLT 2002)*.

Eric Jang, Shixiang Gu, and Ben Poole. 2017. Categorical Reparametarization with Gumbel-Softmax. In *Proceedings of The 5th International Conference on Learning Representations (ICLR 2017)*.

An Nguyen Le, Ander Martinez, Akifumi Yoshimoto, and Yuji Matsumoto. 2017. Improving Sequence to Sequence Neural Machine Translation by Utilizing Syntactic Dependency Information. In *Proceedings of the The 8th International Joint Conference on Natural Language Processing (IJCNLP 2017)*, pages 21–29.

Jiwei Li, Michel Galley, Chris Brockett, Jianfeng Gao, and Bill Dolan. 2016. A Diversity-Promoting Objective Function for Neural Conversation Models. In *Proceedings of The 15th Annual Conference of the North American Chapter of the Association for Computational Linguistics: Human Language Technologies (NAACL-HLT 2016)*, pages 110–119.

Ryo Nakamura, Katsuhito Sudoh, Koichiro Yoshino, and Satoshi Nakamura. 2019. Another Diversity-Promoting Objective Function for Neural Dialogue Generation. In *Proceedings of The Second AAAI Workshop on Reasoning and Learning for Human-Machine Dialogues (DEEP-DIAL)*.

Kishore Papineni, Salim Roukos, Todd Ward, and Wei-Jing Zhu. 2002. BLEU: A Method for Automatic Evaluation of Machine Translation. In *Proceedings of the 40th Annual Meeting of the Association for Computational Linguistics (ACL 2002)*, pages 311–318.

Ilya Sutskever, Oriol Vinyals, and Quoc V Le. 2014. Sequence to sequence learning with neural networks. In *Proceedings of The Twenty-eighth Conference on Neural Information Processing Systems (NeurIPS 2014)*, pages 3104–3112.

Jörg Tiedemann. 2009. News from opus-A collection of multilingual parallel corpora with tools and interfaces 1 Index of Subjects and Terms 13 vi News from OPUS-A Collection of Multilingual Parallel Corpora with Tools and Interfaces. *Recent advances in natural language processing*, 5:237–248.

Oriol Vinyals and Quoc V Le. 2015. A Neural Conversational Model. In *Proceedings of the 32nd International Conference on Machine Learning (ICML 2015)*.

Chen Xing, Wei Chung Wu, Yu Ping Wu, Jie Liu, Yalou Huang, Ming Zhou, and Wei-Ying Ma. 2017. Topic Aware Neural Response Generation. In *Proceedings of the Thirty-First AAAI Conference on Artificial Intelligence (AAAI 2017)*.

Kaisheng Yao, Baolin Peng, Geoffrey Zweig, and Kam-Fai Wong. 2016. An Attentional Neural Conversation Model with Improved Specificity. *arXiv preprint arXiv:1606.01292*.

Yizhe Zhang, Michel Galley, Jianfeng Gao, Zhe Gan, Xiujun Li, Chris Brockett, and Bill Dolan. 2018. Generating Informative and Diverse Conversational Responses via Adversarial Information Maximization. In *Proceedings of 32nd Conference on Neural Information Processing Systems (NeurIPS 2018)*.

Responsive and Self-Expressive Dialogue Generation

Kozo Chikai
SHIMANO INC.
tokoroten0401@gmail.com

Junya Takayama and **Yuki Arase**⋆
Osaka University
⋆Artificial Intelligence Research Center (AIRC), AIST
{takayama.junya,arase}@ist.osaka-u.ac.jp

Abstract

Generic responses frequently generated by neural models are a critical problem for user engagement in dialogue systems. For a more engaging chit-chat experience, we propose a response generation model motivated by the interpersonal process model for intimacy. It generates responsive and self-expressive replies, which are implemented as domain-awareness and sentiment-richness, respectively. Experiments empirically confirmed that our model outperformed the sequence-to-sequence model; 68.1% of our responses were domain-aware with sentiment polarities, which was only 2.7% for responses generated by the sequence-to-sequence model.

1 Introduction

Dialogue systems that conduct non-goal-oriented chat, *i.e.*, chit-chat, is an active research area. The sequence-to-sequence model (SEQ2SEQ) (Vinyals and Le, 2015; Shang et al., 2015) is commonly used for implementation, however, recent studies, *e.g.*, (Li et al., 2016a), point out that SEQ2SEQ frequently generates overly generic responses. Among different approaches to address this problem, previous studies propose to generate more engaging responses by reacting to topics in users' utterances (Xing et al., 2017) or embodying emotions (Zhou et al., 2018; Huang et al., 2018). Herein we make a step further to generate responsive and self-expressive replies simultaneously.[1]

The interpersonal process model for intimacy (Reis and Shaver, 1988) indicates that *conversational responsiveness* (Miller and Berg, 1984), *i.e.*, showing concern for what was said, and *self-expression*, *i.e.*, sharing thoughts and feelings, are primary factors to create intimacy. Motivated by this theory, we believe that the con-

---

[1] In this study, we focus on single-turn conversations, *i.e.*, generating a response to a single utterance from the user.

Domain: Baseball

User: Sugano will be the ace for Japan!
　　　（菅野は日本のエースになるよ）

Seq2Seq: Really? （そうなの？）
Our model (+): Sugano is cool!
　　　（菅野は良いですよね！）
Our model (-): No way? There is no hope for Sugano!
　　　（菅野は無理ですね！）

Domain: Pokémon GO

User: Caught my first Pikachu! So cute!!
　　　（初めてピカチュウ捕まえた！可愛い！！）

Seq2Seq: Wow, awesome! （え、まじでいいよ！）
Our model (+): Shiny Pikachu is pretty cute.
（ピカチュウの色違いがなかなか可愛いですよね）
Our model (-): Shiny Pikachu is pretty hard, indeed.
（ピカチュウの色違いが、なかなか難しいですよね）

Figure 1: Responses generated by our model and SEQ2SEQ ((+) represents a positive response and (-) represents a negative response.)

versational responsiveness and self-expression are also valid for a dialogue system to generate engaging responses. We implement the conversational responsiveness as *domain-awareness* because it effectively conveys an impression that the dialogue agent is listening to the user by responding about mentioned topics. Also, we implement the self-expression as *sentiment-richness* by representing sentiment polarity to generate subjective responses with feelings.

Specifically, the encoder predicts the domain of a user's utterance and integrates domain and utterance representations to tell the decoder the target domain explicitly. Then the decoder embodies sentiment polarity in its generation process. Fig. 1 shows real responses generated by our model. You may find that our responses react to the domains of input utterances while showing salient sentiments. On the other hand, SEQ2SEQ ends up generating generic responses.

To the best of our knowledge, this is the first study that simultaneously achieved both domain-

Proceedings of the 1st Workshop on NLP for Conversational AI, pages 139–149
Florence, Italy, August 1, 2019. ©2019 Association for Computational Linguistics

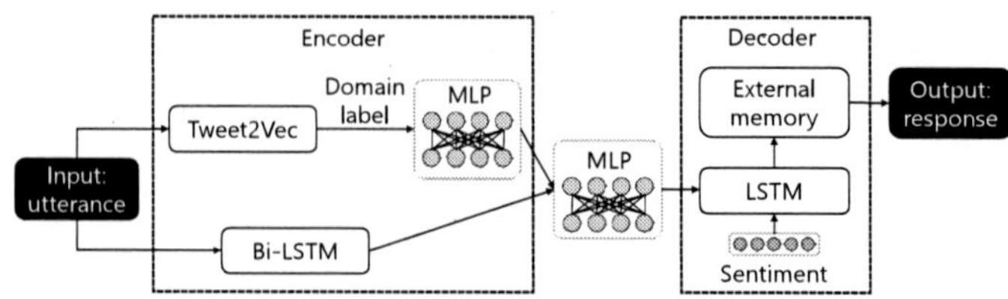

Figure 2: Architecture of the proposed model, on which the encoder is responsible for domain-awareness and the decoder takes care of embodying sentiment polarity.

aware and sentiment-rich response generation. Our contributions are twofold. First, we achieve these features in a simple architecture integrating existing methods on top of SEQ2SEQ in order to make it easily reproducible in existing dialogue systems. Second, our model utilizes fine-tuning to compensate for the training data scarcity, which is essential because there is a limited amount of domain-dependent and sentiment-rich dialogues. Our codes and scripts are publicly available.[2]

Evaluation results empirically confirmed that our model significantly outperformed SEQ2SEQ from the human perspective. Annotators judged that responses generated by our model are consistent with the utterances' domains and show salient sentiments for 89% and 72% of cases while preserving fluency and consistency. Furthermore, they judged 68.1% responses by our model as *both* domain-aware and sentiment-rich, which was only 2.7% for responses by SEQ2SEQ.

2   Related Work

The generic response problem in SEQ2SEQ is a central concern in recent studies. Different approaches have been proposed to generate diversified responses; by an objective function (Li et al., 2016a; Zhang et al., 2018b), segment-level reranking via a stochastic beam-search in a decoder (Shao et al., 2017), or by incorporating auto-encoders so that latent vectors are expressive enough for the utterance and response (Zou et al., 2018). In these approaches, balancing the diversity and coherency in a response is not trivial. Zou et al. (2018) show that metrics to measure the diversity are not proportional to human evaluation.

Another group of studies tackles the generic response problem by improving coherence in the response, which is relevant to conversational responsiveness. Approaches include reinforcement

learning (Zhang et al., 2018a) and prediction of a keyword that will be the gist of a response given an input utterance and its generation in the decoder (Mou et al., 2016; Yao et al., 2017; Wang et al., 2018). In our study, we consider domain-level coherency to achieve the conversational responsiveness similar to (Xing et al., 2017).

Several studies focus on self-expression in responses. Some add persona in dialogue agents to generate consistent responses to paraphrased input utterances (Li et al., 2016b; Zhang et al., 2018c; Qian et al., 2018). Zhou et al. (2018) conducted the first study that controls emotions in dialogue agents using two factors. The first is embedding of a desired emotion label as in (Li et al., 2016b; Huang et al., 2018). The second is internal and external memories, which control the emotional state and the output of the decoder, respectively. These previous studies propose methods to achieve *either* conversational responsiveness or self-expression. Herein we aim to achieve *both* features simultaneously.

3   Proposed Architecture

To be easily implemented on existing dialogue systems, our model design aims to be simple. We integrate TWEET2VEC (Dhingra et al., 2016) and the external memory (Zhou et al., 2018) with SEQ2SEQ (Fig. 2). While sentiments in texts are well-understood in natural language processing, emotions need more studies to be considered in practical applications. Besides, determining the appropriate emotions for a specific utterance remains problematic (Hasegawa et al., 2013). In our model, we focus on sentiments and input the embedding of a sentiment label s to the decoder, which specifies the desired sentiment to represent in a response.

3.1   Encoder

Fig. 3 shows the design of our encoder, which integrates the input utterance and its domain.

---

[2]https://github.com/KChikai/
Responsive-Dialogue-Generation

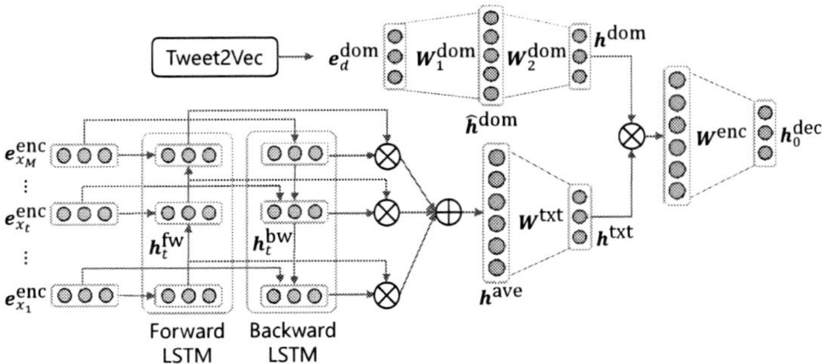

Figure 3: Design of the encoder ($\otimes$ concatenates input vectors and $\oplus$ averages them)

Input Utterance Encoding The input utterance is represented as a vector. Bi-directional recurrent neural networks empirically show superior performance in generation tasks (Bahdanau et al., 2015) because they refer to the preceding and subsequent sequences. We apply bi-directional Long Short-Term Memory (LSTM) (Hochreiter and Schmidhuber, 1997) networks to encode an input utterance into a vector. Given the input utterance $X = \{x_1, x_2, \cdots, x_M\}$ of length M, the forward LSTM network encodes the input at time step t as

$$\mathbf{c}_t^{\mathrm{fw}}, \mathbf{h}_t^{\mathrm{fw}} = \mathrm{LSTM}(\mathbf{e}_{x_t}^{\mathrm{enc}}, \mathbf{c}_{t-1}^{\mathrm{fw}}, \mathbf{h}_{t-1}^{\mathrm{fw}}).$$

$\mathbf{h}_t^{\mathrm{fw}} \in \mathbb{R}^\lambda$ is the representation output, which is computed based on the embedding of x_t (denoted as $\mathbf{e}_{x_t}^{\mathrm{enc}} \in \mathbb{R}^\omega$) and the previous representation output $\mathbf{h}_{t-1}^{\mathrm{fw}}$. $\mathbf{c}_{t-1}^{\mathrm{fw}} \in \mathbb{R}^\lambda$ is a cell state vector that works as a memory in LSTM. The backward LSTM works in the same fashion by reading the input in the reverse order. The final vector representation $\mathbf{h}^{\mathrm{txt}} \in \mathbb{R}^\lambda$ is computed by averaging the concatenated forward and backward outputs

$$\mathbf{h}^{\mathrm{ave}} = \frac{1}{M} \sum_{t=1}^{M} [\mathbf{h}_t^{\mathrm{fw}}; \mathbf{h}_t^{\mathrm{bw}}],$$
$$\mathbf{h}^{\mathrm{txt}} = \sigma(\mathbf{W}^{\mathrm{txt}} \mathbf{h}^{\mathrm{ave}}),$$

where $[\cdot; \cdot]$ concatenates two vectors, $\sigma(\cdot)$ is a sigmoid function, and $\mathbf{W}^{\mathrm{txt}} \in \mathbb{R}^{\lambda \times 2\lambda}$. In this way, $\mathbf{h}^{\mathrm{txt}}$ encodes the summaries of both the preceding and subsequent words.

Domain Estimation & Representation Another task of the encoder is predicting the domain of the input utterance and integrating the domain label with the utterance. For domain estimation, we apply TWEET2VEC due to its superior ability to predict a label of short and colloquial text,

which should be the case for input utterance to dialogue agents. Although the original paper predicted hashtags of tweets, we predict domains of utterances. Another advantage of TWEET2VEC is that it is language-independent and easily adapted to different languages.

Specifically, TWEET2VEC encodes the input utterance using bi-directional recurrent neural networks adapting gated recurrent units (GRUs) (Cho et al., 2014). The final vector representation of input $\hat{\mathbf{h}}^{\mathrm{txt}}$ is computed by integrating the forward and backward outputs using a fully-connected layer. Then $\hat{\mathbf{h}}^{\mathrm{txt}}$ is passed through a linear layer, and the posterior probabilities of the domains are computed in a softmax layer.

Domain d of the highest posterior probability is converted into dense vector representation $\mathbf{h}^{\mathrm{dom}} \in \mathbb{R}^\delta$. Specifically, a two-layer multilayer perceptron (MLP) is employed where a rectifier is used as the activation function

$$\hat{\mathbf{h}}^{\mathrm{dom}} = \mathrm{relu}(\mathbf{W}_1^{\mathrm{dom}} \mathbf{e}_d^{\mathrm{dom}}),$$
$$\mathbf{h}^{\mathrm{dom}} = \mathrm{relu}(\mathbf{W}_2^{\mathrm{dom}} \hat{\mathbf{h}}^{\mathrm{dom}}),$$

where $\mathbf{e}_d^{\mathrm{dom}} \in \mathbb{R}^\delta$ is the embedding vector of d, $\mathbf{W}_1^{\mathrm{dom}} \in \mathbb{R}^{\eta \times \delta}$, and $\mathbf{W}_2^{\mathrm{dom}} \in \mathbb{R}^{\delta \times \eta}$.

Utterance & Domain Label Integration Finally, the utterance and domain representations pass through another fully-connected layer and are integrated into a vector $\mathbf{h}_0^{\mathrm{dec}} \in \mathbb{R}^\lambda$

$$\mathbf{h}_0^{\mathrm{dec}} = \mathbf{W}^{\mathrm{enc}} [\mathbf{h}^{\mathrm{txt}}; \mathbf{h}^{\mathrm{dom}}], \tag{1}$$

where $\mathbf{W}^{\mathrm{enc}} \in \mathbb{R}^{\lambda \times (\lambda + \delta)}$. $\mathbf{h}_0^{\mathrm{dec}}$ is then passed to the decoder for response generation.

3.2 Decoder

Given $\mathbf{h}_0^{\mathrm{dec}}$ encodes the input utterance and the predicted domain, the decoder generates a response embodying the desired sentiment. Input utterance X is paired with a sequence of outputs to predict $Y = \{y_1, y_2, \ldots, y_N\}$ of length N.

We apply the external memory to SEQ2SEQ in order to proactively control the sentiments in the outputs. Fig. 4 shows the detailed design of the decoder. First, we concatenate the output sequence with the embedding of the desired sentiment label as a soft-constraint to instruct the decoder of the desired sentiment for response generation (Li et al., 2016b). The external memory then directly controls response generation by switching outputs between words with sentiment polarities (hereafter referred to as *sentiment words*) and generic ones. Specifically, in the external memory, vocabulary V is divided into two subsets: $V = \{V_s \cup V_g\}$. V_s contains only sentiment words, such as `cool` and `terrible`, while V_g contains other generic words, such as `day` and `me`. The weight of a switcher, which determines the priority of the sets of vocabulary is computed based on the representation output from an LSTM network.

Embedding of s (denoted as $\mathbf{e}^s \in \mathbb{R}^\delta$) is concatenated with output y_{t-1} at the previous time step and then input into the LSTM network as

$$\mathbf{c}_t^{\text{dec}}, \mathbf{h}_t^{\text{dec}} = \text{LSTM}([\mathbf{e}_{y_{t-1}}^{\text{dec}}; \mathbf{e}^s], \mathbf{c}_{t-1}^{\text{dec}}, \mathbf{h}_{t-1}^{\text{dec}}),$$

where $\mathbf{c}_t^{\text{dec}} \in \mathbb{R}^\lambda$ is the cell state vector in the LSTM, $\mathbf{h}_t^{\text{dec}} \in \mathbb{R}^\lambda$ is the representation output from the LSTM, and $\mathbf{e}_{y_{t-1}}^{\text{dec}}$ is the embedding of y_{t-1}. Recall that the initial input to the decoder $\mathbf{h}_0^{\text{dec}}$ is computed in Eq. (1).

Then $\mathbf{h}_t^{\text{dec}}$ is passed to the external memory to sequentially predict output as

$$a_t = \sigma(\mathbf{W}^a \mathbf{h}_t^{\text{dec}}),$$
$$\mathbf{o}_g = \text{softmax}(\mathbf{W}^g \mathbf{h}_t^{\text{dec}}),$$
$$\mathbf{o}_s = \text{softmax}(\mathbf{W}^s \mathbf{h}_t^{\text{dec}}),$$
$$y_t \sim \mathbf{o_t} = [(1 - a_t)\mathbf{o}_g; a_t \mathbf{o}_s],$$

where $\mathbf{W}^a \in \mathbb{R}^{1 \times \lambda}$, $\mathbf{W}^g \in \mathbb{R}^{\lambda \times |V_g|}$, and $\mathbf{W}^s \in \mathbb{R}^{\lambda \times |V_s|}$. $a_t \in [0, 1]$ weighs either the probabilities of generic words or sentiment words based on context represented in $\mathbf{h}_t^{\text{dec}}$. $\mathbf{o}_g \in \mathbb{R}^{|V_g|}$ and $\mathbf{o}_s \in \mathbb{R}^{|V_s|}$ are the posterior probabilities to output a word in each vocabulary. $\mathbf{o}_t \in \mathbb{R}^{|V|}$ is the final probability of each word adjusted by a_t. At run-time, a beam-search with a beam-size of 5 is conducted to avoid outputting an unknown tag.

Our model optimizes the cross-entropy loss between predicted word distribution $\mathbf{o}_t$ and gold distribution $\mathbf{p}_t$. In addition, a regularizer constrains

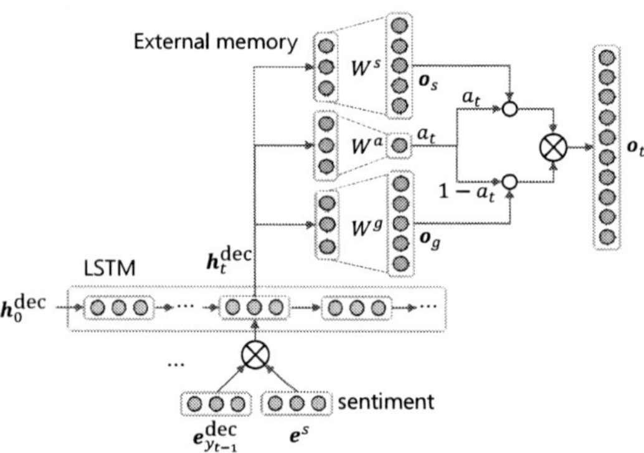

Figure 4: Design of the decoder ($\otimes$ concatenates input vectors and $\circ$ multiplies a vector and scalar.)

the selection of a sentiment or generic word

$$-\sum_{t=1}^{N} \mathbf{p}_t \log(\mathbf{o}_t) - \sum_{t=1}^{N} q_t \log(a_t), \qquad (2)$$

where $q_t \in \{0, 1\}$ is the gold choice of a sentiment word or a generic word.

4 Training Framework

Because our model aims to generate domain-aware responses with sentiments, it should be trained on in-domain conversations with sentiments. Although either in-domain conversations or conversations with sentiments are available, their intersections are scarce. Furthermore, our model integrates TWEET2VEC and external memory. Thus, training errors propagate from each sub-model to the final response.

Consequently, we designed a training framework that pre-trains sub-models independently and then conducts fine-tuning on the connected model, where a model is trained using the pre-trained parameters as the initial weights. The training process uses not only a small-scale conversational (in-domain) corpus of specific domains but also a large-scale conversational corpus of general domain.

4.1 Sentiment Annotation

Training requires sentiment annotations on the general and in-domain corpora. Because it is cost prohibitive to annotate sentiments to these corpora manually, we rely on automatic sentiment analysis. Given that input utterances to dialogue agents are short, incomplete, extremely casual, and potentially noisy, we need a robust method to predict sentiments with guaranteed accuracy.

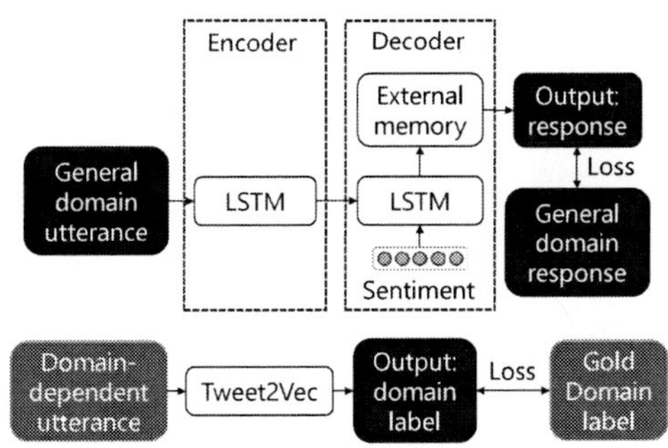

Figure 5: Pre-training process (Gray boxes denote data from the in-domain corpus.)

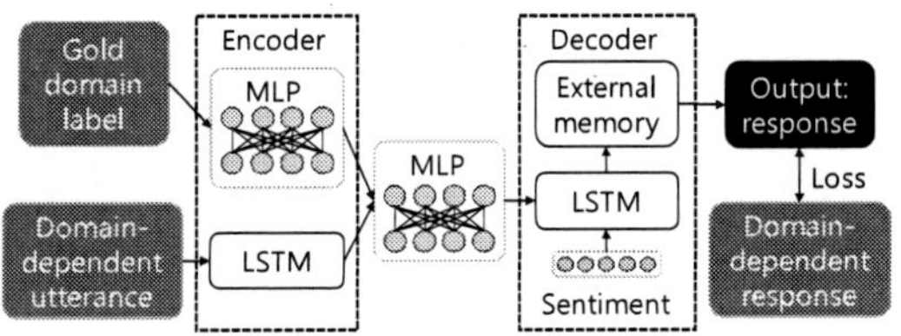

Figure 6: Fine-tuning process (Gray boxes denote data from the in-domain corpus.)

Although we tried several state-of-the-art methods for sentiment analysis (Severyn and Moschitti, 2015; Zhu et al., 2015), our preliminary evaluation showed that they were easily confused by colloquial styles in conversational texts. Hence, we used a simple heuristics based on a sentiment lexicon to prioritize the robustness in analysis. Specifically, a sentence is annotated as positive (negative) if there are more positive (negative) words. If there is an equal number of positive and negative words, then the sentence is annotated as neutral.

We extracted words with strong polarities from existing sentiment lexicons (Kobayashi et al., 2005; Takamura et al., 2005). Besides, we collect casual and recent sentiment words by crawling Twitter.[3] This sentiment lexicon is used for the above sentiment analysis and the external memory as V_s after the filtering described in Sec. 5.2. More details of lexicon construction are in Sec. A.

4.2 Pre-Training on Sub-Models

After annotating sentiments on the general and in-domain corpora, we conducted pre-training. In the pre-training step, sub-models are independently trained (Fig. 5).

SEQ2SEQ requires large-scale training data for fluent response generation. Thus, we used the general corpus here. We directly connected the bi-directional LSTM in the encoder and the LSTM in the decoder to train this sub-model. The loss function (Eq. (2)) is computed by referring to the gold-responses in the corpus. Embeddings to represent sentiments are trained at this stage.

TWEET2VEC is independently trained using the in-domain corpus for domain prediction. The model optimizes the categorical cross-entropy loss between the predicted and gold domain labels.

4.3 Fine-Tuning on the Entire Model

After pre-training, fine-tuning is conducted using the in-domain corpus to train MLPs that integrate the domain label and input utterance (Fig. 6). Additionally, embeddings of domain labels e_d^{dom} are trained at this stage. To avoid error propagation from the pre-trained TWEET2VEC, gold domain labels are inputted into the MLP to learn correct representations of domain labels.

Once fine-tuned, these sub-models are connected to generate domain-aware responses with sentiments (Fig. 2).

5 Evaluation Design

Because the effectiveness of each component for embodying emotions have been evaluated in (Zhou et al., 2018; Huang et al., 2018), we focus on evaluating whether *both* domain-awareness and sentiment-richness are achieved *simultaneously* by our model compared to SEQ2SEQ.

5.1 Data Collection

To train our model, we collected both general and in-domain conversational texts in Japanese. The general corpus is constructed by crawling conversational tweets using Twitter API.[4] We also crawled conversational tweets used in the NTCIR Short Text Conversation Task (Shang et al., 2016). In total, the general corpus contains about 1.6M utterance-response pairs.

The in-domain corpus crawls conversations in public Facebook Groups using Facebook Graph API.[5] Because members are fans of specific products, organizations, and people, we expect that their conversations are domain-dependent.[6] Specifically, we used two domains, Japanese pro-

---

[3]https://twitter.com/

[4]https://developer.twitter.com/en/docs
[5]https://developers.facebook.com/docs/graph-api
[6]We also tried to collect in-domain conversations using hashtags on Twitter, but they were too noisy.

Type	Domain	# of Pairs
General	Mixture	1.1M
In-domain	Baseball	24k
	Pokémon Go	23k

Table 1: Training data profile

	Summary	Setting
ω	Dimension of word embedding	256
λ	Dimension of the representation output in the LSTM network	512
δ	Dimension of the embedding and representation output of labels	64
η	Dimension of the hidden layer in the MLPs	512
$|V|$	Vocabulary size	45k
$|V_s|$	Vocabulary size of the sentiment words	1,387

Table 2: Hyper-parameters and their settings

fessional baseball leagues and Pokémon Go[7], anticipating that salient sentiments are easily manifested in sports and game domains. Experiments using a wider range of domains is our future work. We crawled conversations since a group's inception to November 2017. In total, the in-domain corpora contain about 29k baseball-related conversations and 28k game-related conversations. We assume that sentiments can be embodied in domains with weaker sentiment tendencies due to pre-training in the general domain corpus. Verification of this assumption is a future task.

After crawling, we preprocessed the corpora to remove noise and standardize texts (details are described in Sec. B). Table 1 shows the amount of our training data after the preprocessing step.

As a validation set of pre-training, 1k conversation pairs were sampled from the general corpus. Similarly, 1k pairs for validation and another 1k as a test set were sampled from the in-domain corpus for the automatic evaluation. The training set excluded these validation and test sets.

5.2 Model Setting

Table 2 summarizes the hyper-parameters in our model and their settings. The vocabulary size was

45k, which consisted of frequent words in the general and in-domain corpora. The general and in-domain corpora contained $1,387$ sentiment words, which were used as V_s in the external memory.

In both pre-training and fine-tuning, submodels, except for TWEET2VEC, were trained at most 100 epochs with early stopping using the validation set. Batch size was set to 200, dropout was used with a rate of 0.2, and Adam (Kingma and Ba, 2015) with a learning rate of 0.01 was applied as an optimizer.

During pre-training and fine-tuning, an out-of-vocabulary (OOV) word in input utterances was replaced with a similar word in the vocabulary to reduce the effects of data sparsity (Li et al., 2016c). We generated word embeddings using the fastText (Bojanowski et al., 2017) with the default settings feeding Wikipedia dumps[8] as training data. When a word is OOV, the top-50 similar words are detected using cosine similarities between their embeddings. If one of these similar words is in the vocabulary, it replaces the original OOV word. Otherwise, the original word is replaced with an unknown word tag.

TWEET2VEC was trained on the in-domain corpus using the official implementation[9] with the default settings. We crawled 200 new domain-dependent conversational pairs as a validation set. The prediction accuracy was 89.0%, which is reasonable considering that our texts are colloquial.

We compare our model to SEQ2SEQ that was implemented using bi-directional LSTM networks as an encoder and an LSTM network as a decoder. Our model has the same hyper-parameters and training procedures, except that SEQ2SEQ was trained using both general and in-domain corpora. For SEQ2SEQ, a validation set of 1k pairs was randomly sampled from the combined corpus excluding from the training and test sets described in Sec. 5.1.

5.3 Human Evaluation

Because each utterance has many appropriate responses, an automatic evaluation scheme has yet to be established. To assess the quality of the generated responses from the human perspective, we designed two evaluation tasks. Task 1 evaluates the overall quality of our model compared to SEQ2SEQ from the perspectives of

---

domain-awareness and sentiment-richness. Task 2 evaluates if an intended sentiment is embodied as desired without being affected by domain-awareness.

We recruited five graduate students majoring in computer science that are Japanese native speakers (hereafter called annotators). After an instruction session to explain judgment standards, they annotated Task 1 and Task 2. As a token of appreciation, each annotator received a small stipend.

Test Set Creation To exclude external factors, *e.g.*, word segmentation failures, that may affect the evaluation results, we manually created a test set consisting of 300 utterances in the baseball domain and another 300 utterances in the Pokémon Go domain.

First, we crawled new conversational pairs from the same Facebook Groups from November to December 2017. Next, we manually excluded conversations in the general domain (*e.g.*, greetings). We then cleaned sentences in the same manner with the general and in-domain corpora. Besides, we manually replaced OOV words within vocabulary words that preserve the original meanings of sentences. Slang and uncommon expressions were also manually converted to standard expressions to avoid impacting the accuracy of word segmentation. Half of the test set (150 conversations for each domain) was used for Task 1 and the other half was used for Task 2. Note that all annotators annotated the same conversations, in total 600 pairs of utterances and responses.

Task 1: Overall Evaluation Annotators judged triples of an input utterance and responses by our model and by SEQ2SEQ. The order of responses was randomly shuffled to ensure a fair evaluation. Annotators assessed the following aspects:

- Fluency: Annotators judged if a response is fluent and at an acceptable level to understand its meaning (1 = fluent, 0 = influent).

- Consistency: Annotators evaluated whether a response is semantically consistent with the utterance (1 = consistent, 0 = inconsistent). Generic responses can be regarded as consistent if they are acceptable for given utterances. Responses judged as influent are automatically annotated as inconsistent.

- Domain-awareness: Annotators compared the two responses and determined which one better matched the domain of the input utterance (1 = model that generated the better response, 0 = the other model).

- Sentiment-richness: Annotators compared the two responses and determined one showing salient sentiments like Domain-awareness annotation. Only positive or negative responses were considered for our model.

For Domain-awareness and Sentiment-richness, we conduct a pairwise comparison of our model and SEQ2SEQ, which enables reliable judgments for subjective annotations (Ghazvininejad et al., 2018; Wang et al., 2018), rather than independently judging different models.

Task 2: Evaluation of Sentiment Control Our model takes a sentiment label that is desired to be expressed in a generated response as input, which we refer to as *intended* sentiment. This task evaluates if such an intended sentiment is embodied in a response by comparing the intended sentiment and a sentiment that annotators perceive in practice.

Annotators were shown a pair of input utterance and generated response by our model, and then asked to judge if the response was positive, negative, or neutral. We evaluated the agreement between the intended and perceived sentiments.

6 Evaluation Results

As an automatic evaluation measure, we computed the BLEU score (Papineni et al., 2002) following evaluations in (Li et al., 2016a; Ghazvininejad et al., 2018). Our model achieved the higher BLEU score (1.54) than SEQ2SEQ (1.39). However, as discussed in (Liu et al., 2016; Lowe et al., 2017), current automatic evaluation measures show either weak or no correlation with human judgements, or worse, they tend to favor generic responses. Hence, we focus on human evaluation in the following.

First of all, the agreement level of annotations is examined based on Fleiss' κ. All annotations have reasonable agreements ($\kappa \geq 0.37$) except the annotation of fluency for SEQ2SEQ whose κ value is as low as 0.21 (all the κ values are shown in Sec. C). This phenomenon may be because SEQ2SEQ tends to output generic responses that are less dependent on the utterances, making judgments difficult due to the limited clues to evaluate fluency.

Table 3 shows the macro-averages and the 95% confidence intervals of the scores obtained by the

Metrics	SEQ2SEQ	Our model
Fluency	**0.995** ± 0.006	0.955 ± 0.023
Consistency	**0.773** ± 0.094	0.753 ± 0.127
Domain-awareness	0.109 ± 0.044	**0.890** ± 0.044
Sentiment-richness	0.282 ± 0.133	**0.717** ± 0.133

Table 3: Evaluation results of Task 1

annotators in Task 1. Our model achieved significant improvements over SEQ2SEQ; 89% and 72% of the responses generated by ours were deemed as consistent with the utterance domain and showing salient sentiments, respectively. Furthermore, 68.1% responses by our model were judged as *both* domain-aware and sentiment-rich, which was only 2.7% for responses by SEQ2SEQ.

As for fluency and consistency, SEQ2SEQ yields slightly more fluent (99.5%) and consistent (77.3%) responses compared to our model (95.5% and 75.3%, respectively). SEQ2SEQ benefits from the generic responses because such responses apply to various inputs, making it easier to achieve a high consistency compared to our model that generates domain-dependent responses. Additionally, generic responses are easier to generate because they are typically short. The average numbers of characters in responses when inputting the test set were 19 and 32 for SEQ2SEQ and our model, respectively. This result reveals that our model achieves a reasonably high fluency even when generating significantly longer responses. Another reason is the side-effect of external memory that influences the internal state of the decoder as reported in (Zhou et al., 2018).

As a result of Task 2, the macro-average of the agreement between the intended and perceived sentiments is 64.5 ± 2.3%, where Fleiss' κ of annotation is 0.52. Fig. 7 is a confusion matrix showing the distribution of the obtained 1,500 annotations. Neutral responses tend to be judged as either positive (28.5%) or negative (15.6%). One reason is our simple sentiment annotation, which assigns a neutral label when the numbers of positive and negative words in a sentence are equal. Improving the polarity strength is a future task.

The annotators perceived 17.6% of the intended negative responses as positive. Detailed analyses of generated responses revealed that this category contained sentiment words whose polarities

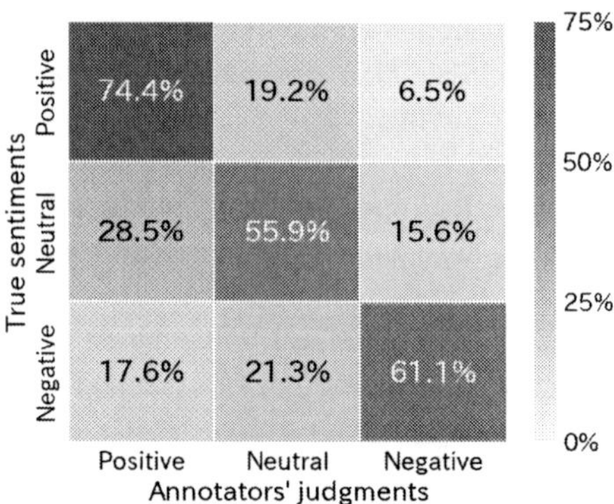

Figure 7: Confusion matrix of intended (true) sentiments and the sentiments that annotators perceived

depend on the context, *e.g.*, `envy`, `great`, and `surprising`. These words are considered negative in our sentiment lexicon because they tend to be used with negative emoticons to show humor in Twitter. In the future, we will develop post-processing to clean our lexicon and consider the self-attention (Vaswani et al., 2017) to resolve such context-dependent cases.

Fig. 1 shows real examples of generated responses. While SEQ2SEQ produces generic responses like "`Really?`", our model generates domain-aware responses with sentiments like "`Sugano is cool!`" (positive response) and "`No way? There is no hope for Sugano!`" (negative response) for the baseball domain. Sec. D provides more examples that show how our model achieved domain-awareness and sentiment-richness.

7 Conclusion

As a solution to the generic response problem in SEQ2SEQ, we implemented conversational responsiveness and self-expression to a neural dialogue model. Different from previous studies, our model achieves these features simultaneously in forms of domain-awareness and sentiment-richness, respectively. Evaluation results empirically demonstrated that our model significantly outperformed SEQ2SEQ. In the future, we will improve the accuracy in embodying sentiments and extend our dataset to cover diverse domains.

Acknowledgments

This project is funded by Microsoft Research Asia, Microsoft Japan Co., Ltd., and JSPS KAKENHI Grant Number JP18K11435.

References

Dzmitry Bahdanau, Kyunghyun Cho, and Yoshua Bengio. 2015. Neural machine translation by jointly learning to align and translate. In *Proc. of ICLR*.

Piotr Bojanowski, Edouard Grave, Armand Joulin, and Tomas Mikolov. 2017. Enriching word vectors with subword information. *Transactions of the Association for Computational Linguistics*, 5:135–146.

Kyunghyun Cho, Bart van Merrienboer, Dzmitry Bahdanau, and Yoshua Bengio. 2014. On the properties of neural machine translation: Encoder–decoder approaches. In *Proc. of the Workshop on Syntax, Semantics and Structure in Statistical Translation (SSST)*, pages 103–111.

Bhuwan Dhingra, Zhong Zhou, Dylan Fitzpatrick, Michael Muehl, and William Cohen. 2016. Tweet2Vec: Character-based distributed representations for social media. In *Proc. of ACL*, pages 269–274.

Marjan Ghazvininejad, Chris Brockett, Ming-Wei Chang, Bill Dolan, Jianfeng Gao, Scott Wen-tau Yih, and Michel Galley. 2018. A knowledge-grounded neural conversation model. In *Proc. of AAAI*.

Takayuki Hasegawa, Nobuhiro Kaji, Naoki Yoshinaga, and Masashi Toyoda. 2013. Predicting and eliciting addressee's emotion in online dialogue. In *Proc. of ACL*, pages 964–972.

Sepp Hochreiter and Jürgen Schmidhuber. 1997. Long short-term memory. *Neural Computation*, 9(8):1735–1780.

Chenyang Huang, Osmar Zaiane, Amine Trabelsi, and Nouha Dziri. 2018. Automatic dialogue generation with expressed emotions. In *Proc. of NAACL-HLT*, pages 49–54. Association for Computational Linguistics.

Diederik P. Kingma and Jimmy Ba. 2015. Adam: A method for stochastic optimization. In *Proc. of ICLR*.

Nozomi Kobayashi, Kentaro Inui, Yuji Matsumoto, Kenji Tateishi, and Toshikazu Fukushima. 2005. Collecting evaluative expressions for opinion extraction. In *Proc. of IJCNLP*, pages 596–605.

Taku Kudo, Kaoru Yamamoto, and Yuji Matsumoto. 2004. Applying conditional random fields to japanese morphological analysis. In *Proc. of EMNLP*, pages 230–237.

Jiwei Li, Michel Galley, Chris Brockett, Jianfeng Gao, and Bill Dolan. 2016a. A diversity-promoting objective function for neural conversation models. In *Proc. of NAACL-HLT*, pages 110–119.

Jiwei Li, Michel Galley, Chris Brockett, Georgios Spithourakis, Jianfeng Gao, and Bill Dolan. 2016b. A persona-based neural conversation model. In *Proc. of ACL*, pages 994–1003.

Xiaoqing Li, Jiajun Zhang, and Chengqing Zong. 2016c. Towards zero unknown word in neural machine translation. In *Proc. of IJCAI*, pages 2852–2858.

Chia-Wei Liu, Ryan Lowe, Iulian Serban, Mike Noseworthy, Laurent Charlin, and Joelle Pineau. 2016. How not to evaluate your dialogue system: An empirical study of unsupervised evaluation metrics for dialogue response generation. In *Proc. of EMNLP*, pages 2122–2132.

Ryan Lowe, Michael Noseworthy, Iulian Vlad Serban, Nicolas Angelard-Gontier, Yoshua Bengio, and Joelle Pineau. 2017. Towards an automatic turing test: Learning to evaluate dialogue responses. In *Proc. of ACL*, pages 1116–1126.

Lynn C. Miller and John H. Berg. 1984. Selectivity and urgency in interpersonal exchange. In Valerian J. Derlega, editor, *Communication, Intimacy, and Close Relationships*, chapter 7, pages 161–205. Elsevier.

Lili Mou, Yiping Song, Rui Yan, Ge Li, Lu Zhang, and Zhi Jin. 2016. Sequence to backward and forward sequences: A content-introducing approach to generative short-text conversation. In *Proc. of COLING*, pages 3349–3358.

Kishore Papineni, Salim Roukos, Todd Ward, and Wei-Jing Zhu. 2002. BLEU: a method for automatic evaluation of machine translation. In *Proc. of ACL*, pages 311–318.

Qiao Qian, Minlie Huang, Haizhou Zhao, Jingfang Xu, and Xiaoyan Zhu. 2018. Assigning personality/profile to a chatting machine for coherent conversation generation. In *Proc. of IJCAI*, pages 4279–4285.

Harry T. Reis and Phillip Shaver. 1988. Intimacy as an interpersonal process. In S. Duck, D. F. Hay, S. E. Hobfoll, W. Ickes, and B. M. Montgomery, editors, *Handbook of personal relationships: Theory, research and interventions*, pages 367–389. John Wiley & Sons.

Aliaksei Severyn and Alessandro Moschitti. 2015. UNITN: Training deep convolutional neural network for twitter sentiment classification. In *Proc. of the Int'l Workshop on Semantic Evaluation (SemEval)*, pages 464–469.

Lifeng Shang, Zhengdong Lu, and Hang Li. 2015. Neural responding machine for short-text conversation. In *Proc. of ACL-IJCNLP*, pages 1577–1586.

Lifeng Shang, Tetsuya Sakai, Zhengdong Lu, Hang Li, Ryuichiro Higashinaka, and Yusuke Miyao. 2016. Overview of the NTCIR-12 short text conversation task. In *Proceedings of the 12th NTCIR Conference on Evaluation of Information Access Technologies*, pages 473–484.

Yuanlong Shao, Stephan Gouws, Denny Britz, Anna Goldie, Brian Strope, and Ray Kurzweil. 2017. Generating high-quality and informative conversation responses with sequence-to-sequence models. In *Proc. of EMNLP*, pages 2210–2219.

Hiroya Takamura, Takashi Inui, and Manabu Okumura. 2005. Extracting semantic orientations of words using spin model. In *Proc. of ACL*, pages 133–140.

Ashish Vaswani, Noam Shazeer, Niki Parmar, Jakob Uszkoreit, Llion Jones, Aidan N. Gomez, Lukasz Kaiser, and Illia Polosukhin. 2017. Attention is all you need. In *Proc. of NIPS*, pages 5998–6008.

Oriol Vinyals and Quoc V Le. 2015. A neural conversational model. In *ICML Deep Learning Workshop*.

Yansen Wang, Chenyi Liu, Minlie Huang, and Liqiang Nie. 2018. Learning to ask questions in open-domain conversational systems with typed decoders. In *Proc. of ACL*, pages 2193–2203.

Chen Xing, Wei Wu, Yu Wu, Jie Liu, Yalou Huang, Ming Zhou, and Wei-Ying Ma. 2017. Topic aware neural response generation. In *Proc. of AAAI*, pages 33351–33357.

Lili Yao, Yaoyuan Zhang, Yansong Feng, Dongyan Zhao, and Rui Yan. 2017. Towards implicit content-introducing for generative short-text conversation systems. In *Proc. of EMNLP*, pages 2190–2199.

Hainan Zhang, Yanyan Lan, Jiafeng Guo, Jun Xu, and Xueqi Cheng. 2018a. Reinforcing coherence for sequence to sequence model in dialogue generation. In *Proc. of IJCAI*, pages 4567–4573.

Hainan Zhang, Yanyan Lan, Jiafeng Guo, Jun Xu, and Xueqi Cheng. 2018b. Tailored sequence to sequence models to different conversation scenarios. In *Proc. of ACL*, pages 1479–1488.

Saizheng Zhang, Emily Dinan, Jack Urbanek, Arthur Szlam, Douwe Kiela, and Jason Weston. 2018c. Personalizing dialogue agents: I have a dog, do you have pets too? In *Proc. of ACL*, pages 2204–2213.

Hao Zhou, Minlie Huang, Tianyang Zhang, Xiaoyan Zhu, and Bing Liu. 2018. Emotional chatting machine: Emotional conversation generation with internal and external memory. In *Proc. of AAAI*.

Xiaodan Zhu, Parinaz Sobhani, and Hongyu Guo. 2015. Long short-term memory over recursive structures. In *Proc. of ICML*, pages 1604–1612.

Meng Zou, Xihan Li, Haokun Liu, and Zhihong Deng. 2018. Memd: A diversity-promoting learning framework for short-text conversation. In *Proc. of COLING*, pages 1281–1291.

A Construction of the Sentiment Lexicon

We used two sentiment lexicons created by Kobayashi et al. (2005) and Takamura et al. (2005). The former is manually created, while the latter is automatically created by estimating the strengths of semantic orientations of words in the range of $[-1.0, 1.0]$. We only used words with a strong polarity. Specifically, words with scores of $[-1.0, 0.9]$ or $[0.9, 1.0]$. These lexicons contain only formal words like headings in dictionaries. Therefore, we extended our sentiment lexicon to collect casual and recent sentiment words.

We searched tweets that are expected to contain sentiments by querying Twitter with positive and negative emoticons. In total, we crawled 400k potential positive and negative tweets and generated word embeddings from these tweets using the fastText (Bojanowski et al., 2017) with the default setting. We then manually selected 57 sentiment words from the vocabulary as seeds. The top-15 similar words per seed were extracted as sentiment words, which were ranked by the cosine similarity between embeddings of the seed and a candidate. In total, we collected $1,621$ negative and $2,666$ positive words as our sentiment lexicon.

B Preprocessing

We employed conversational text crawled from Twitter and Facebook, which are inherently noisy. We conducted data cleaning before training our model.

First, line breaks, emoticons, Japanese emoticons (kaomoji), URLs, and consecutive duplicate symbols were removed. Then texts less than or equal to 25 words were obtained after word segmentation using Mecab (Kudo et al., 2004). Table 4 shows detailed statistics of our training data after this preprocessing.

C Annotation Agreement

Table 5 shows the Fleiss' κ for each annotation result in our human evaluation. It confirms that reasonably high agreements were achieved.

D Example Responses

Fig. 8 shows real responses generated by our model and SEQ2SEQ using input utterances from our test set. Our method successfully generates

Data (Source)		Total # of pairs	Positive	Neutral	Negative
General (Twitter)		$1,081,500$	$218,322$	$760,451$	$102,727$
In-domain (Facebook)	Baseball	$24,666$	$6,011$	$16,623$	$2,032$
	Pokémon GO	$22,734$	$7,633$	$13,299$	$1,802$

Table 4: Detailed statistics of training data

Annotation			κ
Task 1	Fluency	SEQ2SEQ	0.21
		Our model	0.45
	Consistency	SEQ2SEQ	0.41
		Our model	0.37
	Domain-awareness		0.78
	Sentiment		0.46
Task 2			0.52

Table 5: Fleiss' κ on annotation results

Input utterance	Model		Generated response
Ohtani wants to try hand at pitching in the majors. (大谷選手のメジャー移籍の可能性はあります)	Seq2Seq		I like him better now. (俺は今からの方が好きです)
	Our model	Positive	Really? I was expecting that! (そうなんですか!それは、期待してるんですよね!)
		Neutral	Really! I didn't know that! (そうなんですか!それは知りませんでした!)
		Negative	Really? He'll be rude to any team. (そうなんですか!それは、どこの球団にも失礼ですね!)
I'm expecting the head coach, Kanemoto, to develop fresh talent. (金本監督は若手をどんどん育てて欲しいですね。)	Seq2Seq		Agreed, but I like him. (私もそう思うけど、私は好きです。)
	Our model	Positive	I expect the Giants head coach to develop talent. (巨人の監督に期待してますね)
		Neutral	Maybe, if he becomes the Giants head coach. (巨人の監督になったら、そうですね。)
		Negative	Giant players are difficult, too. (巨人の選手も、怖いですね。)
I wanted to exchange a 2km-egg. LOL! (この時ばかりはニキロタマゴと交換してあげたかったですわら)	Seq2Seq		Uh, nice! (あ、よかったです!)
	Our model	Positive	That shiny Magikarp had a good profile. (金コイは個体値良かったですね)
		Neutral	They were a shiny Magikarp and Eevee. (金コイとイーブイでしたね)
		Negative	A shiny Magikarp is disappointing. (金コイはキツイですね)

Figure 8: Example responses generated by our model and SEQ2SEQ

domain-aware and sentiment-rich responses compared to SEQ2SEQ.

Author Index